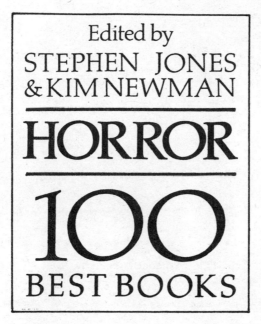

Edited by
STEPHEN JONES
& KIM NEWMAN

HORROR

100

BEST BOOKS

CARROLL & GRAF

For Mum and Dad, for all their love
and continued support   STEVE

For Meg, much love   KIM

This edition first published in Great Britain by Xanadu Publications Ltd.
1988
First published in the United States of America by
Carroll & Graf Publishers, Inc. 1988

Carroll & Graf Publishers, Inc.
260 Fifth Avenue
New York, NY 10001

Library of Congress Cataloguing in Publication Data
  Horror: the 100 best books/edited by Stephen Jones and Kim Newman.
  p. cm.
  Includes index
  ISBN 0–88184–417–9: $15.95
  1. Horror tales, English—History and criticism   2. Horror tales, American—History and criticism 3. Bibliography—Best books—Horror
tales 4. Horror tales—Bibliography 5. Authors—Books and reading.
    I. Jones, Stephen II. Newman, Kim

  PR830.T3H67 1988
  823'.0822—dc19

Manufactured in Great Britain

Foreword

by Ramsey Campbell

Horror fiction is the branch of literature most often concerned with going too far. It is the least escapist form of fantasy. It shows us sights we would ordinarily look away from or reminds us of insights we might prefer not to admit we have. It makes us intimate with people we would cross the street to avoid. It shows us the monstrous and perhaps reveals that we are looking in a mirror. It tells us we are right to be afraid, or that we aren't afraid enough. It also frequently embraces, or at least is conterminous with, the ghost story. It flourishes here and there in the fields of science fiction and crime fiction, and not infrequently it bobs up in the mainstream, whatever that is. Despite its name, it is often most concerned to produce awe and terror in its audience, but it is not unusual for a horror story to encompass a wider emotional range.

Some of what I've said so far (even when it is understood as seeking to define good horror fiction) will doubtless prove controversial. For instance, not only ignorant critics but some horror writers (generally bad ones) will dismiss the notion that this field has anything to do with literature. However, there are remarkably few mainstream writers (especially of short fiction) who have not attempted the horror story. A good many mainstream writers are best known, or remembered only, for their horror fiction, and some of these examples are among the classics of the field. The present book will go some way toward displaying the scope of the field and the diversity of its creators.

Diversity breeds conflict, in this field as in any other. Both M. R. James and Montague Summers deplored the *Not at Night* series, as Robert Aickman did the later *Pan Books of Horror Stories*. Algernon Blackwood found Lovecraft's work 'lacking in spirituality', Russell Kirk convicted Blackwood's of a lack of Christianity. H. Russell Wakefield, nearly at the end of his career, was disappointed enough to foresee no future at all for the ghost story (a knell frequently tolled during this century). Skirmishes most often flare between practitioners of the graphically gruesome and the subtle, as if they were mutually exclusive or even mutually destructive but, oddly enough, until recently almost all the public statements came from the second camp. Not long ago a writer of gruesomely violent horror fiction was dismissed by someone subtler as having nothing to do with horror. This nonsensical suggestion provoked a defence, whose voicing I take to be a healthy sign. I cannot see that a field, often blamed for causing what it has the courage to

3

examine, can call itself honest if it rushes to make scapegoats of its own less respectable writers. Let them be allowed to make themselves clear and be seen for what they are.

For these and other reasons, I welcome the range of subjects and contributors which the list of contents promises. May it broaden the reading of whoever uses it.

Merseyside
23 February 1988

Contents

FOREWORD by Ramsey Campbell   3

INTRODUCTION by Stephen Jones and Kim Newman   9

1   CLIVE BARKER on *Doctor Faustus*, by Christopher Marlowe (*c.* 1592)   11

2   JOHN BLACKBURN on *The Tragedy of Macbeth*, by William Shakespeare (1606)   14

3   DIANA WYNNE JONES on *The White Devil*, by John Webster (1612)   15

4   SCOTT BRADFIELD on *Caleb Williams*, by William Godwin (1794)   17

5   LES DANIELS on *The Monk*, by Matthew Gregory Lewis (1796)   19

6   JOHN SLADEK on *The Best Tales of Hoffman* (1814–16)   21

7   DAVID PIRIE on *Northanger Abbey*, by Jane Austen (1817)   23

8   JANE YOLEN on *Frankenstein*, by Mary Wollstonecraft Shelley (1818)   25

9   PETER TREMAYNE on *Melmoth the Wanderer*, by Charles Maturin (1820)   27

10   GARRY KILWORTH on *The Confessions of a Justified Sinner*, by James Hogg (1824)   29

11   JOHN M. FORD on *Tales of Mystery and Imagination*, by Edgar Allan Poe (1838)   30

12   EDGAR ALLAN POE on *Twice-Told Tales*, by Nathaniel Hawthorne (1938)   32

13   THOMAS TESSIER on *The Black Spider*, by Jeremias Gotthelf (1842)   34

14   THOMAS M. DISCH on *The Wandering Jew*, by Eugene Sue (1844–5)   36

15   MICHAEL McDOWELL on *The Confidence Man*, by Herman Melville (1857)   39

16   M. R. JAMES on *Uncle Silas*, by J. Sheridan Le Fanu (1864)   41

17   JACK WILLIAMSON on *Dr Jekyll and Mr Hyde*, by Robert Louis Stevenson (1886)   43

18   TIM STOUT on *She*, by H. Rider Haggard (1887)   45

19   H. P. LOVECRAFT on *The King in Yellow*, by Robert W. Chambers (1895)   47

20   GENE WOLFE on *The Island of Dr Moreau*, by H. G. Wells (1896)   49

21   COLIN WILSON on *Dracula*, by Bram Stoker (1897)   51

22   R. CHETWYND-HAYES on *The Turn of the Screw*, by Henry James (1898)   53

23	DOUGLAS E. WINTER on *Heart of Darkness*, by Joseph Conrad (1902)	55
24	RICHARD DALBY on *The Jewel of Seven Stars*, by Bram Stoker (1903)	59
25	GEOFF RYMAN on *Ghost Stories of an Antiquary*, by M. R. James (1904)	61
26	T. E.D. KLEIN on *The House of Souls*, by Arthur Machen (1906)	64
27	HILAIRE BELLOC on *John Silence*, by Algernon Blackwood (1908)	67
28	DAVID LANGFORD on *The Man Who Was Thursday*, by G. K. Chesterton (1908)	70
29	TERRY PRATCHETT on *The House on the Borderland*, by William Hope Hodgson (1908)	71
30	MILTON SUBOTSKY on *The Collected Works of Ambrose Bierce* (1909)	73
31	MIKE ASHLEY on *Widdershins*, by Oliver Onions (1911)	75
32	BASIL COPPER on *The Horror Horn*, by E. F. Benson (1912–34)	77
33	GEORGE HAY on *A Voyage to Arcturus*, by David Lindsay (1920)	79
34	STEVE RASNIC TEM on *The Trial*, by Franz Kafka (1925)	81
35	ROBERT E. HOWARD on *Something About Eve*, by James Branch Cabell (1929)	83
36	KARL EDWARD WAGNER on *Medusa*, by E. H. Visiak (1929)	85
37	MARVIN KAYE on *The Werewolf of Paris*, by Guy Endore (1933)	86
38	JESSICA AMANDA SALMONSON on *The Last Bouquet*, by Marjorie Bowen (1933)	88
39	ROBERT BLOCH on *The Cadaver of Gideon Wyck*, by Alexander Laing (1934)	89
40	HUGH LAMB on *A Second Century of Creepy Stories*, ed. Hugh Walpole (1937)	92
41	LIONEL FANTHORPE on *The Dark Tower*, by C. S. Lewis (c. 1938)	93
42	DENIS ETCHISON on *Johnny Got His Gun*, by Dalton Trumbo (1939)	95
43	DONALD A. WOLLHEIM on *The Outsider and Others*, by H. P. Lovecraft (1939)	96
44	HARLAN ELLISON on *Out of Space and Time*, by Clark Ashton Smith (1942)	99
45	GERALD W. PAGE on *Conjure Wife*, by Fritz Leiber (1943)	102
46	MAXIM JAKUBOWSKI on *Night Has a Thousand Eyes*, by Cornell Woolrich (1945)	104
47	GRAHAM MASTERTON on *The Lurker at the Threshold*, by H. P. Lovecraft & August Derleth (1945)	106
48	FORREST J ACKERMAN on *Deliver Me from Eva*, by Paul Bailey (1946)	107
49	DAVID G. HARTWELL on *And the Darkness Falls*, ed. Boris Karloff (1946)	109
50	PETER HAINING on *The Sleeping and the Dead*, ed. August Derleth (1947)	110

51   ROBERT R. MCCAMMON on *Track of the Cat*, by Walter Van Tilburg Clark   113

52   SUZY MCKEE CHARNAS on *The Sound of His Horn*, by Sarban (1952)   115

53   JOE HALDEMAN on *Lord of the Flies*, by William Golding (1954)   117

54   RICHARD CHRISTIAN MATHESON on *I Am Legend*, by Richard Matheson (1954)   119

55   JOE R. LANSDALE on *The October Country*, by Ray Bradbury (1955)   121

56   STEPHEN GALLAGHER on *Nine Horrors and a Dream*, by Joseph Payne Brennan (1958)   123

57   HUGH B. CAVE on *Psycho*, by Robert Bloch (1959)   126

58   STEPHEN LAWS on *Quatermass and the Pit*, by Nigel Kneale (1959)   127

59   MICHEL PARRY on *Cry Horror!*, by H. P. Lovecraft (1959)   130

60   LISA TUTTLE on *The Haunting of Hill House*, by Shirley Jackson (1959)   131

61   TAD WILLIAMS on *The Three Stigmata of Palmer Eldritch*, by Philip K. Dick (1964)   134

62   JACK DANN on *The Painted Bird*, by Jerzy Kosinski (1965)   136

63   CRAIG SHAW GARDNER on *The Crystal World*, by J. G. Ballard (1966)   140

64   COLIN GREENLAND on *Sub Rosa*, by Robert Aickman (1968)   142

65   BRIAN ALDISS on *The Green Man*, by Kingley Amis (1969)   144

66   NEIL GAIMAN on *The Complete Werewolf*, by Anthony Boucher (1969)   146

67   DAN SIMMONS on *Grendel*, by John Gardner (1971)   149

68   F. PAUL WILSON on *The Exorcist*, by William Peter Blatty (1971)   151

69   JOHN SKIPP on *The Sheep Look Up*, by John Brunner (1972)   154

70   FRANCES GARFIELD on *Worse Things Waiting*, by Manly Wade Wellman (1973)   157

71   STEPHEN KING on *Burnt Offerings*, by Robert Marasco (1973)   159

72   AL SARRANTONIO on *'Salem's Lot*, by Stephen King (1975)   161

73   CRAIG SPECTOR on *Deathbird Stories*, by Harlan Ellison (1975)   163

74   BRIAN LUMLEY on *Murgunstrumm and Others*, by Hugh B. Cave (1977)   165

75   CHARLES L. GRANT on *Sweetheart, Sweetheart*, by Bernard Taylor (1977)   167

76   DAVID J. SCHOW on *All Heads Turn When the Hunt Goes By*, by John Farris (1977)   169

77   PETER STRAUB on *The Shining*, by Stephen King (1977)   171

78   WILLIAM F. NOLAN on *Falling Angel*, by William Hjortsberg (1978)   173

79   CHARLES DE LINT on *The Wolfen*, by Whitley Strieber (1978)   175

80   SHAUN HUTSON on *The Totem*, by David Morrell (1979)   177

81   PETER NICHOLLS on *Ghost Story*, by Peter Straub (1979)   178

82   CHRISTOPHER EVANS on *The Land of Laughs*, by Jonathan Carroll (1980)   181

83   DAVID S. GARNETT on *The Cellar*, by Richard Laymon (1980)   182

84 CHET WILLIAMSON on *Red Dragon*, by Thomas Harris (1981) 184
85 J. N. WILLIAMSON on *The Keep*, by F. Paul Wilson (1981) 186
86 SAMANTHA LEE on *The Dark Country*, by Dennis Etchison (1982) 189
87 RAMSEY CAMPBELL on *In a Lonely Place*, by Karl Edward Wagner (1983) 191
88 JOHN CLUTE on *The Anubis Gates*, by Tim Powers (1983) 193
89 BRIAN STABLEFORD on *The Arabian Nightmare*, by Robert Irwin (1983) 195
90 MALCOLM EDWARDS on *The Wasp Factory*, by Iain Banks (1894) 197
91 THOMAS F. MONTELEONE on *The Ceremonies*, by T. E. D. Klein (1984) 199
92 MICHAEL MOORCOCK on *Mythago Wood*, by Robert Holdstock (1984) 200
93 IAN WATSON on *Who Made Stevie Crye?*, by Michael Bishop (1984) 203
94 EDWARD BRYANT on *Song of Kali*, by Dan Simmons (1985) 205
95 ADRIAN COLE on *The Damnation Game*, by Clive Barker (1985) 207
96 R. S. HADJI on *Hawksmoor*, by Peter Ackroyd (1985) 208
97 ROBERT HOLDSTOCK on *A Nest of Nightmares*, by Lisa Tuttle (1986) 210
98 GUY N. SMITH on *The Pet*, by Charles N. Grant (1986) 212
99 EDDY C. BERTIN on *Swan Song*, by Robert McCammon (1987) 214
100 JACK SULLIVAN on *Dark Feasts*, by Ramsey Campbell (1987) 216
    NOTES ON THE CONTRIBUTORS 219
    LIST OF RECOMMENDED READING 249
    ACKNOWLEDGEMENTS 255

INTRODUCTION

It seemed like a simple idea at the time . . .

There are plenty of critical guides clogging the shelves, particularly in the science fiction and fantasy categories. Some are interesting, idiosyncratic selections, others are narcissist tomes. The problem is that the titles chosen and dissected can only reflect the author's own tastes, and even genre specialists cannot always embrace the entirety of a complex and varied field. Thus, a devotee of the Classic English Ghost Story will decline to include anything written after the First World War, while a disciple of the Cthulhu Mythos might omit any mention of the 18th-century Gothic novel. Even worse, an editor might include works *not* to his personal taste simply in order to be 'representative'. How many times have you come across: '*The Castle of Otranto* is turgid and unreadable, but we wouldn't be here without it, so here's an in-depth analysis of how important it is . . . '?

Our solution was to invite one hundred of the world's top horror, science fiction and fantasy authors and critics to contribute a brief essay on his or her favourite horror book. This, we thought, would make for a genuinely representative, though eclectic and controversial selection. Writers could acknowledge a debt of gratitude to those titles or authors that first inspired them to reach for the pen or switch on the word-processor. Or put forward a case for an unjustly neglected work, or even for an out-of-genre book that struck them as too horrific to escape our categorisation. We sent out rough guidelines, and they could pick any book from any date. It might have been long out-of-print or a recent best-seller. We expected people to suggest novels, anthologies or collections, we didn't mind plays or published screenplays, and we would have accepted poetry if anyone had lighted on Coleridge, Beaudelaire of Poe (no one did). We forgot to include the word 'fiction' in our original letter, and so one cleverclogs (it was John M. Ford) tried to slip in Herman Kahn's *On Thermonuclear War*. We are pleased that our final representation includes Jacobean Revenge Tragedies, gothic novels, literary classics, science fiction, detective stories, westerns, war novels, surrealist fantasies, pulp horror and major works of modern fiction. William Shakespeare, Herman Melville, Joseph Conrad, William Golding, John Brunner, C. S. Lewis and Peter Ackroyd may be surprised to find themselves in company with Edgar Allan Poe, Bram Stoker, Arthur Machen, Richard Matheson, Stephen King, Richard Laymon, and Clive Barker, but read the pieces and you'll see how they earned their places there.

We started by approaching considerably more than the 100 contributors we needed, and got predictably mixed results. Many never replied. Others were too busy to contribute. Some wrote polite letters thanking us for the invitation, but declining on the basis that they knew nothing about horror (a number of those will find their own novels discussed in the text). A couple were just plain rude. If your favourite horror writer isn't here, we're sorry. But the majority of people did get back to us, and that's when the real problems began. It's surprising to learn just how many authors retain a lifelong affection for the stories of M. R. James or H. P. Lovecraft, or such books as *Dracula* and *The Haunting of Hill House*. We could easily have put out a volume containing ten different appreciations of each of these. Also, there were contributors who hinted—often not too subtly—that perhaps *their* books should have been included in our preliminary list of suggestions. One American writer was terribly enthusiastic about the project until he discovered we didn't want him to write about his *own* best book. Harlan Ellison re-read his childhood favourite novel (*The Edge of Running Water* by William Sloane) and now blames us for destroying his beautiful memory of a book that he now thinks is pretty rotten. Rob Holdstock kept re-reading books that influenced him and finding they weren't that horrific after all. We learned that being an editor also involves a working knowledge of diplomacy.

Then, putting aside such mundane considerations as contracts, sub-clauses and deadlines, there was the problem of those classics of the genre that none of our 100 wanted to write about. As you might expect, the random method of asking people for their favourites meant that a number of books everyone would put in their Top Ten didn't quite make it. So major books like *Rosemary's Baby*, *The Vampire Tapestry* and *Fevre Dream*, and prominent authors like James Herbert, Thomas Tryon and Michael McDowell sadly don't get a look in. It's also why we've compiled a Recommended Reading list and fairly inclusive notes on the works of our contributors. Once you've finished reading all 100 of the books discussed in the main text, you should start working your way through our secondary list. *Then* you'll be an expert. You can be excused *The Castle of Otranto* if you've got a note from your mother.

We hope this book is informative, and fun. It should offer a guide for the relative newcomer to the subject, but also some meat for the veteran afficionado. It was a logistical nightmare to compile, but we hope we've succeeded in giving a working overview of an often-maligned field of literature.

Anyway, the *real* problem was getting all the contributor's signatures for the special limited edition . . .

Stephen Jones and Kim Newman
London, March 1988

CHRISTOPHER MARLOWE

The Tragical History of Dr Faustus

Dr Faustus *is generally believed to have been written in the last year of Marlowe's life, well after his* Tamburlaine *(1587) and* The Jew of Malta *(1589?). Marlowe based his work on what was supposed to have happened to a German necromancer of the 16th century. It's a legend that has inspired many other works of art, most notably Goethe's play* Faust *(1808), the operas by Arrigo Boito (*Mefistofele, *1868) and Charles Gounod (1860), and various pieces of music by Berlioz, Wagner, Liszt, Schumann and Louis Spohr. Marlowe's play, directed by Richard Burton and Neville Coghill, was filmed in 1967, with Burton as Faustus and Elizabeth Taylor as a silent Helen of Troy. Notable performances in the play in the 20th century, either as Faustus or Mephistophiles, have been given by D. A. Clarke-Smith, Noel Willman, Robert Harris, Hugh Griffith, Cedric Hardwicke, Paul Daneman, Michael Goodliffe, Orson Welles, Jack Carter and Ben Kingsley.*

It is not that the old stories are necessarily the *best* stories; rather that the old stories are the *only* stories. There are no new tales, only new ways to tell. Such, at least, is the conviction of many who have studied narrative. I'd count myself amongst their clan.

For the writer this presents certain challenges, not the least of which is the shaping of a fresh and original interpretation of a structure which may have been cast and re-cast several hundred times down the centuries. The problem is particularly acute when working in a *genre* that boasts a very clear line of tradition, as does horror. Write a vampire story and you may be certain it will be compared with countless others in the family, and if you've failed to bring anything new to the lineage you'll be judged accordingly.

In that challenge, of course, lies the greatest spur to invention, and high times can follow, as the writer drives his imagination to new extremes of form and content, honing his vision so that whatever else may be said of the resulting work it can at least be called uniquely *his*.

But there's a greater pleasure yet. In travelling the road of a particular story—along which every town will have streets and squares in common, yet none looks quite like the other—the writer may see, with a backward glance, the way the essentials of the tale have been reinterpreted over the years, subtly changing to reflect the interior lives of those who've gone before. The road becomes an index to the blossoming and decay of belief-systems; a book, if you will, of books, in which the subject is both the history of story and the story of history.

Perhaps, if he's far-sighted, the writer, looking back along the road he's travelling, may even glimpse its beginnings (or at least the rocky place from which it emerged), and be enriched by recognition of why the tale he's reinterpreting was first created.

The story of the ambitious man, brought down through an excess of pride, or curiosity, or half a dozen other sweetly human qualities, is one part of the story I'm celebrating here. The other part concerns intercourse with hellish divinities. It tells of a shaman who touches an inner darkness—a forbidden place that promises dangerous knowledge—and is snatched off by the very forces he's hoped to control. Put together, these elements form the Faust myth. Baldly put, Faust's (or Faustus's) story is that of a brilliant, ambitious academic who sells his soul to the Devil in exchange for insights and experiences he believes he can gain no other way, and later—as the time for payment approaches—regrets the terms of the deal, and attempts to escape damnation.

I first encountered this story in Marlowe's variation, and though I later read other versions—Goethe's, most significantly—it is that first meeting that claims greatest hold on my affections. I was as ravished by the splendours of the play as Marlowe's Doctor is by magic, which he believes will show him the secrets of the stars, and of men's souls. I had the same hopes of art; still do, in fact. But while a book is readily bought, a play or a painting easily viewed, Faustus—to gain *his* magic—must sign in blood, and give his soul over to Lucifer for all eternity. Not so hard. This is a man who has studied until study can reward him no longer. A man to whom science has become a cul-de-sac, philosophy a dead library, and who wants to drag the walls and the words down and see the world for himself. It's little wonder that Mephistopheles' warnings cannot deter this hungry adventurer from the trip.

To evoke the pleasure of what follows, Marlowe uses his prodigious poetic gifts (which were silenced too quickly: he died at twenty-nine, stabbed in the eye in a brawl that may have been staged to conceal an assassination). Here Faustus looks on the beauty of Helen of Troy, raised from the past for his delectation:

> 'Was this the face that launch'd a thousand ships,
> And burnt the topless towers of Ilium?
> Sweet Helen, make me immortal with a kiss.'

It's the word-music that ensured Marlowe's immortality, not the kisses. (There's a lesson there, damn it.) Later in the play that same genius conjures Faustus' terror as damnation approaches:

> 'You stars that reign'd at my nativity,
> Whose influence hath allotted death and hell,

> *Now draw up Faustus like a foggy mist*
> *Into the entrails of yon labouring cloud.'*

He is not drawn up, needless to say. *'Ugly hell'* gapes, and the Devil claims his due, leaving Faustus' servants and ex-students to pick up the pieces, literally. Whereas Goethe saves his adventurer with love and metaphysics, Marlowe has his Doctor beg for forgiveness—

> *'See, see, where Christ's blood streams in the firmament!*
> *One drop would save my soul. . . .'*

—but here his pleas go unanswered.

The play thus moves through a strikingly diverse series of modes, from the early scenes of debate, to invocation, and temptation; then through masque, high poetry and low comedy as Faustus' years of experience pass; finally into melancholy and despair. Behind it all Marlowe's subversive vision is at work. This is the man reputed to have claimed that 'whoso liketh not tobacco and boys is a fool', and who would die as he lived, in a passion. That heat—that sense of momentum—turns his version of the Faust story into a headlong plunge, as exhilarating as it is tragic. Goethe's treatment may be more philosophically complex, and arguably contains characters more sensitively drawn; it is *certainly* the more humane of the two interpretations. But Marlowe's variation values theatricality and poetic dazzle over moral texture, and the kid I was when I first read it liked the choice. He still does. Maybe in my dotage I'll be more profoundly moved by Goethe's brilliantly argued case for the redeemability of the human spirit (indeed, I may need its reassurances), but I'm still too close to Marlowe in age and temper to relinquish my first love.

What delights me, finally, is to have a choice of versions. I've even added a few variations to the canon of Faust tales myself. 'The Damnation Game', 'The Hellbound Heart' and 'The Last Illusion' are all conscious strivings to make sense of the story for a late-20th-century readership. *Hell*, I point out in 'The Damnation Game', *is reimagined by each generation*. So are the pacts, and the pact-makers. But the story will survive any and all reworkings, however radical, because its roots are so strong. That far-sighted backward glance I spoke of earlier—the one that leads back to the rocky place—shows us in the Faust tale one of the most important roads in all fantastic fiction. At its centre is a notion essential to the horror genre and its relations: that of a trip taken into forbidden territory at the risk of insanity and death. With the gods in retreat, and the idea of purgatorial judgments less acceptable to the modern mind than new adventures after death as dust and spirit, all imaginative accounts of that journey become essential reading. In their diversity lies testament to the richness of our literature's heritage. In their experiencing, a sense of how the human perspective changes. And in their wisdom—who knows?—a guide to how we, adventurers in the forbidden magic of our *genre*, may behave when the last Act is upon us.

—CLIVE BARKER

2   [1606]

WILLIAM SHAKESPEARE

The Tragedy of Macbeth

Scotland. Macbeth, Thane of Glamis, a loyal subject of King Duncan, meets three Witches on a blasted heath. They prophesy that he will become Thane of Cawdor and then King, and that his comrade Banquo will sire a line of kings. Macbeth is immediately made Thane of Cawdor by Duncan, and is inspired—partly by the witches, partly by his wife, partly by his own ambition—to plot the murder of Duncan. He becomes king, but tries to prove the witches false by murdering Banquo and thus ensuring his own family will succeed him. Visiting the witches again, he receives further prophecies that suggest he is invincible—he cannot be killed by a man born of woman, and he will not be unthroned unless Birnam Wood marches upon Dunsinane castle. However, while his wife is driven mad by guilt, Macbeth sees each of the further prophecies come true—Banquo's sons escape him to become the ancestors of James I of England (recently crowned when the play was being written), his enemies use the cut-down trees of Birnam as shields when they advance on the castle, and he faces in battle Macduff, who was born by Caesarian.

A really serious crime, in the long run, leads to temporal retribution and possible damnation.

I have tried to use such a theme many times personally, and though I am no Shakespearean scholar, I believe that one must realize how grave the Macbeths' crimes were. In Shakespeare's day, regicide was regarded as the worst crime of all, as the king or queen was God's consort on Earth. Duncan was also a good ruler who

> 'Hath borne his faculties so meek,
> Hath been so clear in his great office
> That his virtues
> Will plead like angels, trumpet-tongued against
> The *deep damnation* of his taking-off.'

Macbeth was assured by the witches that he need fear nothing unless

14

Birnam Wood came to Dunsinane and he was opposed by a man not born of woman. The witches were equivocators and this point is explained by the drunken porter at the castle gate: 'Lechery, it provokes and unprovokes; it provokes the desire, but it takes away the performance. Therefore much drink may be said to be an equivocator with Lechery: it makes him, and it mars him . . .'

By the witches' own forecast, Banquo was ordained the father of a line of kings and this prediction is repeated after his murder, so Macbeth sees his original crime as fruitless, and he and Lady Macbeth are driven mad by guilt. His wife commits suicide and he accepts the news briefly. 'She should have died hereafter. There would have been time for such a word . . .' Only at the very end, when the witches' falsehood is finally revealed, does Macbeth come to terms with reality and realize the truth.

> 'Though Birnam Wood be come to Dunsinane
> And though opposed being by no woman born
> Yet will I try the last. Before my body
> I throw my warlike shield. Lay on, Macduff,
> And damned be he who first cries "hold, enough".'

According to Aristotle, the word 'tragedy' means 'arousing pity and terror'. The play succeeds in both respects. To my mind, *Macbeth*'s plot makes the play one of the best thrillers in our language and to this is added some of the finest poetry ever written. A truly magnificent feast.

—JOHN BLACKBURN

3   [1612]

JOHN WEBSTER

The White Devil

The White Divel, or, The Tragedy of Paulo Giordano Urfini, Duke of Brachiano, with The Life and Death of Vittoria Corombona the famous Venetian Curtizan *is a Jacobean Revenge Tragedy complete with poisonings, multiple murders, a scheming villain, a tragic villain, ghosts, intrigues, a crime-busting Pope, and a vengeance-crazed pirate. Webster (1580–1634) was also the author of* The Duchess of Malfi *(1614), an even more gruesome tragedy, and skull* The Devil's Law-Case *(1620), a twisted comedy. A gloomy misanthrope who complains in his preface about the rabble's lack of enthusiasm for the play, Webster was characterized famously by T. S. Eliot as seeing 'the skull beneath the skin'.*

I have always found your actual werewolves, vampires and devils rather boring. *The White Devil* is to me true horror because all these creatures are present in it, and ghosts too, but as human beings. It is also full of graveyard humour which is hysterically funny, much of it centering on Flamineo, who is my favourite villain—witty, neurasthenic and utterly selfish.

There are only two 'good' characters: Vittoria's brother Marcello, who is too stupid to be otherwise, and the boy Giovanni. All the others go in for quasi-virtuous acts that damn them. At the start of the play Corinna curses her children with a big display of outrage, and the curse works (this is the main undercover supernatural theme). Isabella, with an equal display of virtue, pretends to hate her husband and gets murdered for it—with justice because she talks witchcraft. The talk is always a giveaway. It flickers by, savage and vivid, subliminally dubbing Isabella a witch, Corinna a witch, invoking arcane herb lore, linking Brachiano with the devil and calling Flamineo wolf, wolf, wolf, until it rises to the spell Corinna chants over her dead son, in which she all but names Flamineo the werewolf he is.

Under the influence of Vittoria, the Pope reveals himself fascinated with vice and the Duke of Florence ends up (literally) black. Brachiano, basically a coarse-grained man bored with his wife, commits murder and then dabbles in Satanism by employing a conjuror. His death—*On pain of death, let no man name death to me; It is a word infinitely terrible*—surrounded by imaginary horrors—*Look you, six grey rats that have lost their tails Crawl up the pillow*—is a real spine-chiller.

By a bold stroke, Vittoria herself, the vampire woman at the centre, is decidely understated. Her character emerges mostly from the disgusted reactions of the rest, even her brother Flamineo, who behave as if they are trying to detach a leech. But the talk is again a giveaway. As her lover dies, all she can say is *I am lost for ever!* Everything else she says is equally self-centred. And vampire she is. Right at the end when she has run out of victims and is about to be killed, she says she is pale *from want of blood*.

And the boy Giovanni? He becomes Duke of Padua at the end and orders the murderers tortured with sanctimonious relish. As Flamineo remarks, his talons will grow out in time, and here we see them sprouting.

—DIANA WYNNE JONES

WILLIAM GODWIN

Things As They Are; or: The Adventures of Caleb Williams

Caleb Williams, an honest young man, takes a position as secretary to Ferdinando Falkland, the landowner upon whose property the Williams family resides. Although treated kindly by Mr Falkland, Caleb is warned to stay away from a certain room in which the master keeps a mysterious trunk. Unable to contain his curiosity, Caleb investigates and learns that Falkland is a murderer. However, their respective social positions ensure that Falkland goes uncharged and Caleb is ruined. Caleb loses his job and becomes an outcast, persecuted by his former master, and is thrown in with thieves and murderers. His ordeal takes him from the melodramatic Gothic horrors of Falkland's gloomy old house with its terrible secret to the all-too-real hell of the underside of 18th-century England. Godwin, a reformer best known for his Enquiry Concerning Political Justice (1793), here prefigures Dickens by straddling the genres of gruesome thriller and social exposé. His daughter was Mary Shelley, author of Frankenstein.

> There is a sort of domestic tactics, the object of which is to elude curiosity, and keep up the tenor of the conversation, without the disclosure of our feelings or opinions. The friends of justice will have no object more deeply at heart, than the annihilation of this duplicity.... It follows, that the promoting the best interests of mankind, eminently depends upon the freedom of social communication....
>
> William Godwin, *An Enquiry Concerning Political Justice*

During the year he finished writing *Things As They Are; or: The Adventures of Caleb Williams*, many of William Godwin's radical friends and associates were either in jail or awaiting trial for treason. While these radicals advocated democratic equality, aristocratic government deployed its privileged machinery of coercion and law. Radicals believed men found the Truth inside their own classless human heart, but aristocratic government preferred its exterior distinctions of family name, property and station. Radicals sought to unveil the common 'nature' of democratic Man, while government sought to veil that nature, if not immure it.

For Godwin, as for Caleb, truth does not belong to the world of appearances, but to the world's repressed heart; in order to achieve justice, one must penetrate the corrupt duplicity of government and gaze into the hearts of the men who run it. As Godwin wrote in his *Enquiry* only a few years before completing *Things As They Are*:

> One of the most essential ingredients in a virtuous character, is undaunted firmness; and nothing can more powerfully tend to destroy this principle than the spirit of monarchical government. The first lesson of virtue is, Fear no man; the first lesson of such a constitution is, Fear the King.

In Godwin's universe, terror belongs to the surface world of politics, not to the dark primitive world of Man's unconscious. Prisons, disguise, and aristocratic reputation pursue Caleb across a landscape made horrible by the very absence of man's super-natural Reason. Political corruption for Godwin is not, as our modern age might try to argue, a thing of the human heart, but rather of the human heart's confinement; Caleb is never pursued by evil men so much as he conspires with the scheme of his own persecution. By refusing to disclose his knowledge of Falkland's crimes, Caleb commits himself to a prison of silence. By adopting disguise, Caleb makes himself subject to criminals disguised as police and government officials. Like the prison reformer Jeremy Bentham, Godwin believes even prisons should be made accessible to public inspection, just as the secrets of Falkland's padlocked trunk implicitly demand Caleb's compulsive investigation.

Godwin's great novel does not designate heroes and villains, but rather widespread political conditions. Repressed by political injustice, individual selves diminish and collapse; in a corrupt world, all men suffer, regardless of class or distinction. 'I began these memoirs with the idea of vindicating my character,' Caleb concludes. 'I have now no character that I wish to vindicate.' Caleb cannot 'win' his final confrontation with Falkland while the political world which created Falkland endures. Without the freedom of open democratic discourse, individual 'character' lacks meaning or definition. When for two hundred years critics reduced *Things As They Are* to a 'psychological romance' entitled *Caleb Williams*, they disregarded Godwin's most fundamental belief: that terror is not a product of the human mind, but of political men.

—SCOTT BRADFIELD

MATTHEW GREGORY LEWIS

The Monk: A Romance

Madrid, c. 1600. Ambrosio, the impossibly saintly abbot of the Capuchin order, is visited by a demon in the form of Matilda, a young and lovely woman who enters the monastery disguised as a novice. She seduces Ambrosio, and encourages him to plumb the depths of degradation. He is led unknowingly to rape his sister and murder his mother, and a final confrontation with Lucifer himself leaves Ambrosio's broken and bleeding corpse to the insects. Sub-plots, essential to a Gothic novel, feature the Wandering Jew and a sad spectre known as the Bleeding Nun. By going beyond the comparatively polite horrors of Mrs Radcliffe and Horace Walpole, Lewis earned the admiration of such figures as Byron and de Sade, the displeasure of many 'respectable' folks, and a nickname, 'Monk', that stayed with him to the grave. The Monk, his first novel, was written before Lewis' 21st birthday; he followed it with a succession of lesser romances, tales and plays, including The Castle Spectre *(1797),* Tales of Terror *(1799),* The Bravo of Venice *(1805), and* One O'Clock, or The Knight and Wooddemon *(1811).*

*T*he Monk, although it was published almost two hundred years ago, in 1796, may legitimately claim to be the first modern horror novel in the English language. Predecessors like Horace Walpole and Ann Radcliffe had pioneered the Gothic tale, but the stories they told tended to be distressingly genteel and moralistic. This was not enough for Matthew Gregory Lewis, who, while little more than a boy, produced a work that was outrageous, offensive, and obnoxious, one that still demonstrates its power to dismay. A standard history of English literature claims that it exhibits 'the perverted lust of a sadist'. Can there be a higher recommendation?

Set in the early 17th century, *The Monk* was a period piece even in 1796, yet it contains enough bad attitudes to raise a few hackles even today. Attacked for obscenity and blasphemy, the book was censored in its later editions, in no small measure because it had been revealed that the writer, who penned the novel at the tender age of nineteen, had recently become a Member of Parliament. The author's youth is ultimately more important than his government credentials, for this is a work of enthusiasm and excess, its audacity and adolescence speaking to and for the audience that has always eagerly embraced the horrific.

The Monk sneers at convention: its episodes include dead babies, mangled nuns, murdered mothers, deflowered virgins, and sex-crazed clergymen. This is the sort of material that 20th-century artists have frequently flaunted to provide their own emblems of emancipation, but Lewis had staked out the territory long before the grandparents of his followers were born.

Such calculated bad taste made Lewis a celebrity in his time, yet he also embodied the essential paradox of the horror writer: contemporaries from Lord Byron to Sir Walter Scott describe him as an honorable and kindly man. Literary historians have reduced him to the catalyst whose personal influence inspired Polidori's *The Vampyre* and Mary Shelley's *Frankenstein*, but in his lifetime he was recognized for his own achievements, and rightly so. Lewis cut to the bone.

In the depraved monk Ambrosio, Lewis created a character that speaks uneasily to readers centuries later. Ambrosio is Faustian, in the traditional mode, but he represents not the lust for power, or the lust for money, or even the lust for knowledge. What he displays, embarrassingly but importantly, is the lust for lust. He is the forefather of a roster of lascivious villains from Dracula through Norman Bates to Freddy Krueger.

Despite its overblown language and its overstrained coincidences, *The Monk* is a revolutionary work. It defies polite society, and it also challenges the limits of its genre. The evil in this tale is not exterior, an outside outrage to be subdued by the representatives of civility and good taste. Rather, the evil is within its protagonist, and there is no bland embodiment of virtue to stand in his path. The evil runs its course, consuming itself rather than facing defeat from the forces of conformity. This is not melodrama, but tragedy, and as such it shames most of the popular 20th-century terror tales whose only drive is to enforce the status quo.

Lewis wanted to see how far he could go, and he went there. In a time when we are confronted with a flood of reassuring horror stories, each one promising its readers that everything awful exists only in others, the courage that Lewis displayed shines like a bloody beacon.

And any book with a character called The Bleeding Nun can't be all bad.

—LES DANIELS

E. T. A. HOFFMANN

The Best Tales of Hoffmann

Ernst Theodor Amadeus Hoffmann never put his name to a collection under the title Tales of Hoffmann, *but since the success of Jacques Offenbach's opera* Les Contes d'Hoffmann *(1881), there have been several competing volumes under variations of the name, including R. J. Hollingdale's* Tales of Hoffmann *(1932), Leonard J. Kent and Elizabeth C. Knight's* Tales of E. T. A. Hoffmann *(1972), and Victor Lange's* Tales *(1982). The volume discussed here is E. F. Bleiler's selection,* The Best Tales of Hoffmann. *In Hoffmann's lifetime (1776–1822), his short horror pieces appeared in* Fantasiestücke in Callots Manier *(4 vols, 1814–15) and* Nachtstücke *(1816), although several of his best-known works — 'The Golden Flowerpot', 'The Sand-Man' — were not published until after his death. Hoffmann's major horror novels are* Die Elixier des Teufels *(1815–16) and* Lebensansichten des Katers Murr *(1821– 22). Offenbach's opera was marvellously filmed in 1951 by Michael Powell and Emeric Pressburger, with Moira Shearer outstanding as Olimpia the Automaton.*

This collection includes 'The Sand-Man', the best-known of Hoffmann's stories, as well as 'The Golden Flowerpot', a lavish alchemical tale whose passages of vivid fantasy brought grudging praise from Goethe. These and most of the remaining eight tales are unrolled like dreams, with all of the humor, horror, and superreality dreams require.

In 'Rath Krespin', a man collects rare violins only to dismantle them. A miser meets his doppelgänger ('Signor Formica'). A machine whispers prophecies ('Automata'). A divinity student falls under the spell of a blue-eyed snake ('The Golden Flowerpot'). A miner is lured to his death by the glowing face of the Metal Queen ('The Mines of Falun'). In a comic-horrific tale 'The King's Betrothed', a woman finds herself engaged to a carrot.

But the deepest nightmare here is the 'The Sand-Man'. This dark tale was written in 1816, two years before Mary Shelley's *Frankenstein*, in a similar spirit of horrified fascination with science and its application to artificial life. Hoffmann is concerned with the horror of automata indistinguishable from real people.

In 'The Sand-Man', the nightmare is relentless. It begins with a child's confusion. A cruel nurse tells young Nathanael that the Sand-man 'comes to little children when they won't go to bed and throws handfuls of sand in their eyes, so that they jump our of their heads all bloody'. He believes the Sand-man is the lawyer Coppelius, who comes to the house nightly to visit his father on some mysterious errand.

Later the child realizes the Sand-man is only a story, but he also senses that Coppelius has some unpleasant hold over his parents. The child hides and sees the men engaged in some secret experiment involving a forge and glowing metal. When Nathanael is discovered, Coppelius threatens to put out his eyes.

In a later, 'last' experiment, the secret forge explodes, killing Nathanael's father. Coppelius disappears.

Grown-up Nathanael attends a distant university. One day a peddler comes to his room, selling barometers and thermometers. The peddler looks like the sinister Coppelius and calls himself Coppola. All the old nameless fears are aroused.

Nathanael quarrels with his fiancée. He soon becomes intrigued by the vision of Olimpia, the rather inert, beautiful daughter of his physics professor, Spalanzani. The professor lives across the street, and Nathanael can see Olimpia through a window. The peddler returns, offering to sell him spectacles, which he calls 'eyes, fine eyes'. He lays out hundreds of glittering samples—fiery glass lenses like eyes staring back at the horrified Nathanael. He buys a telescope, which he uses to spy on Olimpia. His interest deepens to obsession.

Finally Nathanael meets Olimpia at a ball. She plays piano, sings, and dances well, if soullessly, but she hardly speaks. Others at the ball decide that she is either a wooden doll or simpleminded.

Nevertheless, Nathanael pursues his fatal obsession. One night as he is paying a visit to give her a ring, he overhears a quarrel between Spalanzani and Coppelius. He walks in to find them ripping Olimpia apart: Spalanzani reclaims the clockwork he constructed, while Coppelius owns her beautiful glass eyes. After a fight, Coppelius departs with the doll—leaving its glass eyes on the floor. In frustration, Spalanzani picks up the eyes and throws them at Nathanael.

Nathanael goes mad, but his fiancée Clara nurses him back to health. Later they go up to a clock tower to look at the city. Nathanael puts the accursed telescope to his eye, and goes mad once more. He tries to kill Clara, and finally throws himself from the tower.

As in a dream, it is never clear whether Coppelius and Coppola are one man or two; are they split in reality, or only in the divided mind of Nathanael? We are never sure what the mysterious alchemical experiment might be, nor what hold Coppelius had over Nathanael's parents. Facts become lost in Nathanael's mad dream, in which we share. And perhaps that is what is most horrifying about this tale—we dream it ourselves. Hoffmann's mixture of magic and madness is experienced from inside.

Ernst Theodor Amadeus Hoffmann (1776–1822) was the first Late

Romantic writer. His tales profoundly influenced European and American literature, and that most literary of medical arts, psychoanalysis. He was also a composer and conductor, an influential music critic (the first to appreciate J. S. Bach), and a judge. Many of his tales were appropriated for operas and ballets, including *Coppelia*, *The Nutcracker*, and *Tales of Hoffmann*. The *Sand-Man* theme of heartless automata appears in the film *Metropolis* and in much modern science fiction.

—JOHN SLADEK

7   [1817]

JANE AUSTEN

Northanger Abbey

Catherine Morland, a sensitive young girl much given to devouring sentimental Gothic romances of the type popularized by Mrs Radcliffe, comes to Bath to stay with family friends. In the whirl of society, she meets two sets of duplicitous people—the parvenu fortune-hunting Thorpes and the more mysterious, romantic Tilneys. Although she soon sees through the Thorpes, she is lured by her fanciful notions of the romantic life to spend some time at Northanger Abbey, the gloomy ancestral home of the Tilneys. Misled by the likes of Necromancer of the Black Forest *(1794) and* Horrid Mysteries *(1796), Catherine comes to see General Tilney as a villain in the Radcliffian sense and suspect that he has murdered his wife, but eventually a more prosaic—if still ignoble—motive emerges for his attentions. However, the General's son Henry proves a suitable romantic hero and does finally win Catherine's hand. Written sometime in the 1790s under the title* Susan *and sold in 1803 (for £10) to a publisher who didn't bother to issue it,* Northanger Abbey *did not appear in print until a few months after the author's death. It has been adapted for the stage, radio and television several times, most notably as a BBC-TV film with Robert Hardy and Katherine Schlesinger in 1987.*

At the end of the 1970s, when I was struggling to write the novel that would get me into screenwriting, I scrawled in a notebook in huge capitals: NORMAL!TY FOR HORROR! DETAIL, RESEARCH, CHARACTER, BACKGROUND. THE ABNORMAL ONLY HAS

23

MEANING WITHIN THE CONTEXT (DETAILED, PRO-
LONGED) OF THE NORMAL.

I still believe it. I was reading *'Salem's Lot* at the time and it amazed me
how Stephen King's astonishing capacity for endless ordinary details
enabled him to make such a huge success out of what was an almost
indecently ancient vampire plot. It was obvious that when the man
adapted the technique to a really good plot he would produce a classic
and he did it with *The Shining*.

Almost by definition horror needs rules, because it thrives on the
breaking of rules. It needs a sharp sense of everyday reality so that when
the lights go off you really take notice. This is why so many of the
greatest horror writers have made a detour into the genre from other
kinds of writing and perhaps the most distinguished recruit of all was
Jane Austen.

No writer in literary history observed the rules and regulations of
polite society as acutely as Austen, so it's not surprising that she was also
the first writer to see the subversive potential in horror fiction. She
deliberately plotted *Northanger Abbey* so that the notions of Gothic
horror fiction and of civilized society come into direct collision. Her
heroine Catherine Morland is a horror fan whose imagination keeps
running away with her. She sees the most innocuous Sunday afternoon
walk as a potential abduction, laundry lists become secret manuscripts,
country houses turn into Gothic castles. Austen milks the suspense and
the humour to superb effect, but then steers the book to a point where
Catherine's horrific perception is truer than anyone else's. 'In suspecting
General Tilney of either murdering or shutting up his wife', she
concludes, 'Catherine had scarcely sinned against his character or
magnified his cruelty.'

Northanger Abbey is often portrayed wrongly as a spoof. It obviously
gave Austen a lot of fun but it was nothing of the kind. Not only does the
author step out of the novel to deliver a ringing endorsement of Gothic
fiction. But all the book's humour, all its thrills, all its truth comes from
the Gothic world's conquest of the everyday. Women may not regularly
be abducted to ruined abbeys by villains in black cowls but Austen is
intent on showing us just how well that metaphor conveys the emotional
cruelty of polite society. The Gothic perception wins.

—DAVID PIRIE

MARY WOLLSTONECRAFT SHELLEY

Frankenstein: or, The Modern Prometheus

In the Arctic, Captain Walton, an English explorer, takes aboard ship a manic young man, Victor Frankenstein, who recounts the circumstances that have brought him to the ends of the earth. Frankenstein tells of his experiments with the creation of life, and his construction of a huge, manlike creature whose repulsive aspect leads his creator to reject him. The Monster later returns to Frankenstein and tells of his sufferings at the hands of humanity and begs the scientist to make him a mate to ease his loneliness. Frankenstein agrees but abandons the project in horror, and the Monster retaliates by murdering his maker's friends and family. Frankenstein pursues the Monster north, but dies on the ship after his story is finished. The Monster pays his last respects and then vanishes into the wastes. Frankenstein is at once a Gothic horror tale and the first important science fiction novel. Its sustained popularity and place in modern myth is probably as much due to the innumerable stage, film, television, comic book and radio adaptations of it—most of which depart completely from the text—as to the strengths of the work itself.

Subtitled *The Modern Prometheus*, Mary Shelley's masterwork is a remarkable book. Blending as it does allegory with Gothic elements, storytelling with philosophy, it is all the more remarkable because Mary Shelley completed it before her 20th birthday.

Stated bluntly, this 'pseudoscientific novel', as it has been called, is about a scientist usurping nature and God's creative powers, and the terrible consequences that follow that act. Written as a gloss on or as a rejoinder to Milton's *Paradise Lost*, the book is full of grotesque, dreamlike imagery, and the wild chase across the Arctic that ends the novel is a phantasmagoric journey of the lost soul.

Mary Shelley, desiring to create a ghost story, wrote instead what Brian Aldiss calls 'the first ... science fiction', a novel which Shelley herself wanted to 'speak to the mysterious fears of our nature'. The novel was conceived in a dream in which she saw 'the hideous phantasm, of a man stretched out, and then, on the working of some powerful engine, show signs of life, and stir with an uneasy, half vital motion....' That dream followed long late night conversations with her husband, the poet Shelley, Lord Byron, and John Polidori, Byron's doctor. The conversations ranged through vampires, Darwin, and the supernatural and, at Byron's suggestion, they were to have a contest with the four of them writing ghost stories.

Mary Shelley's *Frankenstein* is an epistolary novel with overtones of the Gothic and the Romantic. While the implication is that the hero of the piece (or the anti-hero) is the young doctor Frankenstein, it is to the monster the modern reader more naturally turns. He has the most compelling speeches, is the wiser of the characters, and is the most noble in his own strange way. As Joyce Carol Oates has written of him, 'Surely one of the secrets of *Frankenstein*, which helps account for its abiding appeal, is the demon's patient, unquestioning, utterly faithful, and utterly *human* love for his irresponsible creator.'

Together Frankenstein the creator and the monster, his creation, are a whole: shadow selves. One does not exist without the other. It is why neither the monster nor Frankenstein's brides can last. The two—man and giant—need, deserve, and find one another. *'I shall be with you on your wedding night,'* the monster cries. It is a promise, horrendous in its outcome, but tauntingly sexual in its undertones.

Frankenstein was published anonymously in 1818 and republished—with some changes—under Mary Shelley's name and with an introduction in 1831. Movies, musicals, comic book versions, bowdlerized editions, have all made their mark on the *Frankenstein* story. In 1984, Barry Moser, America's premier wood engraver, created a limited illustrated version for his Pennyroyal Press based on the first edition. The book was later reprinted for the ordinary buyer by the University of California Press. The pictures provide an intelligent, handsome, and powerful gloss on the book. (There is also a fine if academic afterword by Joyce Carol Oates.) The strong black and whites of the main text are dark and brooding, with unremitting shadows and stark contrasts. But the central conversation with the monster—who owes nothing to the overused movie image of the creature with zipper scars and an oversized, blocky head but is rather the novel's charnel-house composite—is where Moser's illustrations show their greatest power. We see a skull with skin stretched over old bones, wisps of hair, protruding teeth. Taken together, the pictures give the impression of a monologue (which in fact is what that section of the book is). The viewer can all but smell the powerful stench of the monster's breath as its words spill out across the page. Strong book-making for one of the world's strongest and most remarkable books.

—JANE YOLEN

CHARLES MATURIN

Melmoth the Wanderer

Young John Melmoth attends the deathbed of his miserly uncle and is informed that a member of the family, also called John Melmoth, has been alive since the 16th century, wandering the Earth in search of someone willing to lay down their soul for him. This Melmoth has made a pact with the Devil, exchanging his soul for immortality, but can get out of it if he finds someone miserable enough to sell Melmoth his/her own soul. Young John examines manuscripts and seeks out old stories, and the novel presents several episodes in which Melmoth appears to those in need of aid and is rebuffed. During his quest, Melmoth encounters a sane man imprisoned in a vile insane asylum, a Spaniard entrapped by the Inquisiton, an Indian maid marooned on a desert island, a young girl forced to marry against her will, a German couple reduced to poverty and a pair of lovers dominated by a greedy mother. Finally, Melmoth returns to his estate and the Devil comes to collect his due. Maturin also wrote The Fatal Revenge, or the Family of Montorio *(1807) and* Albigenses *(1824).*

I was fourteen years old when I first discovered a copy of *Melmoth the Wanderer* in my father's library and tried to read it. 'Tried' because I was obviously not sufficiently mature to understand the complexities of that masterpiece of Gothic horror. I merely skipped a lot of pages to get down to the 'spooky bits'! However, since then I have read and re-read *Melmoth* many times and each time extracted nuggets of pure literary gold from what I have come to regard, with many others, as one of the great works of the horror genre of any generation.

Melmoth the Wanderer was published in 1820 when its author, Charles Robert Maturin, an Irish clergyman living in Dublin, was 40 years old. Maturin, who was to die four years later, had already established his reputation with several novels and plays which had brought him praise from literary luminaries such as Lord Byron and Sir Walter Scott. *Melmoth* was initially seen by its publisher Archibald Constable, as a competitor to Mary Shelley's *Frankenstein*, published two years earlier. However, the literary world soon realized that here was a work that needed no comparison with any other.

Melmoth combines all the Gothic terrors. It is replete with dungeons, castles, ghosts, cannibalism, monsters (both real and imaginary) and some truly monumental instances of terror. Walter Scott, Thackeray, Baudelaire, Rossetti and Honoré de Balzac were quick to hail it as a milestone of literature in any genre. Balzac, in those days before copyright, immediately wrote a sequel to the novel entitled *Melmoth Reconciled*, which was a little too whimsical to stand comparison with its progenitor.

The book was an instant success. Numerous editions, translations and a long-running dramatization quickly followed the initial publication.

H. P. Lovecraft, in acknowledging it as a masterpiece, has said that it made 'the Gothic tale climb to altitudes of sheer spiritual fright which it had never known before'. Professor Leonard Woolf has written that it has 'the most sustained and certainly the most complex vision of any Gothic fiction—not excepting *Dracula*.'

The Irish literary critic, Aódh De Blacam, in his *First Book of Irish Literature*, sees Maturin as 'manifestly in the tradition of Swift', another Dubliner. He goes on to say 'in works like this we see a definite vein of Irish genius, a horrific imagination which dramatizes the insane universe of the sceptic'. De Blacam went further and saw Maturin as the founder of the Irish school of horror fantasy writing in which he included later horror writers such as Fitzjames O'Brien, Sheridan Le Fanu, Bram Stoker and, much later, Dorothy Macardle (author of the classic *The Uninvited*). He argues that were it not for Maturin, then there might not have been such classics as *Carmilla*, or *Dracula*.

To this I would argue that were it not for *Melmoth the Wanderer*, there might not have been the classic *The Picture of Dorian Gray* (1891). Oscar Wilde, yet another Dubliner, was a great admirer of Maturin's work. In *Melmoth* there is reference to a portrait of 'J. Melmoth, 1648' hanging in an obscure closet in the ancient Melmoth mansion in Co. Wicklow. The portrait is the hidden reminder that Melmoth has lived nearly two centuries. Wilde took this theme and imbued it with his own genius to write his own vivid contribution to weird literature. Indeed, Wilde paid Maturin an unusual tribute in the fact that, during his last sad days in exile in Paris, he chose the name 'Sebastian Melmoth' as a pseudonym.

Melmoth is only fitfully in print. Critics and literary morticians often pay tribute to it but it seems that it is hardly ever read nowadays except by ardent fans of the genre. That is exceedingly sad. Even in my re-readings of it, there are passages which never fail to make my scalp itch, make a cold tingle send shivers down my back, make me peer nervously at the rattling windows and door of my room and make me edge nearer the cold circle of light from my reading lamp. *Melmoth*, even with the passage of time, remains an enduring masterpiece. It is a book which ought to be read by every aspiring writer in the genre, particularly today when so many are substituting technicolor gore for more literary qualities, such as the slow build up of tension and psychological fear, which seem so lacking in the genre today.

—PETER TREMAYNE

JAMES HOGG

The Private Memoirs And Confessions Of A Justified Sinner

17th-century Scotland. George Colwan, the well-liked heir of the Laird of Dalcastle, is systematically persecuted, abused and finally murdered by his half-brother Robert Wringhim. Wringhim becomes the Laird, but later hangs himself. A hundred years later, his strangely-preserved body is found, along with a written confession. Wringhim, a fanatical Calvinist, believes in his own predestined salvation and thus in his right to commit any atrocity and go unpunished. In this belief he is encouraged by Gil-Martin, a doppelgänger who may be the Devil. After Wringhim becomes Laird, he starts to be blamed for many crimes committed in his person by Gil-Martin and is finally driven to suicide. A powerful, ambiguous and surprisingly 'modern' novel, The Private Memoirs *(which has been published in abridged editions as* The Suicide's Grave *or* The Confessions of a Fanatic*) has been highly influential upon the visions of many, including Edgar Allan Poe and Robert Louis Stevenson. Innumerable 'doppelgänger' or 'duality of man' stories can trace their lineage back to Hogg, including incidentally Garry Kilworth's 'Dop*el-gan*er'.*

Central to *The Confessions Of A Justified Sinner* is the main character's belief in the pre-ordination of an élite group which, taken to extremes, provides him with an unassailable justification to commit murder without sinning. Since Robert Wringhim's life follows a predestined path, laid by God, all that he does has been sanctioned in heaven and is therefore 'right'. Thus, to kill one of the unchosen is merely to send a sinner to early judgement. Wringhim has a shapechanging adviser in these nefarious activities: his doppelgänger, Gil-Martin, the personification of the evil side of his own nature. Fratricide, matricide and just plain, ordinary homicide are rationalized by Gil-Martin and accepted by Wringhim as necessary *good works*, carried out in the Lord's name.

One of the effects of horror fiction is to give the Devil a face and a name, but still retain credibility of character. This is a difficult thing to do, without creating a monster which appears ridiculous. The Devil might be absurd and grotesque, but he must not appear foolish or invite laughter. With Gil-Martin, Hogg manages to instil dread without the loss of a demonic personality. Like many Gothic horror novels with a psychological base, this one immerses the reader in a dark well of chaos, where it is difficult to separate reason from insanity, and reversals of good and evil are backed by persuasive argument.

Certainly, the novel is chaotic. The narrative is erratic and, superficially at least, undisciplined, and it has more wildness and savagery than *Wuthering Heights*. What makes it stand out from other horror novels however, is its structure: a complicated, fractured affair, designed by Hogg to give the tale an appearance of authenticity. Hogg went to extraordinary lengths to make it appear as if the contained events actually occurred. A year before publication, which was initially anonymous, he wrote a letter to *Blackwood's Magazine* stating that a corpse, clutching a manuscript in its bony fingers, had been exhumed from a Scottish peat bog. An unnamed 'editor' was later supposed to have investigated this claim, relocated the grave and secured the document. Having read it, the editor questioned locals as to its authenticity. The editor even tells us he asked Hogg to lead him to the grave, but the author shut the croft door in his face.

The novel then, consists of *The Editor's Narrative*, covering half the book, followed by the *Sinner's Memoirs*, the manuscript found with the body, and following these, Hogg's original letter to *Blackwood's*. All of these 'documents' were of course written by Hogg himself.

The uneven, eccentric nature of the writing, the contradictions in the text, the conflicting testimonies of 'witnesses' to various murders, which appear in *The Editor's Narrative*, and the strangeness of the book's structure, all serve (whether intentionally or not) to immerse the reader in a tale of insanity, creating an atmosphere of dread and horror which gives the genre its name.

It was Hogg's best novel by far and he was even accused of being helped by another writer: a claim which his critics found difficult to prove and which has been subsequently discredited by modern-day academics.

—GARRY KILWORTH

11 [1833–47]

EDGAR ALLAN POE

Tales of Mystery and Imagination

The stories collected under the title Tales of Mystery and Imagination *first appeared in a variety of periodicals between 1833 and 1847 and mainly saw their first book publication in Poe's collections* Tales of the Grotesque and Arabesque *(1840) and* Tales of Edgar A. Poe *(1845). Besides the three C. Auguste Dupin detective stories and such classic tales of horror as 'The Fall of the House of Usher', 'The Black Cat', 'The Pit and the Pendulum', 'The Tell-Tale Heart', 'The Masque of the Red Death' and 'The Cask of Amontillado', the book includes a series of variations on the theme of the dead/deadly woman ('Ligeia', 'Morella', 'Berenice', 'Morella'), some classic adventures in the Verne mould ('The Gold Bug', 'A Descent into the Maelstrom'), a few philosophical pieces, two or three quaint but strained attempts at crackerbarrel humour and 'trick' tales of the type then popular ('The Sphinx', 'The Thousand-and-Second Tale of Scheherazade'). This diversity demonstrates that Poe was not only a major horror writer, but an important figure in American literature and a formative influence on both science fiction and the detective story.*

The raven remains on the door. The axe will not be drawn from the brain. The beat beneath the floorboards keeps getting louder.

There isn't anywhere you can go in this overcast, weedgrown, blood-fertilized field of ours that he hasn't been first: the chilly blue-lit corners, the arena of onstage violence, Poet's Corner, the comedy sideshow, the Vale of Things Man Was Not Meant to Know. In the perfumed, moldy halls of horror, he is the doorkeeper, the cartographer, and the resident ghost. (Edgar, now be still: we swiped not from Walpole or Stoker with half so good a will.)

There is no real fear, you see, in that which does not exist. The Elder Whats'ernames, the vampire or werewolf cinedenatured of their human origins, the retarded adolescent boogeyperson with all the world's cutlery at his disposal—who cares? But Edgar was scared of what was there. More importantly, he was scared of what hadn't arrived yet, but would.

Jeremy Bentham and his merry pranksters said that locking bad people up made them into good people. Edgar knew better, knew that one ought to be very sure that one's *anima* is dead before burying it. And now whole nations hear the scratch of bloody fingernails wanting Out, about to bring their houses down around the haunted palaces of their skulls.

Violence was something that low forms did, ugly hairy monstrosities, probably foreign and of peculiar religions. Edgar gave us ordinary people, the house-owners next door doing a bit of DIY remodelling: nervous, with their little tics, but certainly not mad, or at least ethically mad. (And when he *does* give us the hairy thing, it is a logical hairy thing, an innocent thing with its master's razor.)

Exploration was an adventure, and if the adventurers died it was boldly and clear-eyed. Edgar descended the Maelstrom and confronted Arthur Gordon Pym with something white beyond reason.

It was Edgar who exposed the elegant system of Dr Tarr and Professor

Fether, telling us that we would not always be able to tell the loonies from their keepers. It was Edgar who pointed out that Scheherezade was safe only as long as she spun fictions for the King.

Since even Edgar's black vision did not plumb the horrors of the bestseller system, he wrote whatever he pleased. Tales of Mystery? And *Imagination?* My God, Eddie, what rack of the bookstore are we gonna put *that* in? You're never going anywhere unless you get out of genre. . . .

He was also, when he felt like it, funny as hell. (Something that seems generally true of fear's fine technicians. The idiom may cut closer than it seems: if you don't see what's funny about hell, you'll never make it back to type up your report.)

Edgar told us what horror was, and where it comes from, and in terms that will carry the message as long as horror and its source exist: which is to say, as long as we are human. Here we sit, and the Raven has told us what to expect. We walk the decks, waiting for the tarred canvas to unfurl and spell out something meaningful. On we dance, against the arrival of the guest who wears no mask.

—JOHN M. FORD

12   [1837, expanded 1842]

NATHANIEL HAWTHORNE

Twice-Told Tales

Following in the literary footsteps of Washington Irving and Charles Brockden Brown, Nathaniel Hawthorne was instrumental in establishing a distinctively American tradition of ghost, horror and supernatural fiction. Twice-Told Tales features stories of apparitions, madness, revenge, witchcraft and proto-science fiction experimentation. His later collections in a similar vein were Mosses From an Old Manse (1846) and The Snow Image and Other Twice-Told Tales (1850), which contain such much-anthologized tales as 'Young Goodman Brown' and 'Ethan Brand'. Edgar Allan Poe praised Hawthorne's short stories well before the author attained prominence as a novelist with The Scarlet Letter (1850) and The House of the Seven Gables (1851). The 1963 film Twice-Told Tales, a Vincent Price vehicle conceived as an imitation of the Poe-derived Tales of Terror (1962), features adaptations of 'Dr Heidegger's Experiment', 'Rappacini's Daughter' and the prologue to The House of the Seven Gables.

W e have very few American tales of real merit—we may say, indeed, none, with the exception of *The Tales of a Traveller* of Washington Irving, and these *Twice-Told Tales* of Mr Hawthorne. Of Mr Hawthorne's Tales we would say, emphatically, that they belong to the highest region of Art—an Art subservient to genius of a very lofty order. We had supposed, with good reason for so supposing, that he had been thrust into his present position by one of those impudent *cliques* which beset our literature, and whose pretensions it is our full purpose to expose at the earliest opportunity; but we have been most agreeably mistaken. We know of few compositions which the critic can more honestly commend than these *Twice-Told Tales*. As Americans, we feel proud of the book.

Mr Hawthorne's distinctive trait is invention, creation, imagination, originality—a trait which, in the literature of fiction, is positively worth all the rest. But the nature of the originality, so far as regards its manifestation in letters, is but imperfectly understood. The inventive or original mind as frequently displays itself in novelty of *tone* as in novelty of matter. Mr Hawthorne is original in *all* points.

It would be a matter of some difficulty to designate the best of these tales; we repeat that, without exception, they are beautiful. 'Wakefield' is remarkable for the skill with which an old idea—a well-known incident—is worked up or discussed. A man of whims conceives the purpose of quitting his wife and residing *incognito* for twenty years in her immediate neighbourhood. Something of this kind actually happened in London. The force of Mr Hawthorne's tale lies in the analysis of the motives which must or might have impelled the husband to such folly, in the first instance, with the possible causes of his perseverance. Upon this thesis a sketch of singular power has been constructed. 'The Wedding Knell' is full of the boldest imagination—an imagination fully controlled by taste. The most captious critic could find no flaw in this production. 'The Minister's Black Veil' is a masterly composition of which the sole defect is that to the rabble its exquisite skill will be *caviare*. The *obvious* meaning of this article will be found to smother its insinuated one. The *moral* put into the mouth of the dying minister will be supposed to convey the *true* import of the narrative; and that a crime of dark dye (having reference to the 'young lady') has been committed, is a point which only minds congenial with that of the author will perceive. 'Mr Higginbotham's Catastrophe' is exceedingly well imagined, and executed with surpassing ability. The artist breathes in every line of it. 'The Old White Maid' is objectionable, even more than 'The Minister's Black Veil', on the score of its mysticism. Even with the thoughtful and analytic, there will be much trouble in penetrating its entire import.

'The Hollow of the Three Hills' we would quote in full, had we space;—not as evincing higher talent than any of the other pieces, but as affording an excellent example of the author's peculiar ability. The

33

subject is commonplace. A witch subjects the Distant and the Past to the view of a mourner. It has been the fashion to describe, in such cases, a mirror in which images of the absent appear; or a cloud of smoke is made to arise, and thence the figures are gradually unfolded. Mr Hawthorne has wonderfully heightened his effect by making the ear, in place of the eye, the medium by which the fantasy is conveyed. The head of the mourner is enveloped in the cloak of the witch, and within its magic folds there arise sounds which have an all-sufficient intelligence. Throughout this article also, the artist is conspicuous—not more in positive than in negative merits. Not only is all done that should be done (what perhaps is an end with more difficulty attained), there is nothing done which should not be. Every word *tells*, and there is not a word which does *not* tell.

—EDGAR ALLAN POE

13   [1842]

JEREMIAS GOTTHELF

The Black Spider

In an attempt to save her neighbours from the violence threatened by a band of tyrannical knights who rule the valley, Swiss midwife Christine strikes a bargain with the Devil. The Devil's kiss on Christine's cheek seals the agreement and the people are spared. However, the price—a newborn child—is too much for the woman to pay, and when the Devil is denied his due, he extracts a grisly revenge. A burning mark develops on Christine's cheek where she was kissed. It grows, swelling frightfully, taking the shape of a black spider. Finally, it erupts, unleashing masses of spiders that carry plague and hideous death throughout the valley. The horrid climax of the novel is strikingly similar to a sequence in John Schlesinger's film The Believers (1987), in which a spider-disgorging boil appears on the heroine's cheek.

First published in 1842, *The Black Spider* was largely ignored and forgotten until 1949, when Thomas Mann wrote about it with the highest praise. English translations soon followed and today readers can enjoy it as one of those relatively rare examples of an outstanding horror novel that deservedly ranks among the best of world literature.

The author, Albert Bitzius, was a Swiss pastor who chose to use a pseudonym and gained a measure of success with several lengthy novels of regional life written in a realistic manner. *The Black Spider* is quite different, and very special. Although it's a short novel it combines the plague tale, the historical legend and the religious parable with a quirky, personal style. The result is a work of both epic scope and driving immediacy, and even now it reads as a thoroughly modern piece of fiction.

That the midwife, motivated only by a desire to help, should be forced to act the mother in a bestial travesty of natural birth is one of the more disturbing ironies in this remarkable story. It is also one of the best early examples in literature of the human body being invaded by alien or demonic forces. The devil is eventually trapped, but it is a stalemate rather than a simple victory. Evil remains at hand, a constant threat and a dangerous temptation, as we are shown when there is a reprise of the terror two hundred years later.

There's much more to it than that, of course. *The Black Spider* is actually an artful, highly involved two-fold narrative couched in the kind of literary framework that Henry James used more than fifty years later in *The Turn of the Screw*, one that would become routine in countless tales of terror.

At times the writing is so casual as to appear slapdash, but any minor infelicities have the cunning effect of heightening tension and atmosphere, and the story never lets up, even though it ranges over a period of nearly six centuries. Gotthelf was not a craftsman but he was a spontaneous, intuitive writer who had a sure sense of what he was doing.

When *The Black Spider* first appeared its transparent religious lesson was no doubt taken as the whole point of the novel, and there's no denying it has an almost Biblical quality. That may be the least important side of it, however. *The Black Spider* is a richly suggestive work with clear political and even environmental overtones; it rewards attention at several different levels. But perhaps its greatest strength can be found in its very real, human characters and the emotional intensity of their terrible situation. *The Black Spider* is a macabre, darkly glittering classic.

—THOMAS TESSIER

EUGÈNE SUE

The Wandering Jew

Marie-Joseph Eugène Sue's Le Juif Errant *is perhaps the most sustained literary treatment of the legend of the Jew cursed by Jesus Christ to remain alive until the Second Coming.* The Wandering Jew *has cameo appearances in novels as diverse as Lewis'* The Monk *(1796) and Walter M. Miller Jr's* A Canticle for Leibowitz *(1960). Sue's Jew, influenced perhaps by Maturin's Melmoth, travels a degraded modern world, spreading cholera wherever he goes, and is used by the author to expose various contemporary evils. As in many late Gothics, the perfidious Jesuits come in for a particular bashing. The novel was filmed several times in the early days of the cinema, by French film pioneer Georges Méliès in 1904, and by Italian studios in 1913 (as* L'Ebreo errante) *and 1918 (as* Morok). *Later movies under the same title—including a 'lost' 1933 Conrad Veidt vehicle—are adaptations of a play by E. Temple Thurston. Sue was also the author of the grisly melodramatic novels* Les Mystères de Paris *(The Mysteries of Paris, 1842–43),* Les Septs Péchés Capitaux *(The Seven Cardinal Sins, 1847–9) and* Les Mystères du Peuple *(The Mysteries of the People, 1849–56).*

Publishers call them blockbusters; critics dismiss them as potboilers; in their own time and place—Paris of the 1840s—they were *romans-feuilletons*, or 'newspaper-novels'—and the greatest of them all was Eugène Sue's *The Wandering Jew* (unless that honor belongs to *The Count of Monte Cristo*, which was being serialized at exactly the same time in a rival Paris newspaper). *The Wandering Jew* has got, as the form demands, everything: an heiress falsely accused of madness and incarcerated in a lunatic asylum; a destitute hunchbacked seamstress of the highest moral character hopelessly in love with a blacksmith (who is a patriotic poet on the side); bloodthirsty panthers, telepathic twins, debauchery, murder, suicide, duels, supernatural manifestations, blazing passions, wild mobs, a plague of cholera, scenes in Java and the Arctic, the *two* best Reading-of-the-Will scenes that ever were, *and* towering over all these attractions, the nastiest crew of villains ever brought together in one book, presided over by the fiendish, the insidious, the wholly diabolic Jesuit priest and arch-hypocrite, Père Rodin, who is hell-bent on becoming the next Pope.

My first acquaintance with Sue's genius came at about age 10 when, like stout Cortez upon his peak in Darien, I stared in wild surmise at the

Classics Illustrated comic-book of *The Mysteries of Paris*, wherein the hero had been trapped, among frantic rats, in a cellar rapidly being flooded to the rafters. Here was an absolutely Basic Truth about human destiny that no other Classics Illustrated author had ever revealed to me. It was to be another ten years before I found the Modern Library Giant of *The Wandering Jew* (no longer in print, alas) and consumed its 1,337 pages of faded purple prose like so many kilograms of popcorn, since when I have remembered its main outlines and best scenes with the seared after-image recall that some few paintings of the same era achieve—Géricault's *Raft of the Medusa* or Delacroix's *Liberty Leading the People*, paintings that could be dismissed as clichés if they had not established themselves as archetypes.

While that part of the novel-reading public that includes some classics as a staple in their diet can usually enjoy the glorious excesses of painters and composers, they tend to shy away from books that purvey the equivalent pleasures of Too Much and Far Out. Melodrama and an eye peeled for box office success are accounted mortal sins by academics, and it is academia that has been left in charge of which books of the past are to be accounted classics, taught, and kept in print.

Yet I doubt the neglect of Sue's novel can be ascribed entirely to highbrow snobbery, since any number of comparable novels by Scott, Hugo, Dumas, and Wilkie Collins have managed to stay in print without much assistance from academia. Nor need the book's length tell against it, for in the great pageturners, from *Clarissa* to *The Godfather*, length becomes a positive virtue: no one wants the fun to stop.

I suspect that the root of the problem may be that *The Wandering Jew* is a vehemently anticlerical parable ('vituperative', one reference book calls it), while the tenor of the last forty years has been towards that brand of genteel ecumenicism whose first article of faith is that religion and politics should not be discussed—or if they are, every effort must be made to be fair and impartial. But melodrama is seldom fair: fair isn't fun. Besides, Sue wasn't writing in the age of Bing Crosby but at a time when the Roman church was in the vanguard of political repression. Which is not to say he doesn't stack the deck. Besides the machiavellian Père Rodin and his Jesuit minions, the book's crew of Catholic villains includes a venal Mother Superior whose convent is a prison in disguise, a gluttonous bishop who is regaled by an ultramontane (i.e., rich and right wing) dowager with a lenten repast that includes 'little Calvaries of apricot tartlets', and 'a superb crucifix of angelica with a crown of preserved barberies', together with such lay assistants as sweat-shop operators, wild animal tamers, and Indian thugees. There is not, this side of *Melmoth the Wanderer* (the most lurid of the Gothic novels and my second choice for an anthology of favorite horror novels; it was one of Sue's prime sources), another work of literature better calculated to drive a Catholic Anti-Defamation League into paroxysms of denunciation. To return such a book to print is obviously asking for trouble.

And that's a pity, because despite its glorious excesses (or in addition to them) *The Wandering Jew* represents a considerable literary achievement, especially for the way that Sue is able to weave his many characters into a plot of monolithic unity. To wit: seven descendants of one Marius de Rennespont stand to inherit that gentleman's fortune, which has mounted at 5% interest over 150 years to a sum of 212,175,000 francs (or 8,487,000 pounds sterling). These seven, whom the Jesuits are determined to despoil of this fortune, represent a cross-section of all that is sexy, virtuous, and left-wing: Blanche and Rose Simon, twin daughters of one of Napoleon's marshals, lately escaped from Siberia; a utopian-minded industrialist; the dashing Prince Djalma; an 18-year-old heiress of exquisite refinement; a debauched but good-hearted workman called Couche-tout-Nud; and the saintly young priest Gabriel, whom the Jesuits have tricked into making over his share of the fortune as a deed of gift. For the first half of the novel the bad guys conspire to see that only Gabriel will be present at the reading of the will, thus becoming sole legatee. Just as their scheme seems to have succeeded, the female counterpart of the Wandering Jew of the title appears as *dea ex machina* to uncover a hidden codicil that sets the plot in motion for another 600+ pages. I am sworn not to reveal how it all ends, but take my word, the final tableau is a lulu, and anything but *vivante*.

For some readers that synopsis may suggest that the book is no more than a classic of camp humor, and indeed there are chapters when the extravagance of the plot can be discombobulating, especially if they have been bullied by the schoolmarms of Serious Literature into believing that grand gestures and bold colors are necessarily in bad taste. However, anyone who can enjoy Griffith's *Birth of a Nation* or a well-sung *Il Trovatore* should have no trouble achieving total immersion in Sue's story, while readers on friendly terms with Dickens and Balzac will feel a kindred sympathy for Sue. More to the point, perhaps, in terms of resurrecting this book from the limbo of used book stores, readers of such current melodramatists as Stephen King or Anne Rice ought to be highly receptive to Sue's grand excesses (especially if his novel were to appear in a slightly condensed version). With just a bit of spit-and-polish the old warhorse could be a best-seller all over again.

—THOMAS M. DISCH

HERMAN MELVILLE

The Confidence Man: His Masquerade

The Mississippi steamer Fidèle *departs from St Louis for New Orleans, bearing a wide cross-section of mid-19th-century American society. Among the passengers is an individual who appears and reappears in a variety of disguises—a crippled black, a charity fund-raiser, a stock speculator, an employment agent, a bogus philosopher—and rooks the venal and gullible of much more than their money. Neither a piece of Mark Twain-style Americana nor a simple tale of a cunning criminal,* The Confidence Man *is a masterpiece of misanthropy, in which Melville takes swipes at a wide variety of Americans, including figures like Emerson, Thoreau and Fenimore Cooper. The Confidence Man himself is a diabolic, perhaps supernatural, being whose methods of disguise are never rationally explained: his* modus operandi *has been reworked in novels as different as Grant Allen's* An African Millionaire *(1898) and Steve Gallagher's* Valley of Lights *(1987). The poor reception of the book convinced the 38-year-old Melville to give up writing and devote the rest of his working life to a solid job as a customs inspector. Many of his works, most famously* Moby-Dick *(1851), contain horrific, bizarre or semi-supernatural incidents; his relatively few overt tales of horror—which touch upon vampirism, robots and ghosts—appear in* The Piazza Tales *(coll. 1966).*

*T*he Confidence Man is not generally regarded as a novel of horror or fantasy, but I say without hesitation that it is the most fundamentally unsettling, powerful, and influential book I have ever opened. Melville's narrative was born of a cynicism so profound and twisted his story-telling makes Kafka seem a bliss ninny in comparison. The book—what is in it and what I was taught by it—became then, and remains, the catechism of my irreligion. Perhaps, if I'd never read the book, I'd have become a writer anyway—but by no means would I be the same writer. I still find it astonishing how many crucial lessons *The Confidence Man* taught me. The instruction was bleak but invaluable.

First, I realized that the most potentially dangerous and subversive of fictional characters is the narrator who speaks in a confiding, authoritative, and supposedly neutral third-person voice. It is unsettling enough to read a book written in first-person, where we come to mistrust the truth, the motives, and the candor of the narrator. But what happens when the anonymous third-person narrator of a novel is untrustworthy?

It seemed to me, reading in awe, that not Melville, but the God of Lies himself had written the book. A narrator, I understood then, was every bit as much a creation of the writer as were the characters whose stories the narrator told us. This lesson I took to heart. Now I find myself frequently asked how it is possible I write books that seem totally different from one another: Southern Gothic Horror, Historical Thriller, Boy–Girl Romantic Adventure, Gay Detective Novels, Right-Wing Men's Adventure. I'm told it appears as if wholly different people had composed and told stories in the various genres. That is essentially correct—I don't so much create characters and a story as create a particular narrator who creates characters and a story. My narrators are variously cold, close, indulgent, condescending, admiring, jolly, warm-hearted, caustic, and clinical. *The Confidence Man* bears a sub-title: *His Masquerade*—but no one in the story wears so many costumes as he who tells the story.

The second lesson I got from Melville's book is contained in the three chapters with disconcertingly circular titles: [Ch. 14: 'Worth the consideration of those to whom it may prove worth considering'; Ch. 33: 'Which may pass for whatever it may prove to be worth'; and Ch. 44: 'In which the last three words of the last chapter are made the text of the discourse, which will be sure of receiving more or less attention from those readers who do not skip it']. These ironic discourses—ironically dedicated to readers—are coded messages with meaning only to other writers. I write and I work by the observations contained in these cold yet scalding passages. One single dictum propels my typing fingers: '. . . in books of fiction, [readers] look not only for more entertainment, but, at bottom, even for more reality, than real life itself can show.' If there were ever harsher, crueler, more demanding, but finally more comforting words for a novelist, I have never read them.

Finally, what *The Confidence Man* gave me was a straight-walled definition for what I had always felt about life and existence. It is my philosophy today, and I mean this in a straightforward plebeian manner—it is the basis on which I speak, and act, and feel. According to Melville (and now according to me, too), the universe and existence are only a joke but dimly discerned. The punchline is garbled and all we know, while the cosmos' laughter clamors in our fevered brains, is that we are the butt of that joke.

The Confidence Man is a book about deception, lies, obscure jests, undeserved misery, gratuitous fortune, connivance, philistine victories, and off-the-cuff evil. I felt after reading it that the lids of my eyes had been ripped away. Thereafter I saw existence and humanity and my own life with a galling amused embarrassing clarity, perceiving in dark unambiguous outline its doomed unpitied helplessness. This is the horror—finally—which prompts and imbues every tale I have ever put to paper. It is why I always write with humor, because we are the confused

40

victims of this obscure impractical joke we call life. And the laughter will echo when neither we nor those we love are around to hear it.

—MICHAEL McDOWELL

16   [1864]

J. SHERIDAN LE FANU

Uncle Silas: A Tale of Bertram-Haugh

Austin Ruthyn, father of the seventeen-year-old narrator Maud, firmly believes that his disgraced brother Silas is innocent of the crimes everyone else attributes to him. On Silas' recommendation, he takes into his house Madame de la Rougièrre, a sinister governess who terrorizes Maud and is expelled when Austin finds her prying into his private papers. Austin realizes that Silas is plotting to gain the fortune he intends to leave to Maud, but succumbs to a stroke just as he is about to strike out of his will the clause that gives Maud over into her uncle's care until she reaches her majority. Maud goes to live at Bertram-Haugh, Silas' gloomy pile, and soon realizes that Silas, his reprobate son Dudley and the wicked governess are scheming against her. Although not one of the ghost stories for which its author was famous, Uncle Silas *is a prime example of mid-Victorian post-Gothic melodrama. Unlike* Jane Eyre, *with which it shares many elements, it does not finally resolve into a romance between the put-upon heroine and the saturnine master of the crumbling house but piles on the horrors and reveals Silas to be a villain considerably worse than the world thinks him. In 1947, it was filmed twice, in England as* Uncle Silas *(a.k.a.* The Inheritance*) with Jean Simmons as the heroine, and in Argentina by Carlos Schliepper as* El Mysterioso Tio Silas.

This masterpiece of its kind first appeared in its present form in the *Dublin University Magazine* in 1864 under the title of *Uncle Silas and Maud Ruthyn*. This serial publication was followed by a three-volume edition by Bentley, and one-volume issues since then have been frequent.

When he wrote *Uncle Silas* Le Fanu had already produced four long stories. Two of these, 'The Cock and Anchor' and 'Torlogh O'Brien', were early works, separated by an interval of fourteen or fifteen years from the long series which he began in 1861. In that year he brought out *The House by the Churchyard*, and in 1863 *Wylder's Hand*. I have always thought that in some ways *The House by the Churchyard* is the best of all his books: but it cannot be denied that *Uncle Silas* is the better known and has elisted more suffrages. It is indeed more compact and clearer in plot; its population is more easily grasped; there is not the multiplicity of threads which make the earlier book—some would say confusing, I say rich and attractive. And it does possess very great excellences. Let me reckon up some of the features which I remember to have caught my fancy when I first read the book, some time in the early eighties, I suppose. There was Maud Ruthyn herself. Surely that character is well kept up throughout? Of course there is always the improbability of the recollection of long dialogues spoken many years before they were written down, but that is a convention in which one can very easily acquiesce. What matters is that the girl should write as a sensible pleasant woman would write in later years, when she was able to detach herself enough from her girlish self to be amused at it and critical of it. That I think Le Fanu has made her do, and he has made her sensible and pleasant. It was a role, by the way, which he rather liked: in his last novel, *Willing to Die*, the pen is held by a lady very like Maud Ruthyn, and so it is in the admirable story of 'Carmilla'.

Monica Knollys: I do not know if the wise sharp-tongued humorous lady of mature age has often been better drawn. What good language she uses! How well she tells the story of Charke's murder! for Dr Bryerly too I have a particular respect. His talk to the house-keeper when he comes at dead of night to watch by Austin Ruthyn's body is one of those outbursts in which I think Le Fanu reaches a great height of eloquence, and shows the poet that was in him.

But naturally, among the characters, my chief admiration was centred on Uncle Silas himself and yet more on Madame de la Rougièrre. The horrid veneer of French culture combined with pietism that appears in Silas's talk and letters is inimitable: 'Chaulieu and the evangelists' as Lady Knollys puts it. It is she too who drops a hint about Silas which I think was, in the back of Le Fanu's mind, the key to the situation, though, true to his artistic instinct, he does not dwell on it. 'Perhaps,' she says, 'Other souls than human are sometimes born into the world and clothed in flesh.' 'Venerable, bloodless, fiery-eyed,' Uncle Silas is a figure who stamps himself on the memory.

'On a sudden, on the grass before me, stood an odd figure—a very tall woman in grey draperies, nearly white under the moon, courtesying extraordinarily low, and rather fantastically.' That is the way in which Madame de la Rougièrre is introduced, and from that moment whenever she is on the scene she rivets the attention. It is a most careful study; the language she speaks is but one of many successes in the portrait. What a hideous atmosphere she carries with her! The hints of a dreadful past, the growing certainty that she is an accomplice in an obscure plot, the relief when she vanishes from Knowl, the ghastly shock when she is discovered in the attic at Bertram-Haugh—to me all these episodes seem to be really masterly in the working out.

Throughout the story many little scenes are managed which serve to put us in the right frame of mind, expectant of tragedy. There is the talk of the Swedenborgian in the third chapter, there is the account of the family ghosts of Knowl, the fortune-telling gipsy, the mysterious 'Fly the fangs of Belsarius': but of course it is the march of the main story with its short glimpses of light followed by increasing darkness, the gradual withdrawal of friends and closing up of avenues of escape, that ought to enlist and does enlist our terrified interest. The climax, I have always thought, is in every way worthy of what has gone before, and the swift ending of the book is artistically right, I am sure. Vulgar Victorian curiosity, I confess, always makes me wish to know exactly what Uncle Silas and Dudley said to each other when they discovered their mistake: but this is more than we could reasonably expect to be told; even if Dickon Hawkes heard it and repeated it, years after, Lady Ilbury might well have hesitated to write it down.

There are not many stories which succeed in creating and in sustaining with the right intensity the atmosphere of mystery and the *crescendo* of impending doom, and whose dramatis personae are at the same time so unremote and so easily realized. I wish the book many readers, and I wish that all of them may find in it the same delight that it has often brought to me.

—M. R. JAMES

17 [1886]

ROBERT LOUIS STEVENSON

The Strange Case of Dr Jekyll and Mr Hyde

The friends of Dr Henry Jekyll, a respected chemist, are perturbed and mystified by his association with Edward Hyde, a sinister brute. Mr Utterson, Jekyll's lawyer, witnesses an incident in the street in which Hyde tramples a little girl. Later, Jekyll makes a will leaving his money to Hyde 'in the event of my death or disappearance'. Hyde's crimes descend to murder, and Jekyll becomes more and more tormented. Finally, Hyde is tracked to Jekyll's laboratory and found dead, a suicide. Jekyll's posthumous confession reveals that he is Hyde, thanks to a potion which liberates the baser aspects of the human soul. An instant classic on its first appearance, Dr Jekyll and Mr Hyde has been dramatized and filmed endlessly. Among the many actors to attempt the dual role were Charles Mansfield, John Barrymore, Fredric March, Spencer Tracy, Christopher Lee, Kirk Douglas, David Hemmings and Boris Karloff. Stevenson's original draft was apparently more gruesome and sensationalist than the book is as it stands; he was persuaded—perhaps unfortunately—by his wife to re-write it, emphasizing the moral lesson of the tale.

The chilling idea for *The Strange Case of Dr Jekyll and Mr Hyde*, so Stevenson wrote, came to him in a terrifying dream. First published in 1886, the story did more than any other work to earn his fame. When I discovered it, some forty years later, it shook me with an impact I will never forget.

Such bits of fantasy or science fiction were still rare then, hard to find and precious when you found them. *Weird Tales*, the first magazine devoted to fantasy, did not begin its hard struggle for survival until 1923. *Amazing Stories*, the first science fiction magazine, began publication only in 1926; Hugo Gernsback did not invent the term 'science fiction' until 1929.

Popular tastes have vastly changed since then. The book racks are loaded now with bumper crops of fantasy, science fiction, and horror; Asimov and Heinlein and Stephen King are best-selling authors. Yet *Dr Jekyll and Mr Hyde* still commands attention and builds suspense as it always did, with its atmosphere of long-ago London, its vivid images of Utterson and Lanyon, and the riveting mystery of the good doctor and the sinister Mr Hyde.

Those are merely devices, however, for what Stevenson had to say. His theme, like Poe's in 'William Wilson' and Conrad's in 'The Secret Sharer', is the double self, a symbol as I see it for the universal conflict between the individual and society.

We are all born naked, selfish individualists. At the moment of birth, however, we are tossed into warfare with all the institutions that try to socialize us: family, school, religion, law. So long as we live, however we rebel or submit, compromise or conquer, that tension never ends. Dr Jekyll, as I see him, is the social man, Mr Hyde the rebel soul. I think they reflect the division in Stevenson himself.

Witness his long history of conflict and compromise with his father, who was a sternly pious Calvinist and a prosperous civil engineer. Stevenson was a sickly child, and sickness can be a strategy of unconscious rebellion. Frequent illness interrupted his schooling. He disappointed his father by failing to follow into the family profession of lighthouse engineering, reading law instead; disappointed him again by rejecting religion and choosing a literary career over the practice of law; hurt him a third time with his pursuit of Fanny Osborne, a married women not yet divorced when his courtship began.

His father was kind and tolerant enough in the end, forgiving the marriage, supporting him when he needed support, but the pattern of social rebellion remains a constant in Stevenson's whole career. It appears in such great novels of adventure as *Treasure Island*, in the romantic wandering through the South Seas that ended with his too-early death on Samoa in 1894, and most clearly, I think, in *Dr Jekyll and Mr Hyde*.

When we thrill to the shock and horror of the story, I think it is because we all, at least to some degree, have been torn by that same internal conflict. When we recoil in terror from the selfish savagery of Mr Hyde, I think it is because we fear our own secret selves.

—JACK WILLIAMSON

18   [1887]

H. RIDER HAGGARD

She

Professor Holly and his young friend Leo Vincey, exploring in the African jungle, discover the fabled lost city of Kôr, which is ruled by Ayesha, She-Who-Must-Be-Obeyed, an immortal white queen. Ayesha believes that Leo is the reincarnation of her lost love, Killikrates, and invites him to join her in bathing in the blue flame, the source of her immortality. However, a second exposure robs her of the gift bestowed by the first, and she reverts horribly to her true age. Haggard capitalized on the sensational success of She *with several sequels,* Ayesha (1905), *a direct follow-up,* She and Allan (1921), *in which Ayesha meets his series hero Allan Quatermain (of* King Solomon's Mines, 1885, *and many others), and* Wisdom's Daughter (1923), *a romance of the ancient world which goes into Ayesha's origins.* She *was first filmed in 1899, by George Méliès, as* La Danse de Feu, *and has been remade many times, most memorably by Irving Pichel in 1935 with Helen Gahaghan and Randolph Scott.*

There's a moment in the 1965 film version of *She* when a map showing the way to a legendary lost city is produced, and the would-be young explorer urges his hesitant friend to accompany him with the appeal 'Do you think you'd ever enjoy another good night's sleep, wondering what might have been at the end of it all?'

Thus begins their trek through swamp and mountain, leading at last to the hidden city and a meeting with the eerie sorceress of blinding beauty who dwells there.

The quest theme, that 'beyond the ranges' notion of a great, undiscovered secret, lies at the very heart of Rider Haggard's haunting 1887 romance of the deathless Ayesha, who has waited two thousand years for the reincarnation of her lost love.

Where are they now, those magnificent Victorian yarns of far-off jungles and plateaux tingling with magic and mystery?

Today the horrors all seem to be coming to us—loping through the subway, festering in the creepy old house next door, escaping from the local hospital, even squirming up the plug-hole into the bath.

Back in 1887, though, the world was a bigger place. In those intrepid days, travellers' tales—marvellous phrase!—offered entertainment rather more enlivening than a moan about the water in Majorca.

Zanzibar: the cliff of the Ethiopian's Head: the caves of Kôr ... Thumb through an atlas for the settings Haggard selected for *She* and they're just another part of the hopeless battleground that makes up modern Africa. But read the story and it takes you back a century and more to a time when the ends of the earth were exactly that—realms created by God for the specific use of authors and their imaginations.

And what a tale it is. A broken potsherd with an ancient inscription lures Cambridge scholar Horace Holly and his handsome young ward Leo Vincey to the East African hinterland, home of the savage Amahagger tribe and their all-powerful queen, She-Who-Must-Be-Obeyed.

Long ago, in the days of the pharaohs, She had bathed in the Flame of Life and made herself immortal. Now she leads a lonely, hermit-like existence, living out the weary centuries in the belief that ultimately the lover whom she murdered will be restored to her.

Ayesha—so lovely she must veil her face from those around her. So old that her feet have worn away the stone steps of her mountain palace. So powerful in jealousy that the mere brush of her hand can blast a native girl dead.

As the plot takes hold one has the fancy that she had always existed, in some dark dimension of the imagination, and that Haggard was the fortunate author to whom she chose to reveal herself. He was later to write of the novel: 'It came faster than my poor aching hand could set it down.' After six weeks of sustained, white-hot scribbling he dumped the manuscript on his agent's desk, announcing 'There is what I shall be remembered by.'

Prophetic words. *She* is far and away the best of his many stirring tales of fantasy and high adventure, which include the classic *King Solomon's Mines*.

46

I read it first at the impressionable age of thirteen, when the description of Ayesha's terrible, disintegrating end filled my schoolboy's heart with an overpowering sense of loss.

At forty-one, it still does: even though I know I have only to pick up the sequels, *Ayesha* and *She and Allan*, to meet her again.

A horror story? Not really. Say rather, a romance in its truest sense—a narrative which passes beyond the limits of ordinary life. Fantasy authors shouldn't have to work down among the dead men all the time.

If *She* were written today it would probably emerge as a sado-sexual romp, with its heroine bedding half the Amahagger before lustfully scorching her reincarnated lover Leo to a crisp.

It's a measure of Rider Haggard's skill that, without allowing Ayesha any intimacies beyond the endearments 'thee' and 'thou', he nevertheless conjures up the most vivid female character in supernatural fiction, creating an unattainable feminine ideal against which men dash themselves as moths against a flame.

Unattainable. Isn't that the secret of fantasy's appeal? A longing for the infinite. And Haggard gives us the perfect image—'as the fishes see the stars, but dimly'.

It was his friend Andrew Lang, the Scottish mythographer and poet, who provided the sonnet which might serve as an epitaph for both *She* and Haggard—

> '. . . .Nay, not in Kôr, but in whatever spot
> In town or field, or by the insatiate sea,
> Men brood o'er buried loves and unforgot,
> Or break themselves on some divine decree,
> Or would o'er leap the limits of their lot—
> There, in the tombs and deathless, dwelleth *SHE*.'

That's if immortals need epitaphs.

—TIM STOUT

19 [1895]

ROBERT W. CHAMBERS

The King in Yellow

The King in Yellow collects two sets of linked stories. The second half of the book consists of a batch of sentimental novelettes with titles like 'The Street of the Four Winds' and 'The Street of the First Shell', dealing with the lives and loves of the Bohemian set in Paris. The first series, however, which comprises

47

'The Repairer of Reputations', 'The Mask', 'In the Court of the Dragon' and 'The Yellow Sign', has as a continuing thread a play called The King in Yellow, *which seems to call down a strange doom on anyone who reads it. The stories involve a fascist-run New York of 1925, prophetic dreams and a solution which will turn living flesh into marble. Several of the names— Carcosa, the Lake of Hali, Hastur—were later re-used by Lovecraft to add sinister hints of a continuity between his stories, which also have an evil book as one of their key elements; interestingly, Chambers took a few of these names from the works of his contemporary, Ambrose Bierce. A single tale, 'The Demoiselle D'Ys', links the two halves of the collection: it is a romantic ghost story with a French setting. Besides influencing Lovecraft and—through him—the* Weird Tales *generation, Chambers' book was read by Raymond Chandler, who had Philip Marlowe solve a vaguely related case in his short story of the same title. Chambers wrote a handful of other horror stories, but spent the rest of his successful career producing slick society romances.*

Very genuine, though not without the typical mannered extravagance of the eighteen-nineties, is the strain of horror in the early work of Robert W. Chambers, since renowned for products of a very different quality. *The King in Yellow*, a series of vaguely connected short stories having as a background a monstrous and suppressed book whose perusal brings fright, madness, and spectral tragedy, really achieves notable heights of cosmic fear in spite of uneven interest and a somewhat trivial and affected cultivation of the Gallic studio atmosphere made popular by Du Maurier's *Trilby*.

The most powerful of its tales, perhaps, is 'The Yellow Sign', in which is introduced a silent and terrible churchyard watchman with a face like a puffy grave-worm's. A boy, describing a tussle he has had with this creature, shivers and sickens as he relates a certain detail. 'Well, sir, it's Gawd's truth that when I 'it 'im 'e grabbed me wrists, sir, and when I twisted 'is soft, mushy fist one of 'is fingers come off in me 'and.' An artist, who after seeing him has shared with another a strange dream of a nocturnal hearse, is shocked by the voice with which the watchman accosts him. The fellow emits a muttering sound that fills the head 'like thick oily smoke from a fat-rendering vat or an odour of noisome decay.' What he mumbles is merely this: 'Have you found the Yellow Sign?'

A weirdly hieroglyphed onyx talisman, picked up on the street by the sharer of his dream, is shortly given the artist; and after stumbling queerly upon the hellish and forbidden book of horrors the two learn, among other hideous things which no sane mortal should know, that this talisman is indeed the nameless Yellow Sign handed down from the accursed cult of Hastur—from primordial Carcosa, whereof the volume treats, and some nightmare memory of which seeks to lurk latent and ominous at the back of all men's minds. Soon they hear the rumbling of the black-plumed hearse driven by the flabby and corpse-faced watchman. He enters the night-shrouded house in quest of the Yellow Sign, all bolts and bars rotting at his touch. And when the people rush in, drawn by a scream that no human throat could utter, they find three forms on the floor—two dead and one dying. One of the dead shapes is far gone in decay. It is the churchyard watchman, and the doctor exclaims, 'That man must have been dead for months.' It is worth observing that the author derives most of the names and allusions connected with his eldritch land of primal memory from the tales of Ambrose Bierce. Other early works of Mr Chambers displaying the outré and macabre element are *The Maker of Moons* and *In Search of the Unknown*. One cannot help regretting that he did not further develop a vein in which he could so easily have become a recognized master.

—H. P. LOVECRAFT

20 [1896]

H. G. WELLS

The Island of Dr Moreau

Edward Prendick, a shipwreck victim, is picked up in the South Seas by a boat carrying a cargo of animals to a nameless island. He strikes an acquaintance with Montgomery, who is overseeing the animals, and is put ashore with him. The island is home to Dr Moreau, a scientist intent on proving his evolutionary theories by raising animals through surgery to the status of human beings. Prendick gradually finds out what is going on and realizes that the strange-looking 'natives' are all former animals, very shakily kept in line by an absurd set of jungle laws. Moreau's experiments have been failing because, although he can turn beasts into approximate humans he cannot prevent them reverting to their former state. The Beast Men revolt and destroy Moreau and Montgomery, leaving Prendick alone on the island with creatures who gradually revert to their animal selves. A mix of Swiftian satire, grand guignol horror, Darwinian theory and high adventure, The Island of Dr Moreau is one of the young Wells' most spirited books. It has been much imitated in pulp fiction and cinema, and been officially filmed twice, most notably as The Island of Lost Souls (1932) with Charles Laughton as the mad doctor. Gene Wolfe has written three loosely connected novellas remotely inspired by the book, The Island of Dr Death, The Doctor of Death Island and The Death of Dr Island.

H. G. Wells was still my father's idol, and for just that reason nothing short of a miracle could have impelled me to read him;

49

but the miracle occurred. I should explain that in those faraway and lost days there flourished a truly wondrous breed of magazines called pulps. (We are still living on the capital they left us; but that is another story.) All were at least as magical as a white rabbit pulled from a hat; but a few, such as *Weird Tales, Planet Stories*, and *Astounding Science Fiction*, were easily as magical as any enchanted castle upon a mountain of glass.

Yet there was one that surpassed them all, that was, in any average issue, fully as magical as Aladdin's lamp. Its name was *Famous Fantastic Mysteries*. I don't think anybody ever told me that it reprinted the best, the least tamed and most venomous, science fiction, fantasy, and horror from the past. If somebody had, I would not have believed it; each issue was brand new to me, utterly wild and marvelous, more disturbing and more exotic than—well, for years I sincerely believed that the rest did not run those stories because they were afraid to. And at last the month arrived in which *FFM* reprinted *The Island of Dr Moreau*.

I did not notice that its author was the very one who made my father's eyes shine in that strange way. I plunged straight into the story, as you should, finishing it in a single stifling tropical afternoon. I re-read most of it that night after dinner, and afterward stretched terrified on my bed with the abominable voices of beastmen whining and chattering in my ears. I re-read it again the next day, then set it aside lest eventually it grow stale. (For I am an invariable putter-off of pleasures, one who will at last dance and flirt, I am sure, upon the lid of his own coffin.) I do not think I read it again until I began preparing to write this brief piece.

Nor did I need to. I remembered it, and indeed have been haunted by it. Years later, when I wrote *The Island of Doctor Death and Other Stories*, and wanted a book that would thrill poor little Tackie while shaking him to his core, I put a vapid imitation of *The Island of Dr Moreau* into his hands. It is the ultimate science-fiction novel, and it is the ultimate horror story. It shows us where we are going, and it shows us that we are already there: that we are worse than beasts, and that when we create our final monster, we will find it a fiend nearly as evil as ourselves. Are you religious? Here is what happened in Eden after Adam and Eve had gone. Are you scientific? Peep into this telescope, this microscope, and behold the emptiness and horror of the universe in your own reflected face.

Enough, I read *The Island of Dr Moreau* a fourth time to write this. I did not remember the first line, and indeed it is not memorable. Then: '... *she collided with a derelict when ten days out from Callao.*' Dr Moreau was back, and I could wind my own fear. Note, please, that Prendick never troubles to learn the name of one of the two men who share the boat with him; and permit me one more brief quotation, this too from an early page: '"*Have some of this,*" *said he, and gave me a dose of some scarlet stuff, iced. It tasted like blood, and made me feel stronger.*'

By now you have decided I am mad, and that this book cannot have been to anyone else what it has been to me; so let me close by describing the cover of the used copy I got. You have seen a thousand in which a hero with a broadsword battles some monster. This shows a youngish man, not quite muscular enough to be that sort of hero, but decent-looking and intelligent. Behind him stands an ogre, dark and bullet-headed, with glowing eyes—the brute refuse of nighmare. One of its hands is upon the man's shoulder, in the most friendly, comradely way. The artist is Douglas Rosa; I know nothing about him except that he painted this picture.

—GENE WOLFE

21   [1897]

BRAM STOKER

Dracula

Jonathan Harker, a solicitor's clerk, arrives at the Transylvanian castle of Count Dracula in order to settle some business about the Count's impending move to England. Harker discovers that the Count is a vampire and undergoes many horrors in the castle, while Dracula sets sail for his new home. In England, Mina, Harker's fiancée, and her best friend Lucy are visited nocturnally by the Count, who turns Lucy into a vampire. Jonathan returns, shattered by his ordeal, and joins Dr Van Helsing's group of fearless vampire hunters, which includes Lucy's three suitors. The heroes destroy the undead Lucy and drive the Count from the country, but he retains his hold over Mina. They pursue the vampire back to his castle and there destroy him, thus reuniting Jonathan and Mina. Although told in the now-archaic Wilkie Collins manner—as a succession of interlocking accounts, journals, newspaper clippings and documents—Dracula is probably the first modern horror novel. In its conflict between an ancient evil and the modern world, it sets the precedent for the entire 20th-century development of the form. It has been adapted for stage, film, television, comic books and radio countless times, and several hands—including those of R. Chetwynd-Hayes, Peter Tremayne, Fred Saberhagen, Manly Wade Wellman, Woody Allen, and Ramsey Campbell—have produced sequels.

D*racula* is a paradoxical masterpiece, a work that, in a sense, has no right to exist. Stoker's other fantasy novels—*The Lady of the*

Shroud, The Lair of the White Worm and *The Jewel of Seven Stars*—
reveal a depressing lack of literary talent; they are crude and obvious. Yet
Dracula is one of the most remarkable classics in the whole realm of
horror fiction. When I reviewed Harry Ludlum's biography of Bram
Stoker in 1962, I received a long letter from a highly literate old
gentleman who told me that I had done less than justice to *Dracula*; he
had read it a dozen times, and felt that, as a novel, it had quite simply
everything: excitement, romance, sympathy, warmth, horror, adventure
... And when I re-read the novel in the light of the old gentleman's
letter, I saw he was right. From those opening words in Jonathan
Harker's journal: '3 *May. Bistritz.*—Left Munich at 8.35 p.m. on 1st
May, arriving at Vienna early next morning ...', it grips the attention.
You feel you are in the hands of a man who knows what he is talking
about. And the talk about the British Museum, the study of maps of
Transylvania, the slightly pedantic description of the races of this part of
central Europe, impart a richness of texture that fills the reader with the
feeling a child experiences when someone says 'Once upon a time ...'

Harry Ludlum's biography reveals that Abraham Stoker himself was
hardly the sort of person one might expect to produce a masterpiece. The
son of a Dublin clerk, he seemed in his twenties destined for a career in
the Civil Service. In childhood he had been sickly and introverted, and
dreamed of becoming a writer. At the age of twenty he discovered the
works of Walt Whitman, and went to the other extreme, becoming a
muscular, healthy and apparently completely normal young man. Deeply
impressed by the actor Henry Irving when the latter came to Dublin,
Stoker became an unpaid theatre critic simply for the satisfaction of
praising his idol; as a result, he and Irving became friends, and in 1878,
Irving asked him to become his general manager. Stoker accepted
immediately, and neither ever had reason to regret the decision. Stoker
worked like a dray horse for his brilliant but slightly crazy employer,
answering fifty letters a day, reading plays and engaging actors. But he
made no attempt to use his new position to lead a Bohemian life; he
remained a stodgily married man, one of those bearded late Victorians
who always looks at life from a loftily moral viewpoint—in one of his
articles, Stoker even advocated the censorship of fiction.

Considering the mad pace of his daily life—his death certificate gave
the cause of death as 'exhaustion'*—it is a mystery how he found time to
write books, let alone a masterpiece like *Dracula*. The novel emphasizes
the importance of allowing oneself to be totally gripped by a subject
before starting to write about it. One evening in 1890, at a midnight
supper, he met a remarkable man named Arminus Vambery, a professor
of Oriental languages from Budapest, who knew twenty languages and
was a student of the occult. Vambery told him about the 15th-century

---

* An Edwardian doctor's euphemism for syphilis (ed.).

ruler of Wallachia, Vlad the Impaler, so named because he enjoyed having people he disliked impaled alive on pointed poles in his dining room. (Any guests who looked sick were in danger of being impaled on another pole.) It may have been after that first meeting with Vambery that Stoker had a horrifying nightmare of a vampire king rising from the tomb. In due course, Vlad became Dracula (dracul means dragon or demon) and Vambery became Van Helsing. It is obvious to any reader that without Van Helsing, the all-knowing expert on the supernatural, the book would be a failure. (Conan Doyle showed the same artistic insight when he created Professor Moriarty as a foil to Holmes.) What seems so extraordinary is that Stoker failed to learn the lesson of *Dracula*, and that his other books are so oddly flaccid and feeble.

When *Dracula* appeared in 1897 it was immediately recognized as the most powerful novel of the supernatural written so far; it has remained in print ever since, and intrigued generations of psychologists, who have speculated how anyone as 'square' as Bram Stoker could create such a horrific rape fantasy. For that is quite obviously what it is all about. These women whose blood Dracula drinks are archetypal symbols of the helpless and violated female. On stage in the Lyceum Theatre, Stoker saw an endless series of Victorian heroines, 'womanly women' who yielded sweetly to manly men at the end of the last act. But in *Dracula*, the gentle Lucy Westenra is not only destroyed by the long-dead Count; she herself becomes a vampire, who has to be destroyed by having a stake hammered into her heart. It seems obvious that strange fires smouldered below the dependable and trustworthy surface of this upright Victorian gentleman. It is because of this touch of paradox—one might almost say this whiff of sulphur—that *Dracula* remains one of the most oddly disturbing novels ever written.

—COLIN WILSON

22   [1898]

HENRY JAMES

The Turn of the Screw

At Christmas, a group of friends are telling ghost stories. One of the company reads from a manuscript penned by a governess. The anonymous narrator arrives at an isolated house to take charge of two orphans, Miles and Flora.

She learns that the children have recently been under the unwholesome influence of Miss Jessell, their former governess, and of Peter Quint, a sinister servant. Both Jessell and Quint are mysteriously dead, and both seem to be extending their influence from beyond the grave, perhaps to take possession of the children. While struggling with Quint's spirit for the soul of Miles, the governess accidentally causes the death of her charge. A classic ghost story, The Turn of the Screw *has been adapted into an opera by Benjamin Britten, into a play,* The Innocents, *by Dalton Trumbo (filmed in 1961 by Jack Clayton) and spuriously 'prequelized' by screen-writer Michael Hastings and director Michael Winner with* The Nightcomers *(1971). It is the most outstanding of James' handful of ghostly stories. The eponymous 'turn of the screw', the involvement of children in the supernatural, might be seen to be at the root of a whole flood of post-*Exorcist *horrors unleashed in the 1970s.*

Courage—real courage—is the ability to see horror on the far side of a crowded room and still have the presence of mind to ask for another cup of tea.

The governess in Henry James's fantasy tale saw the shade of the defunct valet looking down from a tower and was still able to detect that he was not a gentleman. He gave her the sense of looking like an actor—but never—but no never! a gentleman.

I find that after reading this story many times over the years it is extremely difficult to take a firm stand. Did the ghosts of the handsome but base-born valet Peter Quint and the beautiful lady governess Miss Jessel really exist, or were they merely figments created by the unnamed narrator's imagination? It would appear that James intended them to be accepted as evil entities for he wrote to F. W. H. Myers, his brother's fellow researcher into spiritualism, that he had wanted to create the impression of 'the communication to the children of the most infernal imaginable evil and danger—the condition on their part being as *exposed* as we can humanly conceive children to be.'

But exposed to whom? The ghosts? The governess? All communication seems to come from her. She is the only one to see the ghosts; it is she who builds up a most fantastic interpretation of what she has been told by the illiterate housekeeper Mrs Grose. It was assumed that Quint was *evil* and Miss Jessel *infamous*. But were they? The valet certainly seems to have been a lad for the ladies and to have been perhaps a little over partial for a drink at the local. Hence his untimely end. A wrong turning when leaving the pub resulting in a fatal head wound. (A wronged husband taking revenge?)

Poor Miss Jessel may have found it hard to say no and Quint would not be the first man to take advantage of an available situation. Naughty perhaps. But evil? And the children? Miles is sent home from school with the polite request that he does not go back. The reason we are told: That he's an injury to others. What a pity the governess did not demand a detailed explanation of that ambiguous statement. But she assumes it to be some kind of sexual offence—that he was indeed corrupting his school fellows.

Why? He may have organized a midnight raid on the kitchen; a very worthwhile, even necessary operation if my memory of school meals is anything to go by. But not one to find favour in the eyes of any self-respecting headmaster.

Right—wandering around at night clad only in his nightgown suggests an unconventional turn of mind, but could that not have been a boyish prank? An effort to confuse their decidely odd governess? In fact that seems to me more than a possibility. The children leading the governess on—in modern parlance—taking the mickey, and unconsciously bringing her paranoia up to a dangerous level. This is borne out when Flora refuses to see a perfectly visible woman standing on the other side of the lake.

And the governess? The unnamed narrator? Here sex insists on raising its ugly head. She must have been in a rare old state to be so bowled over by the uncle who comes to life as a self-centered, don't-bother-me-I-leave-it-all-to-you monster. Still women do fall for these egoistic brutes, but the governess does seem to have fallen harder than most. Then—in her scene with ten years old Miles she thinks of him and herself as honeymooners at an inn.... Conjecture begins to slide down a very steep, slippery hill and finishes up in a mud-filled ditch.

Now—if only Mrs Grose had also seen those ghosts, then just maybe Miles would not have been frightened to death—for then there would not have been anything for him to be frightened of—being quite accustomed to seeing ghosts—if you get my meaning. Also there would have been no mystery.

—R. CHETWYND-HAYES

23   [1902]

JOSEPH CONRAD

Heart of Darkness

Marlow, Conrad's favoured narrator, forsakes his usual shipping lanes and takes a trip by riverboat up the Congo into the dark heart of Africa in search of Kurtz, a near-mythical entrepreneur who has somehow become possessed by the sinister magic of the continent and become the victim of the mini-empire he has carved out in the uncharted jungle. First published as one of the three stories in Youth: A Narrative, and Two Other Stories, Heart of Darkness *is one of the most substantial thin novels ever written. It takes as its theme the duality of man, as elaborated upon by a variety of dark stories from* The Strange Case of Dr Jekyll and Mr Hyde *to* Lord of the Flies, *and uses the remote setting to create a powerful vision of the quest upriver as a voyage into the soul of humanity. Conrad, born Josef Korzeniowski, is one of the giants of 20th-century literature, and was frequently drawn to bizarre and grotesque subjects.*

I first read *Heart of Darkness* at age fifteen, introduced to its dense and thickly shadowed prose, like almost every other modern reader, via a school assignment. It seemed less a story than a curious travelogue, a river voyage through colonial Africa that was cloaked in an oppressively gloomy atmosphere. There was no telling what it meant (in those innocent days before the massacre at My Lai, my teacher talked about style rather than substance); but its *feeling* was certain: no other fiction before or since has instilled in me such relentless dread.

I returned to *Heart of Darkness* a few years later, this time by choice, drawn back by memories of that emotional power—and a sense of unresolved mystery. Now colored by thoughts of schoolmates maimed and dead, by the daily news from the war in Vietnam, the story, and a very dark truth, seemed to burn from its pages. Conrad captured me forever; I have since read *Heart of Darkness* more times than any other fiction, and it has never failed to challenge, to terrify, and, indeed, to surprise me. I am not alone. This timeless story has inspired artists as diverse as J. G. Ballard (*The Crystal World* and *The Day of Creation*), Francis Ford Coppola (*Apocalypse Now*), and Tim O'Brien (*Going After Cacciato*); and it is rightfully considered one of the greatest horror novels ever written.

'Before the Congo,' Joseph Conrad once told a friend, 'I was a mere animal.'

In 1889, when he was thirty-one, Conrad resigned the command of the *Otago* in Australia and returned to England for reasons that never have been made clear. A few months later, lacking money and a job, he fulfilled a lifelong dream of journeying deep into Africa by agreeing to captain a riverboat for the Belgian Company for Commerce. He spent six months in the Congo, traveling as far as the end of navigation at Stanley Falls; but he soon succumbed to illness—and to the sight of the baseness and degradation of the European intrusion into Africa. He departed for London, never to return ... except in his fiction.

Heart of Darkness, written nearly a decade later, recounts Conrad's experiences in the Congo 'pushed a little (and very little) beyond the facts of the case.' Narrated by Conrad's fictional double, Marlow (the protagonist of *Youth* and narrator of *Lord Jim*, *Chance*, and *The Secret Sharer*), safe in harbor at the mouth of the Thames, its story is deceptively simple.

'I don't want to bother you much with what happened to me personally,' Marlow begins; but his tale is about little else. Hired by 'the Company' to replace a riverboat captain who had been killed by natives, Marlow departs the 'whited sepulchre' of Europe and sails deep into the interior of the dark continent. At the end of his journey awaits a near-legendary agent, Mr Kurtz, the 'Chief of the Inner Station.' From all accounts, Kurtz is the embodiment of enlightened European traditions, a journalist and statesman—indeed, a missionary—who has ventured into the deepest jungle armed only with 'the gift of expression'. Marlow, steaming upriver in his wake, learns that the great man is 'an emissary of pity, of science, of progress, and devil knows what else.'

Devil knows, indeed; for as Marlow follows Kurtz's path deeper and deeper into darkness, the evidence mounts that something has gone wrong. Kurtz, like the ever-darkening jungle, soon takes on the proportions of a terrifying, almost supernatural monster—a violence-breathing icon of the degradation and horror that 'progress' has visited upon Africa: slavery, brutality, exploitation, despoliation, the 'merry dance of death and trade'.

When Marlow reaches the Inner Station, he finds an obscene encampment of war-ready natives, guarded with row upon row of poles that have been topped with severed heads. Inside, Kurtz awaits, grievously ill but with a single regret: the ivory trade has been closed, and Kurtz fears that his method may have failed because it was unsound. Marlow sees no method at all; Kurtz is 'hollow to the core', given over entirely to darkness—living, and now dying, without moral code or stricture. His final words, whether uttered merely in observation or in judgment, come in 'a cry that was no more than a breath: "The horror! The horror!"'

Throughout *Heart of Darkness*, and particularly in its closing section, Marlow's narrative circles around the unexpressed (and perhaps inexpressible) mystery that has left readers and scholars guessing for nearly a century: What horror has seized the Inner Station? Some have suggested cannibalism; but Marlow's own steamer is manned with cannibal tribesmen, whom he lauds for their relatively 'civilized' restraint. No, it is something more—something that renders even the sight of severed heads mundane: 'After all,' Marlow reminds us, 'that was only a savage sight, while I seemed at one bound to have been transported into some lightless region where pure, uncomplicated savagery was a positive relief, being something that had a right to exist—obviously—in the sunshine.'

But that is only Marlow's word. The genius of *Heart of Darkness* lies not only in its insistent atmospherics, deft symbolism, and almost infuriating vagary, but also in the inherent untrustworthiness of its narrative. The story is a labyrinth of unanswered questions: Is Marlow's tale colored with guilt—or, indeed, his own insanity? Was Kurtz in fact real, or merely a projection of Marlow's inner self, confronted at a lonely outpost beyond the purview of society?

Critics of its time, like those in recent years, read *Heart of Darkness* as an indictment of imperialism, a common theme of more explicitly supernatural fiction of the end of the Nineteenth Century. Those were the years of the 'yellow Gothic', whose key novels—*Dr Jekyll and Mr Hyde* (1886), *The Picture of Dorian Gray* (1891), *The Island of Dr Moreau* (1896), and *Dracula* (1897)—all echoed the fears of an era of imperial decline. Like those novels, *Heart of Darkness* speaks profoundly about the thin line between humanity and savagery, the slippery path from enlightenment to primitivism; but Conrad's outraged humanism pushes further, suggesting that there is no line, no demarcation point that separates 'us' from 'them': there is only pretense.

The lessons of *Heart of Darkness* are as real today as they were a century ago, but it is Conrad's singular style of confronting these horrors that has given his story its lasting power. Marlow's journey is a travelogue indeed, not of Africa but of the human soul; and it is for this reason that *Heart of Darkness* is renowned as a symbolist masterpiece, and perhaps the finest depiction of the 'night journey' in all of literature. Marlow's voyage into and out of Africa enacts the mythical descent into the underworld and the return to light, an allegory of death and spiritual rebirth. Marlow has been brought—indeed, he has allowed himself to be brought—to the very face of horror, and has witnessed its bleak nothingness: 'I have wrestled with death,' he tells us; and he has *survived*, emerging whole . . . and human. Like Conrad after the Congo, he is no longer a mere animal, but (for better or worse) a man, nervously alive with a knowledge both terrifying and cleansing.

In his famous preface to *The Nigger of the 'Narcissus'*, Conrad wrote that 'Art itself may be defined as a single-minded attempt to render the highest kind of justice to the visible universe, by bringing to light the truth, manifold and one, underlying its every aspect.' *Heart of Darkness* brings to light a dark and unwelcome truth—the evil innate in all mankind. There is no greater purpose in the fiction of horror.

—DOUGLAS E. WINTER

BRAM STOKER

The Jewel of Seven Stars

After Dracula, The Jewel of Seven Stars is Bram Stoker's best-known novel. Although it has never attained the immense popularity of the earlier novel, it is a much tighter, more controlled work, dealing with the gradual possession of the heroine, Margaret Trelawny, by an ancient Egyptian queen of evil, Tera, whose mummified remains have been brought to an old dark house in London by the girl's archaeologist father. The narrator/hero—Margaret's suitor—delves into the peculiar history of the mummy, and is an appalled witness as Tera's influence is increased through a variety of magical rituals which focus on artefacts found in the queen's tomb. It is one of several Victorian and Edwardian works—Richard Marsh's The Beetle (1897), Arthur Conan Doyle's story 'Lot No. 249'—that reflect public interest in Egyptian archaeology. It was first adapted as Curse of the Mummy, a 1970 segment of the TV series Mystery and Imagination with Isobel Black, and has subsequently been filmed twice: as Blood from the Mummy's Tomb (1971), and as The Awakening (1980).

*T*he Jewel of Seven Stars is Bram Stoker's best-constructed novel after *Dracula*, and revives his themes of immortality through supernatural, and horrific, means. The single-narrator technique is equally as effective and direct in *Jewel* as the multi-narrator, journal/letters format used in *Dracula*, while the degrees of compelling suspense and uncanny complexity are maintained excellently throughout the length of the novel. A feeling of credulity is retained by the liberal descriptions of Egyptian objects and metaphysics in full detail.

The jewel of the title is an enormous ruby carved like a scarab (illustrated on the cover and title-page of the first edition), embellished by hieroglyphics and a clear design of seven stars in the exact contemporary position of the stars in the Plough constellation.

Among the more ghastly artefacts to be found in the London house of Trelawny and his daughter Margaret (where most of the action takes place) are the mummy of a mysterious great Egyptian queen, and her severed, perfectly preserved hand with seven digits. This mummy, found hidden in the remote 'Valley of the Sorcerors', is of a remarkable 'historical' figure adept in magic and ritual, and all the occult Egyptian sciences: 'Tera, Queen of the Egypts, daughter of Antef. Monarch of the North and South. Daughter of the Sun. Queen of the Diadems'. She has suspended herself in time, making all the preparations necessary for her resurrection over forty centuries later; and this is the incredible experiment in which Trelawny is engaged.

Much has been written in recent years about the 'Dracula notes' (sold at auction in 1913, and now housed in Philadelphia), which detail the lengthy research made by Bram Stoker into the occult, historical and geographical background of his great vampire novel.

It is very likely that Stoker undertook similar extended research during 1897–1902 for *The Jewel of Seven Stars*, although these notes have never been discovered or annotated.

The life and times of Vlad the Impaler and his blood-thirsty contemporaries have been very fully documented in various books, whereas the 'original' of Queen Tera has attracted virtually no interest at all.

The only historical character who comes reasonably close to the description of Stoker's Queen Tera is Sebekneferu, also known as Sobknofru, daughter of the great Pharaoh Amenemhat III. She became Queen, and sole monarch, of Egypt after the death of her brother in the closing years of the Twelfth Dynasty.

Cryptically, Stoker describes Queen Tera as a ruler in the Eleventh Dynasty, and her shortened name may have been derived from 'Nebtauira' who (according to Flinders Petrie) followed Antef III in the Eleventh Dynasty. Although described as 'daughter of Antef', there were several pharaohs of this name in quick succession during the same dynasty; but in Stoker's time, Egyptologists were still arguing about the correct dates, sequence and chronology of the earlier dynasties. There were still many 'blank on the map' areas, and Stoker was free to mix fact and fiction to his heart's content.

Some of the leading Egyptologists and archaeologists of the day were among the regular guests entertained by Sir Henry Irving and Bram Stoker at the Lyceum Theatre and the Beefsteak Club in London. Stoker would have had plenty of opportunities to discuss the occult and arcane lore of Ancient Egypt with these men, and numerous acquaintances like his fellow Irish-born writer F. Frankfort Moore (brother-in-law of Mrs Bram Stoker) who had published a weird fantasy novel *The Secret of the Court* in 1895; and Sir William Wilde (father of Oscar) was among those who loved to retell stories of Egypt and Egyptology.

Scarcely a year went by without new discoveries of pharaohs' tombs near Luxor and Thebes, and in remote valleys. By 1902, E. A. Wallis Budge (acknowledged in the novel) had already published an impressive array of books on *The Mummy*, *Egyptian Magic*, *Egyptian Ideas of the Future Life*, and related subjects.

The scholar J. W. Brodie-Innes (Imperator of the Amen-Ra Temple, founded at Edinburgh in 1893), who studied witchcraft and occult Egyptian rituals, wrote to Bram Stoker in 1903 as soon as he had read *The Jewel of Seven Stars*: 'It is not only a good book, it is a *great book* ...

It seems to me in some ways you have got clearer light on some problems which some of us have been fumbling after in the dark long enough . . .' Few could have appreciated the hermetic and metaphysical insights more than Brodie-Innes.

With the compelling and horrific sequence of events related throughout this memorable novel, only a climax of unrelieved tension and finality is possible, and Stoker achieved this perfectly. However, apocalyptic and decidely 'unhappy' endings were entirely out of favour in Edwardian literature, so most of the contemporary criticism was aimed at the horrific nature of the finale, where only the narrator (Malcolm Ross) survives to tell the tale.

When the time came to reprint the book in a cheap or 'popular' edition, the publisher insisted on an entirely different ending, with the survival of the company, complete with wedding bells. (It is not clear whether the new 'bland' ending was written by Stoker himself, or by a publisher's editor—I suspect the latter.) A complete chapter (XVI), 'Powers—Old and New', was also deleted. This revised edition is the one which most readers of the book have sampled in the intervening eighty years; and the revamped somewhat lame ending has always been regarded as weak, a hurried anticlimax, especially when compared to the success of the rest of the novel.

Several more changes were made in the two cinematic versions, *Blood from the Mummy's Tomb* (1971), with Andrew Keir and Valerie Leon, and *The Awakening* (1980), with Charlton Heston and Stephanie Zimbalist; but the modern reader is well advised to go back to the complete, unadulterated text of *The Jewel of Seven Stars* to appreciate the original novel fully.

Not only did Bram Stoker write the greatest vampire novel of all time, he also created one of the best (if not *the* best) horror novels dealing with Ancient Egypt and the mummy's resurrection.

—RICHARD DALBY

25 [1904]

M. R. JAMES

Ghost Stories of an Antiquary

Ghost Stories of an Antiquary was James' first collection. It consists of two previously published pieces and several others 'which were read to friends at

Christmas-time at King's College, Cambridge'. Most feature scholarly protagonists, and many focus on antique items (the whistle of 'Oh, Whistle and I'll Come to You, My Lad', the eponymous objects of 'The Mezzotint' and 'Canon Alberic's Scrap-book'). Although frequently hailed as a master of the suggestive rather than explicit school of horror, James' stories actually contain a surprising amount of physical nastiness—the face sucked off in 'Count Magnus', the heart-ripping of 'Lost Hearts', the spider monsters of 'The Ash-tree'. Ghost Stories of an Antiquary *was followed by* More Ghost Stories of an Antiquary *(1911),* A Thin Ghost *(1919) and* A Warning to the Curious *(1926). James' stories have been adapted for television and (especially) radio many times: Jonathan Miller made a controversial* Whistle and I'll Come to You *for the BBC in 1967, and the Corporation later annually adapted several other James stories more faithfully under the collective title 'A Ghost Story for Christmas'. When we asked over a hundred modern writers to contribute to this book, M. R. James was named far more times than any other author as the most important and influential figure in the horror field.*

M. R. James is one of horror fiction's few class acts. Like Stephen King, he can write about the vile and horrific without seeming to smear it all over himself or you. His stories are rich in atmosphere, inexorable in construction—and describe a world as circumscribed as Jane Austen's.

James's first collection, published in 1904, was called *Ghost Stories of an Antiquary*. The title sums up the balance of elements in the stories. James was a brilliant medievalist and biblical scholar, provost of both King's College Cambridge and, later, Eton.

The main characters are almost always scholars, and almost always bachelors. The world is seen through their eyes. In 'Lost Hearts', the description of a Queen Anne House takes up about 140 words, while a description of the owner's library and published articles takes up another hundred—in a 4,300 word story about a little boy. The narrators in James' stories usually take no part in the action. They piece their stories together as historians would, through old documents or the evidence of friends. The scholarly, slightly fusty tone of voice; the professional characters; and the narrative technique all work together to produce what could be called an air of Cambridge verisimilitude. This air lends credence and charm to the tales, and defines their limits.

The stories are full of unlikely discoveries of old manuscripts or relics, fantasy thrills for historians. In *Canon Alberic's Scrapbook*, for example, a researcher comes across a 16th century collection of pages plundered from illuminated manuscripts. 'Such a collection Dennistoun had hardly dreamed of in his wildest moments.' But the very last page is a drawing of a demon. Here the narrator of the tale intervenes, making a sudden appearance. He describes, not the drawing which has been destroyed, but a photograph of it.

'I entirely despair of conveying by any words the impression this figure makes upon anyone who looks at it,' says the narrator and then describes the figure in great detail:

> 'At first you saw only a mass of coarse, matted black hair; presently it was seen that this covered a body of fearful thinness, almost a skeleton, but with the muscles standing out like wires. The hands were of a dusky pallor, covered, like the body, with long coarse hairs and hideously taloned. The eyes, touched in with a burning yellow, had intensely black pupils ... Imagine one of the awful bird-catching spiders of South America translated into human form and endowed with intelligence just less than human . . .'

M. R. James is thought of as a master of subtle suggestion. He almost never describes physical injury. But his terrors are described in great and very physical detail, and are the focus of the tales. The writing grows more specific when they appear—and there would be no story without them.

The monsters are seldom ghosts. They are curses—spirits of revenge or spite or unrequited longing. They erupt into our world because a scholar has dug them up. James seems to have little interest in the wider implications of his tales either moral or metaphysical. In his fictional world, witches used to be real, as in 'The Ash Tree', until they were all burnt at the stake. The justice of burning witches alive is not questioned. What is of interest is their ability to come back as a crop of large, poisonous spiders. The aims of the stories are modest—to tell a creepy story convincingly and with a measure of elegance. In this aim, he succeeds time after time, but for a historian, he shows little feeling for being haunted by the past, or little interest in what history could really teach us. Like many scholars, his attention is not held by great and central questions.

The stories have the power to unsettle because we are still not sure that our elders were wrong about witches or curses or demons. We don't really believe in electric lights. These are conservative stories, in their means and in their ends, which they do not go beyond. Their aim is to produce a frisson of fear, untainted by disgust or broader concerns. In so limiting his aims and his subject matter, in so restricting the kinds of characters he writes about and the kinds of terrors he describes, it is sometimes as if James is shutting out many other kinds of terror, terrors which his stories sometimes begin to hint at—the terror of loneliness, the terror of the smallness of one's own work, and most of the 20th century, with its wars and more mechanical horrors. It is sometimes difficult to remember that James is a writer of the 20th century. It comes as a surprise to find that his houses even have electric lights. His prose style, his narrators with their letters and documents, even the kinds of people he writes about all seem to belong to a previous era. It is as if James is using old terrors to drive out new ones.

In any event it was a very specific kind of engine that drove James's writing. He produced no other fiction than ghost stories—and those of an antiquary at that.

—GEOFF RYMAN

26   [1906]

ARTHUR MACHEN

The House of Souls

The House of Souls *assembles most of the best of Arthur Machen's occult, ghost and horror fiction. It reprints two-thirds of his linked collection,* The Three Impostors *(1895),* The Novel of the Black Seal *and* The Novel of the White Powder. *The book also includes Machen's best-known, most widely-reprinted stories, 'The White People' and 'The Great God Pan', and several other fine pieces, 'A Fragment of Life', 'The Inmost Light', and 'The Red Hand'. Much of Machen's output draws on folklore and legends, particularly the pre-Christian beliefs found in parts of his native Wales. A teacher, translator, actor, journalist and genuine occult devotee, Machen (1863–1947) also wrote* The Hill of Dreams *(1907),* The Angel of Mons: The Bowmen and Other Legends of the War *(1915),* The Terror: A Fantasy *(1917) and* The Children of the Pool and Other Stories *(1936).*

One of my longest-held ambitions—not a particularly lofty one, but the sort that all too easily gets put off, decade after decade, until one suddenly discovers it's too late—is to spend a year or so motoring around the British Isles, from Penzance to John o' Groats, stopping wherever I please. The back seat of my car would of course be filled with books: with the dozens of travel guides, highway atlases, and gazetteers of haunted houses, prehistoric sites, battlefields, and castles that I've been collecting all my life.

But in addition to the carload of reference works, I'd want to take three volumes of memoirs and a book of supernatural tales. The memoirs are those of Arthur Machen and, together, they constitute a rambling autobiography: *Far Off Things, Things Near and Far*, and *The London Adventure*. The story book is Machen's *The House of Souls*.

Machen (rhymes with 'blacken') was a Welsh clergyman's son who, as a young man, left the countryside behind and moved to London in the hope of becoming a writer, nearly starving in the attempt; later he toured with a company of Shakespearean actors, but for most of his eighty-four years he made his living as a journalist. He was born in Caerleon-on-Usk on March 3, 1863, and died in Amersham, near London, on December 15, 1947. I was privileged to share the earth with him for precisely five months.

Machen is, to my mind, fantasy's pre-eminent stylist. What makes his work so special is the rhythmic quality of his prose: one hears in it the short, seductive cadences of a fairy tale or the Bible. With the eye of a visionary and a language that is, for all its simplicity, at times truly incantatory, he reveals the wonder—and frequently the terror—that lies hidden behind everyday scenes. No other writer's work so perfectly blends the two elements of Walter Van Tilberg Clark's phrase 'the ecstasy and the dread'. (Indeed, Machen's longest foray into literary criticism, *Hieroglyphics*, sees the key attribute of great literature as 'the master word—Ecstasy'.) Jack Sullivan has noted that in Machen's best tales 'beauty and horror ring out at exactly the same moment', and praises Machen for 'his ability to make landscapes come alive with singing prose'. Philip Van Doren Stern saw Machen's imagery as 'rich with the glowing color that is to be found in medieval church glass'. No one is better at evoking the enchantment of the Welsh hills, or the sinister allure of dark woods; no one makes London a more terrifying or magical place, a latter-day Baghdad filled with exotic dangers and infinite possibilities. Wherever he looked, he saw a world filled with mystery. Every word he wrote, from youth to old age, reflects his lifelong preoccupation with 'the secret of things; the real truth that is everywhere hidden under outward appearances'.

But perhaps this 'secret of things' is too shocking for the human mind to accept. That, at least, is the premise of *The House of Souls'* best-known story. 'The Great God Pan', in which a ruthless scientist seeks to rend the 'veil' of everyday reality. ('I tell you that all these things—yes, from that star that has just shone out in the sky to the solid ground beneath our feet—I say that all these are but dreams and shadows: the shadows that hide the real world from our eyes.') In a laboratory set amid 'the lonely hills', he performs a delicate operation on the brain of a young girl, re-awakening atavistic powers and enabling her to glimpse that real world—a process he calls 'seeing the god Pan'. The result is not enlightenment but horror: the child goes mad from what she's encountered and dies 'a hopeless idiot', but not before giving birth to a daughter, a malign being who, decades later, in the form of a seductive woman, causes an epidemic of sin and suicide in Victorian London.

Today, for all its power, the tale's decadent *frissons* may seem rather dated, but at the time, 'Pan' outraged the more prudish English critics.

Machen, who took a perverse pleasure in his bad reviews (he even collected them all in a book, *Precious Balms*), relished 'the remark of a literary agent whom I met one day in Fleet Street. He looked at me impressively, morally, disapprovingly, and said: "Do you know, I was having tea with some ladies at Hampstead the other day, and their opinion seemed to be that . . . 'The Great God Pan' should never have been written."'

Two other stories in the book, 'The Novel of the Black Seal' (part of a longer work, *The Three Impostors*) and 'The Red Hand', can still provoke a shudder, even today. They theorize—as do later Machen tales—that the so-called 'Little People' of British legend, the fairy folk, were in fact the land's original inhabitants, a dark, squat, malevolent pre-Celtic race now driven underground by encroaching civilization, yet living on in caves beneath the 'barren and savage hills' and still practising their unsavoury rites, occasionally sacrificing a young woman or some other luckless wanderer they can catch alone outdoors at night. Writers such as John Buchan have also made use of this theme, but none so chillingly.

The book's most remarkable story is 'The White People'. (It was the direct inspiration, incidentally, for my own novel *The Ceremonies*, which quotes from it at length.) Most of it purports to be the notebook of a young girl who, introduced by her nurse to strange old rhymes and rituals, has a series of nearly indescribable mystical visions involving supernatural presences in the woods. We learn, at the end, that she has killed herself. The girl's stream-of-consciousness style, at once hallucinatory and naive, lends a spellbinding immediacy to the narrative, and for all its confusion and repetitiveness, it remains the purest and most powerful expression of what Jack Sullivan has called the 'transcendental' or 'visionary' supernatural tradition. Most other tales of this sort, such as Algernon Blackwood's 'The Wendigo', E. F. Benson's 'The Man Who Went Too Far', and Machen's own 'Black Seal' and 'Pan', merely *describe* encounters with dark primeval forces inimical to man; 'The White People' seems an actual *product* of such an encounter, an authentic pagan artefact, as different from the rest as the art of Richard Dadd is different from the art of Richard Doyle. Lovecraft, who regarded Machen as 'a Titan—perhaps the greatest living author' of weird fiction, ranked 'The White People' beside Blackwood's 'The Willows' as one of the best horror tales ever written. Machen, who often denigrated his own efforts, and who once wrote, 'I dreamed in fire, but I worked in clay', himself termed the tale merely 'a fragment' of the one he'd intended to write, 'a single stone instead of a whole house', but acknowledged that 'it contains some of the most curious work that I have ever done, or ever will do. It goes, if I may say so, into very strange psychological regions'. E. F. Bleiler's assessment strikes me as more accurate: 'This document is probably the finest single supernatural story of the century, perhaps in the literature.'

Bibliographical note Machen had no love for technology, the modern world, or scientific logic; appropriately, his bibliography is somewhat illogical. English and American editions of various collections are at times dissimilar; two American collections entitled *The Shining Pyramid* have different publishers and largely different contents. Before their appearance in the 1906 *House of Souls*, 'The Great God Pan' and its thematic sequel, 'The Inmost Light'—another tale of inhuman evil, similarly fragmented in form, albeit with a huge opalescent jewel as the source of the horror—had originally been published in 1894 in a separate edition. *The Three Impostors*, containing within it a number of loosely connected stories, had also appeared separately in 1895. It reappeared in the 1906 *Souls* minus one of its chapters, and, in the more commonly seen 1922 Knopf edition, it and 'The Red Hand' were omitted entirely, appearing in a volume of their own.

T. E. D. KLEIN

27   [1908]

ALGERNON BLACKWOOD

John Silence, Physician Extraordinary

This collection features a Sherlockian detective who happens also to be a medical doctor with an interest in the supernatural. His cases—in some of which he plays a relatively minor role—deal with standard ghostliness ('A Psychical Invasion'), a townful of Devil-worshipping shapeshifters ('Ancient Sorceries'), an elemental attracted to violence and blood ('The Nemesis of Fire'), Satanic rites in a secluded German monastery ('Secret Worship'), and lycanthropy in the woods ('The Camp of the Dog'). The last tale features a novel frill on the werewolf legend whereby the fiend can be identified in his human form if the observer has been smoking hashish. Val Lewton and Jacques Tourneur started to adapt 'Ancient Sorceries' when ordered by RKO Pictures to make a film called Cat People *in 1942, but the story was largely abandoned when the team decided to make up their own werecat myth. Although J. Sheridan Le Fanu's Martin Hesselius, the linking character of* In a Glass Darkly *(1872), was a psychic sleuth before John Silence took up the*

67

profession, it was Blackwood's character who set the tone for such followers as William Hope Hodgson's Carnacki the Ghost Finder, Manly Wade Wellman's John Thunstone and Joseph Payne Brennan's Lucius Leffing.

It is the penalty of true literary success that a man who has achieved it shall be seriously criticized. Mr Blackwood's book *The Empty House*, a book of ghost stories, was reviewed in these columns with a praise due to a work of the greatest merit. It was much more worthy of the term 'genius' than are nineteen out of twenty of the books to which this term is applied in a decade of reviewing. It had the quality, inseparable from genius, of conviction; it had the second quality, inseparable from genius, of creation; it had the third quality, inseparable from genius, of art. It was remarked in that former review that if the English people possess one quality more than another remarkable in European letters that quality is the quality of the romantic and the mysterious; and certainly Mr Blackwood presented the English ghost story to his readers in a way that reminded them of the triumphs of the past in this region of literature and which was yet startlingly modern in its methods and in the scientific basis upon which that method reposed. So excellent was the work that some were tempted to see in it the disguise of an older and better known hand. The present writer has heard it suggested (he discarded the suggestion) that Ambrose Bierce, the master of Bret Harte and of all the Californians, was the true author of the work. Indeed, *The Empty House* was so widely and justly discussed that the mere discussion was a true compliment to its powers.

Mr Blackwood has followed that book up by this volume called *John Silence*. It must first be described in what *John Silence* differs from *The Empty House*.

John Silence is a collection of stories dealing with the supernatural. *The Empty House* was a considerable series of short stories, quite a number of them. In *John Silence* the most important stories are lengthy; no story of this description appears in *The Empty House*. In *The Empty House*, therefore, Mr Blackwood was attempting the easier task; the task easier to anyone who desires to be poignant, and especially to be poignant in the sphere of awe. In *John Silence* there is more of the underlying philosophy which has produced this marvellous talent; for, when one says that Mr Blackwood's work approaches genius the phrase is used in no light connection, and when one says that genius connotes conviction one is asserting something which the breakdown of modern dilettante writing amply proves. There is no doubt that the writer of these arresting and seizing fictions most profoundly believes the dogmas upon which they repose; in all there is the supposition (universal before the advent of Christian philosophy) that Evil can capture the soul of a man whether that soul be deserving or undeserving, and in all there is the presupposition that (in the words of St Thomas) 'All things save God have extension,' that spiritual essences can take on, or rather must take on, corporeal form.

What has hitherto been said of this very remarkable book tells the reader little of its intimate character or of its subjects. Its subjects are a case of Possession, a case of Transmutation into another and more evil World, a case of Devil Worship, a case of an old Fire-Curse that went down the ages from Egypt and ended in an English country house, and a case of Lycanthropy. Through all of these runs the personality of a man who has given ample means and leisure to the study of occult things and who has graduated in medicine for the purpose of healing psychic disorders. But this personality, which is that of John Silence, connects rather than dominates the book; what dominates the book is its method. And that method consists in presenting human life (and animal life too, for that matter) as being a close part of one whole, and but a small part of that whole, in which vast Intelligences and vaster Wills stand towards the boundary and control everything within. It is the scheme of the Mystic, but of the Mystic absolute. It is not a mysticism in which the dual solution of Right and Wrong is afforded: it is a sort of Monist Mysticism in which, while Evil and Good are recognized, each is regarded as but one out of two poles attaching to a common substance.

All this would mean very little but for the art in which all of it is involved. Mr Blackwood's writing is of that kind which takes the reader precisely as music takes the listener. It creates a different mood. A man in the middle of one of these stories does not leave it. If he is interrupted he takes it up again where he put it down. It dominates his thought while he is concerned with it; it remains in his mind after he has completed it. In a word, the whole work is a work of successful literary achievement in the most difficult of literary provinces. It is, as its writer must by this time know, a considerable and lasting addition to the literature of our time, and let it be remembered that, tedious and paltry as the literature of our time may be, excellent writing stands in exactly the same place whether it appear among a few, and an elect few, under conditions of high taste, or in a time like ours, when everyone writes, and when most of the best of those who write are less than the worst of other and more worthy generations.

—HILAIRE BELLOC

G. K. CHESTERTON

The Man Who Was Thursday: A Nightmare

After a discussion about anarchy, Lucian Gregory finally convinces his fellow poet Gabriel Syme of his seriousness by taking him to a meeting of the Central Anarchist Council. The members of the Council are named after days of the week, and Syme is persuaded to join in the place of the recently-deceased Thursday. Syme, however, is not the poet he seems to be, but a Scotland Yard man assigned to penetrate the Council. But each member of the Council has his secrets, and it gradually emerges that there are at least as many, if not more, infiltrating detectives as there are genuine Anarchists. Above all, there remains the mysterious, perhaps Satanic, perhaps Divine, secret of Sunday, the almost inhuman President of the Council. G. K. Chesterton was a prolific author whose detective stories, prophetic fantasies and humorous tales often contain bizarre, horrific or supernatural elements. He is best known for the 'Father Brown' mysteries.

We all know some wonder-book that bowled us over in youth and miraculously seems as good or better now. For me it was Methuen's chunky G. K. Chesterton omnibus, comprising *The Napoleon of Notting Hill*, *The Man Who Was Thursday* and *The Flying Inn*. I approached this with the suspicion appropriate to Literature with the capital L, opened it at random, and found myself falling upward through a glittering realm of energy and wit.

Over several years and re-readings, I came to see that for all its grotesque exuberance, *The Man Who Was Thursday* merits the subtitle 'A Nightmare'. Chesterton walked some dark paths before attaining his colossal optimism, and *Thursday's* epigraph to E. C. Bentley observes that 'This is a tale of those old fears, even of those emptied hells, And none but you shall understand the true thing that it tells.' I certainly didn't: the dazzle of the writing, the narrative antics of poetic police, rhetorical anarchists and farcical unmaskings, kept me skating at high speed over some very thin ice.

Underneath, *Thursday* is a metaphysical chiller in which Chesterton, always adept at seeing wonder and comedy in everyday things, now evokes their terror as well. A staircase, a wood, a running man, a smile: each becomes an image of fear. Nihilism first appears as a caricature, but its philosophy is soon defined with horrible precision. 'The innocent rank and file are disappointed because the bomb has not killed the king; but the high-priesthood are happy because it has killed somebody.'

Horror and hilarity mingle in the figure of Sunday, the huge leader who makes jolly little jokes while our approaching hero Syme is 'gripped with a fear that when he was quite close the face would be too big to be possible, and that he would scream aloud.'

A sulphurous reek hangs over the members of the Central Anarchist Council with their weekday codenames. From the moment when the vast stones of the Embankment loom like Egyptian architecture over him, Syme in his spying role of Thursday walks all too close to hell. The hideously aged and decaying Friday pursues him with impossible speed through a London snowstorm; blank-eyed Saturday chills him with a mechanistic vision of scientism ('He was ascending the house of reason, a thing more hideous than unreason itself'); in his sword-duel with Wednesday he meets a demonic opponent who refuses to bleed; eventually the whole earth rises up against his lonely spark of sanity. 'The human being will soon be extinct. We are the last of mankind.'

There are further unmaskings to come: *Thursday* is not only a nightmare but a joke, and Chesterton knew that some of the most breathtakingly effective surprises are happy ones. But when the last mask is stripped away from Sunday (a symbol so vast as to be pictured only in terms of the universe itself), the thing behind is not a joke, and nobody familiar with Chesterton's faith will mistake it.

The Man Who Was Thursday is an extraordinary metaphysical melodrama, an intellectual shocker; its chillier passages have the rare quality of growing more chilly with familiarity. Few horror novels of the raw-liver persuasion have the durability of this 1908 nightmare.

—DAVID LANGFORD

29   [1908]

WILLIAM HOPE HODGSON

The House on the Borderland

In the ruins of a huge old Irish house, two fishermen discover a ragged manuscript that purports to be the journal of an old recluse who lived there with his sister. The old man describes his discovery of a huge cavern that has

*appeared beneath the house and the strange distortions of time and space
which he subsequently experiences. He is projected into a future when the
earth is dying, and to an other-dimensional blasted plain where he finds a
replica of his own house standing amid the desolation. Throughout, he has to
fight off a terrifying horde of porcine demons; finally, the creatures over-
whelm him in mid-word. A vital influence on the works of H. P. Lovecraft,*
The House on the Borderland *is the most concise and effective of Hodgson's
similarly themed novels, which include the interesting* The Boats of the 'Glen
Carrig' *(1907) and* The Ghost Pirates *(1909) and the unreadable* The Night
Land *(1912). In his obsession with entropy and the infinite, Hodgson here
seems to be elaboratingly mystically on the themes presented rationally in
H. G. Wells'* The Time Machine *(1895).*

If I had known, that fateful day in the summer of 195-, what terrors lay
beyond the undistinguished blue cloth binder under my unsuspecting
fingers . . .

My granny thought that occasional doses of mindless terror were just
what a healthy, growing boy needed. She let me work my way along the
Conan Doyles and the Vernes. Just when I thought it was all going well,
she hit me with Hodgson.

A vast cavern under the house, just under the floor, held the
unimaginable horror of the Pit; no wonder I used to go around the place
holding on to the walls. But it turned out that the walls weren't safe,
either, because outside the shadow-thin walls of the world itself there
were dreadful things, looking in and biding their time.

I wore my terror like a medal. My contemporaries watched *Torchy the
Battery Boy* in his sparkler-powered rocket ship, but that was kids' stuff
to me, who had flown on the cinder of the Earth over the interstellar gulf.
Other children hid behind sofas from *Quatermass and the Pit*. I had
grown up. I knew there were no sofas, anywhere.

And yet, and yet, how trite it sounds. Man buys House. House
attacked Nightly by Horrible Swine Things from Hole in Garden. Man
Fights Back with Determination and Lack of Imagination of Political
Proportions (*halfway* through the plot he wonders 'whether I am doing
wisely in staying here'; there's the Pit in his garden, ghastly things trying
to smash the door in at night—this man is perceptive). Estate agent had
not mentioned House is on weak spot in the fabric of reality with hot and
cold running sweat in all rooms.

Then there is the sister, apparently several coupons short of a toaster.
She drifts around the house like a small frightened rodent, and for
perhaps the first third of the book the modern reader excusably takes the
view that this is because she's got a brother who sits up all night shooting
invisible luminous pigs.

And finally, just before the things break through and claim the House,
Hodgson hands us the whole of Time and Space in a couple of chapters.

The journey to the Central Suns sold me infinity. Other people's infinities seem minuscule by comparison.

The language is that stilted, laboured form that makes most elderly horror writing such a tedious business to read. The tiny Tennysonian touches of romance are nauseous. It doesn't matter. These are just scabs on the wound, ignore them. For a day in the summer of 195–, it made me believe that Space was big and Time was endless and that what I thought of as normality was a 30 W lightbulb with only fivepence left in the meter *and there was nothing anyone could do about it.* Forget vampires and gore, it said, this is where the screaming really starts, out in the void, with no-one left to hear.

It was the Big Bang in my private universe as sf/fantasy reader and, later, writer; I can still detect its 2 cm radiation after thirty years.

We live in a cottage on the cave-haunted Mendips. Recently I tried to open up the old inglenook fireplace and found that, after I'd cleaned up the floor, there was a draught blowing *up from between the flagstones.*

Excuse the sloppy typing. I'm holding onto the wall.

Thanks, granny.

—TERRY PRATCHETT

30   [1909]

AMBROSE BIERCE

The Collected Works of Ambrose Bierce

This volume assembles Bierce's two major collections of short stories, Tales of Soldiers and Civilians *(1891, a.k.a.* In the Midst of Life*) and* Can Such Things Be? *(1893). His most famous (and imitated) story remains 'An Occurrence at Owl Creek Bridge', which was filmed by Robert Enrico as* La Rivière d'Hibou *(1961), an Oscar-winning short later transmitted as part of the original* Twilight Zone *series. His other major horror and ghost stories—which range in subject from the American Civil War through lycanthropy, hauntings, vengeful zombies, robots and psychological terror to simple human vileness—include 'The Death of Halpin Frayser', 'The Middle Toe of the Right Foot', 'Moxon's Master', 'The Damned Thing', 'Chickamauga', 'The Man and the Snake' and 'An Inhabitant of Carcosa'. The last named was*

drawn upon by Robert W. Chambers for a few names which crop up in The
King in Yellow *(1895), and were then picked up by H. P. Lovecraft and his
followers for the Cthulhu Mythos.*

Ambrose Bierce, probably the most important and influential American horror writer since Edgar Allan Poe, was born in a log cabin on
a small farm in southwest Ohio on 24 June 1842, grew up in northern
Indiana, suffered a serious head wound as a Union soldier in the
American Civil War, became a prolific journalist and short-story writer,
and was last seen on 11 January 1914 at the battle of Ojinaga in Mexico,
where he was a war correspondent covering Pancho Villa's military
actions.

Bierce's chosen fictional form was the short story. In *The Devil's
Dictionary* he disparaged the 'novel' as 'a short story padded'. He
preferred imagination to realism. He defined realism as 'The art of
depicting nature as it is seen by toads.'

Bierce's stories are cynical, sardonic, ironic, pessimistic, brutal and
filled with black humour. His trademark is the cruel surprise ending. He
was a pioneer in the tale of psychological horror.

The Civil War stories begin realistically and end as imaginative tales of
terror. In 'Chickamauga' a deaf-mute child watches as a group of soldiers
he thinks are playing war games slaughters his family. In 'A Tough
Tussle', a young Union lieutenant guarding a dead Confederate soldier is
killed by his own imagination, as is the soldier in 'One of the Missing',
trapped in a fallen building with what he believes to be a loaded rifle
pointing at him. In Bierce's most famous story 'An Occurrence at Owl
Creek Bridge', an Alabama planter about to be hanged on a bridge for
attempted sabotage escapes and makes his way home only to discover the
real horror. Again and again Bierce uses fantasy to reveal the brutality,
stupidity and horror of war.

Another group of Bierce's stories are poised between natural and
supernatural horror and in them Bierce is often ahead of his time.
'Moxon's Master', in which a chess-playing automaton kills its maker, is
a forerunner of the robot-run-amok story. In 'The Man and the Snake', a
civilian version of 'One of the Missing', a man is killed by imagining a
stuffed snake to be real. 'The Death of Halpin Frayser' in which the
victim is attacked by the ghost of his murderously possessive mother is a
portrayal of an Oedipus complex long before Freud's hypothesis. 'The
Moonlit Road' tells its story from three conflicting points of view,
including that of a murdered woman speaking through a medium, a
narrative device used 42 years later in Kurosawa's film *Rashomon*.

In Bierce's supernatural tales, life is depicted as horrible and the
afterlife as a continuation of the horror. Horror is primarily psychological. In *the Devil's Dictionary*, Bierce defines 'ghost' as 'the outward and

74

visible sign of an inward fear'. Whether dealing with werewolves ('The Eyes of the Panther'), the avenging dead ('The Middle Toe of the Right Foot'), creatures which cannot be detected by human senses ('The Damned Thing'), premature burial ('One Summer Night'), agoraphobia ('An Inhabitant of Carcosa') or corpse-watching ('A Watcher by the Dead'), the ultimate horror is always in the human mind and in man's own capacity for self-destruction.

Among later horror writers influenced by the imagination and techniques of Ambrose Bierce are Clark Ashton Smith, Robert E. Howard, H. P. Lovecraft, August Derleth and Robert Bloch.

—MILTON SUBOTSKY

31 [1911]

OLIVER ONIONS

Widdershins

The centrepiece of this collection is 'The Beckoning Fair One', a much-anthologized novella often cited as one of the best ghost stories in the English language. A writer moves into an old house to finish a novel, and finds a love-hungry female ghost who usurps his heroine, drives him mad, and jealously murders a romantic rival. Many of Onions' best stories combine ghostliness in the M. R. James tradition, with his main characters—often writers or artists—driven to psychological extremes. Widdershins also includes such memorable stories as 'Rooum', 'The Lost Thyrsus', 'The Accident', 'The Cigarette Case' and 'Hic Jacet'. Onions produced two later volumes, Ghosts in Daylight (1924) and The Painted Face (1929); the cream of the three books can be found in his Collected Ghost Stories (1935). The author's preferred pronunciation of his name was 'O-ny-ons'.

Finding titles for books is not easy, but when Oliver Onions called his first collection of ghost stories *Widdershins* he came up with a humdinger. No matter what the word means (and its meaning—contrary to the normal way of things—is singularly appropriate) it sounds right. It conjures up an image of something not quite right, and the reader's in the haunted mood at the very start. The title doesn't describe only the title of the book, it describes its author. George Oliver Onions (1873–1961) was an artist-turned-writer who strove always to do something different,

75

something out of the ordinary. A no-nonsense Yorkshireman, he had no time for spooks and phantoms but that did not stop him turning to the ghost story when the mood hit him. That mood came one crisp winter's night when his wife was combing her long hair, the air crackling with static. Onions became conscious of the unmistakable sound. 'Imagine if one heard that sound without seeing any woman standing there,' he remarked.

That was the catalyst and out of it came the lead story in *Widdershins*, 'The Beckoning Fair One'. Algernon Blackwood thought of it as 'the most horrible and beautiful ever written on those lines'; Robert Aickman claimed it as 'one of the (possibly) six great masterpieces in the field', whilst E. F. Bleiler has said of it, 'in the opinion of many, the best classical ghost story'. It alone is worth the price of admission because Onions created a story that, of its kind, cannot be bettered. With no overt spectral manifestations, but with mere hints and suggestions, he portrays the accelerated mental disintegration of the protagonist, Paul Oleron, whilst establishing an almost suffocating atmosphere of ghostly doom.

Widdershins contains eight further stories and though none is the equal of 'The Beckoning Fair One', all are highly original in theme and treatment. 'Rooum', for instance, is another unsettling story about an engineer who is haunted by something unseen which he claims pursues him and even runs 'through' him. To the reader that unseen pursuer becomes frighteningly real in Onions' portrayal of Rooum's reactions. Writing of this perception does not come easily, but Onions was able to draw upon his skills as a draughtsman and artist, and in a third story, 'Benlian', he creates one of the ultimate in artists' fantasies. Benlian is a sculptor who has created a hideous stone statue which he comes to regard as his god and to which he seeks to transfer his personality. In this story, as in 'The Beckoning Fair One', 'Rooum' and others in the collection, we find a portrayal of madness that leaves the reader uncomfortably unsure about the state of reality and sanity. This was always Onions' aim. In writing his ghost stories he set out to 'investigate the varying densities of the ghostliness that is revealed when this surface of life, accepted for everyday purposes as stable, is "jarred" and, for the time of an experience, does not recover its equilibrium.' In reading *Widdershins* the reader is likewise jarred and never again quite recovers his equilibrium.

—MIKE ASHLEY

E. F. BENSON

The Horror Horn: The Best Horror Stories of E. F. Benson

Drawing on Benson's collections The Room in the Tower and Other Stories *(1912),* Visible and Invisible *(1923),* Spook Stories *(1928) and* More Spook Stories *(1934), editor Alexis Lykiard here presents a fine selection of the more gruesome stories of E. F. Benson, with vampirism and slug-like monstrosities well to the fore. The more recent collection* The Tale of an Empty House and Other Ghost Stories *(1986), edited by Cynthia Reavell, has some overlap with* The Horror Horn, *but concentrates more on the author's gentler ghost tales, most memorably the well-regarded 'Pirates'. Although often adapted for the radio, Benson's horror output has not been much filmed. However, of this selection, 'The Room in the Tower' was the credited but vague inspiration for one of the episodes of* Dead of Night *(1946), which also features the author's 'The Bus-Conductor', and 'Mrs Amworth' became a short TV film with Glynis Johns in 1971.*

Fingers at the window; the cough in the courtyard; the laugh in the darkness at the top of the stairs. The subtle, the restrained; the terror induced by fog, firelight or shadow in which we see little and our imagination supplies the rest.

These are the materials from which are woven the stories of the macabre writers I most admire; those who work within the parameters first set by Edgar Allan Poe, M. R. James, Arthur Machen, H. R. Wakefield, Conan Doyle, Algernon Blackwood, Oliver Onions, W. H. Hodgson, Henry James, Lord Dunsany, Sheridan Le Fanu and H. P. Lovecraft, to name but a few. In this superlative company the name of E. F. Benson must stand high. Yet his work, which has a chilling horror at its very best, has been strangely neglected from the forties onward and it is only in the last 15 years or so that paperback collections of his work have begun appearing.

Edward Frederic Benson came of a distinguished family—his father was a former Archbishop of Canterbury, his elder brother A. C. Benson an essayist and poet, his younger brother Monsignor Robert Hugh Benson also a novelist—and he was a highly regarded classical scholar at Cambridge. His prodigious output as a novelist—he published over 80 books, including his still much acclaimed *Mapp and Lucia* series, recently televised, *Dodo*, and many other works of social comedy—did not prevent him working for the British School of Archaeology in Athens or being Mayor of Rye in Sussex from 1934 to 1937, where he lived at Lamb House, formerly occupied by Henry James.

Yet, for all his humorous output, Benson (1867–1940) had a darker side to his nature and there are striking parallels with W. W. Jacobs and Jerome K. Jerome. The former could turn with ease from comedy to the chill terrors of 'The Monkey's Paw' or 'His Brother's Keeper'; and the latter, while convulsing the world with *Three Men in a Boat*, also produced the horrific 'The Dancing Partner'.

Benson's art in the macabre field was wrought from the same materials. One of his most famous stories, 'The Room in the Tower', first published in 1912, relates in the most prosaic way a recurring dream which haunts the narrator: that he was a guest at a house and his hostess gives him the room in the tower. The dream comes true and at the height of a storm he is in bed when a hand is laid on his shoulder and he smells 'an odour of corruption and decay'. Benson is good at this; he and Lovecraft together with James stand almost alone in their mastery of these effects. There is blood on his shoulder when his host bursts in, and in a nearby room, a shroud spotted with earth. A woman who committed suicide had previously occupied the room. The tale ends with her body being secretly dug up when 'the coffin was found to be full of blood'.

Even more awful in its implications is Benson's celebrated tale 'Caterpillars', which combines the unique terror of the caterpillars' squirming on the victim's bedding with most human beings' everyday fears of falling victim to a dreaded disease. Benson also wrote one of the most celebrated of vampire stories, doubly chilling because it takes place in a modern setting, its focus of evil a smilingly benevolent middle-aged woman, 'Mrs Amworth'. This is one of my all-time favourites and is the perfect expression of the ordinary made terrible, an art which Alfred Hitchcock was to perfect in another medium, that of the cinema.

Equally disturbing is the fourth in Benson's quartet of most powerful stories, 'Negotium Perambulans', rather reminiscent of F. G. Loring's 'The Tomb of Sarah', in which a land-owner in a lonely part of Cornwall inadvertently disturbs a *thing* which eventually wreaks havoc. All this is described in the gentle, measured prose of a scholar, thus making the events both more awful and more plausible, which, after all, is the art which conceals art. The climax involves a giant slug-like creature, which gives off 'a stale phosphorescent light'.

There are many other tales from his gifted pen; most of them with evocative titles which chill even before the reader turns the page: 'The Thing in the Hall', 'The House with the Brick-Kiln', 'The Face', 'The Bed by the Window' and 'The Horror Horn'.

In describing some of my favourites I hope to strike a sympathetic chord in the reader and can only hope that she or he will turn to some of

Benson's neglected masterpieces, whose very pages seem to breathe out the odour of decay. But there are also many delights among the horrors.

—BASIL COPPER

33   [1920]

DAVID LINDSAY

A Voyage to Arcturus

Among the people assembled for a seance in Hampstead are three strangers— Maskull, a rootless man, and Nightspore and Krag, two peculiar visitors from Tormance, a planet orbiting Arcturus. Nightspore and Krag take Maskull with them on their journey back to Tormance, and the Earthman is left to wander the surreal, symbolic landscapes of the new planet, where it becomes obvious that his Pilgrim's Progress *is of a psychological rather than an actual nature. Experiencing everything from love to murder, Maskull is caught between Krag and a rival divinity variously known as Surtur, Shaping and Crystalman, unable to tell which is an angel and which the Devil. An odd refinement of the 'interplanetary voyage' genre of early science fiction, comparable with Wells, Verne, and Burroughs,* A Voyage to Arcturus *has been influential on authors as diverse as Jack Vance and Clive Barker. Lindsay also wrote* The Haunted Woman *(1922),* Sphinx *(1923), and* Devil's Tor *(1932).*

Around 1920, as around 1947, the horror story experienced a sea-change. At both periods, a generation desperate to put behind them the realities of war sought the kind of writing that would justify them and repudiate the ways of their elders. Economics and the psyche were in; destiny and the soul were out. Updated horrors were fine; old-fashioned ones were not. The touch of grue in some of Michael Arlen's stories suited the survivors of Verdun excellently, just as Fritz Leiber's citified ghosts suited the survivors of the Normandy beach-heads.

What was sought was the kind of shudder that might be seen to afflict that peculiar creature, 'the contemporary man' (as if there had ever been born a man who was not 'contemporary'!) At all events, precisely what was *not* wanted was a story about eschatological horror, that kind of

79

horror that has afflicted all the sons of Adam, and no doubt Adam himself in his latter days. Under the circumstances, it was hardly surprising that *A Voyage to Arcturus* was a complete and commercial failure. Had it emerged in 1947, the result would almost certainly have been the same. E. H. Visiak—himself not unaccomplished in this genre—described the novel as inducing 'a state of spiritual terror'. Alas! Such an adjective, at such a time, was a complete no-no.

Well, if Lindsay's novel went down like the proverbial lead balloon, what feature does it have to enable its author to correctly predict that, as long as publishing existed at all, it would always have readers, however few? What was his 'secret ingredient'?

The ingredient is utter honesty in the face of life and of death. The stories of Lindsay's contemporaries in the occult genre—Oliver Onions, E. Nesbit, Sax Rohmer, R. H. Benson, for example—were all dealing with 'entertainments': the terrible things that have happened to Miss M—— or Mr Y——. Miss M—— and Mr Y—— are characters beheld in your mind's eye—they are, in that sense, outside of you. For a moment, as their fate befalls them, you, as one with them, are seized with fear. After that, there remains only the memory of a not-unpleasant thrill. *You* remain untouched (I can think of one exception to this, from the writings of the twenties: May Sinclair's 'Where Their Fire Is Not Quenched').

Lindsay's book, however, is simply not pitched at this level. He is not an entertainer: he is a reporter, bringing you an in-depth account of the interior existence. This account is full of strange colours and eerie sounds: the characters met are often physically bizarre. The superficial reader might call all this 'romantic'. It would be hard to imagine a greater error. The landscape described is actually that of one's own soul, and the characters are ourselves as seen in a distorting mirror. Maskull and Nightspore are you and I. For that matter, we are also Corpang, Tydamin, Spadevil and the rest of the Arcturian crew. But our relationship towards them is different from that we have with Maskull and Nightspore, just as in everyday life we know that we are 'different' from those other bodies we see about us—that we are the centre about which they revolve. Of course, a moment's introspection will destroy this illusion of ours—which is why we are at such pains not thus to introspect.

No, Lindsay was a realist, just as Cabell and Dunsany were realists, whatever the romantic disguises they employed. But he is the more brutal, since he singularly refuses to give us even the most provisional final answer to the riddles he sets. He is, too, at singular pains not to let us off lightly. Has *any* English writer devised a more effective way of describing that certain aspect of life that Lindsay sums in his 'Crystal-man' concept? For myself, I cannot recall a more ice-cold moment of horror than that experienced when reading Nightspore's climactic ascent of the tower of Muspel.

There is no evasion on Lindsay's part in leaving his novel on a suspended ending, for that suspended ending is *us*. It is not Nightspore who has to confront these issues, issues where, as Krag says, 'nothing will be done without the bloodiest blows.' It is you and I. There's terror for you!

—GEORGE HAY

34 [1925]

FRANZ KAFKA

The Trial

Joseph K., an ordinary office worker, is arrested one morning on an unspecified charge and sucked into a vast legal bureaucracy that will never let him go. He tries to reason with a succession of officials, but never does find out what exactly is happening to him. His life is ruined and, after a protracted legal wrangle, the court sends a pair of executioners to put him out of his misery. Mainly written some time before 1920, Der Prozess did not see publication until after the author's death in 1924, and even then was issued against the wishes Kafka expressed in his will. Like The Castle, *it is an unfinished novel: although the last chapter—the execution—was written, Kafka never got around to producing the sections of the book describing the actual trial. It was idiosyncratically filmed in 1963 by Orson Welles, with Anthony Perkins as Joseph K.*

In a passage Kafka deleted from *The Trial* (perhaps because it made his meaning too explicit), Joseph K. tells us that 'waking up was the riskiest moment of the day':

> ... it requires enormous presence of mind or rather quickness of wit, when opening your eyes to seize hold as it were of everything in the room at exactly the same place where you had let it go on the previous evening.

From Kafka's diary during this period:

> My talent for portraying my dreamlike inner life has thrust all other matters into the background; my life has dwindled dreadfully, nor will it cease to dwindle.

It is interesting to keep these statements in mind when reading this dreamlike, paranoiac novel. No modern novel captures the sense of a waking nightmare better than Kafka's *The Trial*. The obsessions of the dream are continued into waking life and embodied in the objects and people which surround the protagonist.

Although the novel's setting is naturalistically detailed, its logic is that of a dream landscape. Joseph K. is never told what he is accused of, and after only a few initial queries he does not ask. He is strangely obsessed by a degenerate sexuality he sees all around him, and is unable to stop himself from seducing his lawyer's maid when he should be discussing his case. He encounters people he should know but he does not recognize them—their identities change from one scene to the next. The Court of Inquiry where he must go is disguised within a tenement and once inside he discovers that this chamber is impossibly large for the structure.

As in a dream, he is at times uncharacteristically brave in his speeches and lacking in impulse control. As in a dream, rooms are impossibly transformed: a bank's storage room suddenly becomes a torture chamber for two of his guards. As in a dream, his body rebels in small ways, he becomes lost easily, and his own self-destructive behavior is frightening to him. His accusers are everywhere; he is acutely aware of faces watching him from windows and keyholes; he senses ears pressed against doors.

He considers compiling a written defense which might have been designed against an unsettling and ambiguous dream reality:

> In this defense he would give a short account of his life, and when he came to an event of any importance explain for what reasons he had acted as he did, intimate whether he approved or condemned his way of action in retrospect, and adduce grounds for the condemnation or approval . . .

Although not the first work to use such techniques, *The Trial* has at least indirectly influenced much of modern horror fiction. Joseph K.'s environment alternatively convinces us with its realism and then is fantastically transformed so that K. is able to see his buried obsessions acted out by the people and city around him. His confidence in reality is thus eroded: this is a harbinger of the paranoid landscapes of such writers as Ramsey Campbell and Dennis Etchison.

The Trial's blurring of the line between character and landscape demonstrates the way characterization functions in much of fantasy fiction. Critics who label Kafka's characters two-dimensional haven't realized that much of this characterization occurs within Kafka's personalized, transformed landscapes. As in a dream, every object and person in the city is a transformed piece of Joseph K.'s character. Consider again Kafka's diary entry mentioned earlier. The fact that his protagonist is named K., and one of K.'s guards is called Franz, might suggest that *The Trial* is a portion of Kafka's own internal landscape and that all its pieces, collectively, characterize *him*.

Kafka maximizes the efficacy of his characterization technique by burying the individual personalities of the subordinate characters within their bureaucratic masks, making them more emblematic of K.'s personal obsessions. Other techniques in *The Trial* which support this approach to characterization (and which have come to typify much of modern horror fiction) are the novel's minimal sense of time passage, and the focus on tone and atmosphere accompanied by a deep probing of internal, subjective states—as opposed to the focus on plot progression found in 'realistic' fiction.

In *The Trial*, Kafka created a landscape in which every detail is potentially significant and a clue to the character of Joseph K. Although more opaque than the many dream narratives which have followed, it stands as a significant precursor to the psychologically informed, contemporary novel of dark fantasy.

—STEVE RASNIC TEM

35   [1927]

JAMES BRANCH CABELL

Something About Eve

In 1805, a Southern gentleman called Gerald Musgrave, wishing to evade the attentions of his married cousin, Evelyn Townsend, strikes a bargain with Glaum of the Haunting eyes, a demon. Glaum agrees to become Gerald's doppelgänger and take over his life, thus freeing the young man to pursue a life of itinerant adventure. Gerald's haphazard quest for the magical city of Antan leads him to encounter a series of peculiar characters, most notably a succession of scheming, charming, seductive and dangerous women. Something About Eve is the eleventh volume in the loosely connected epic romance The Biography of the Life of Manuel, which consists of over twenty books, including Jurgen (1919), The High Place (1923) and The Silver Stallion (1926), and takes the incredibly complicated family of its knightly hero from the imaginary medieval French province of Poictesme to 20th-century America. To put it tactfully, Cabell's writing remains, like that of Robert E. Howard, something of an acquired taste.

Something About Eve is perhaps the crowning achievement of a man who, speaking in a purely literary sense, is undoubtedly the ablest writer of the present age. Here let me remark that there is nothing ambiguous or vague about Cabell's style—there is nothing of the rambling, incoherent maunderings of most of the modern school of writers, who seek to conceal their own ignorance by making the reader feel confused and bewildered. Cabell writes with a diamond pen, if you understand me.

Well, *Something About Eve* would be a masterpiece if for no other reason, because of its perfect English and its juicy morsels of carefully turned obscenity. Cabell has the elegant knack of being beautifully vulgar, and of concealing—from the mass—the most jubilant depravities in innuendo. This alone should be attraction enough for the feminine readers of the nation.

But there is more than this to *Something About Eve*. I was not able to discern whether or not Cabell believed himself in the existence of a Third Truth, but he at least pointed out two minor facts: that most men desire a Third Truth and no man finds it—this side of Hell, at least.

And he shows clearly that women are fatal to endeavour—whether they be the home-loving kind or the butterfly breed. And of the two, Maya is infinitely more to be feared than Evadne of the Dusk. For in the arms of Evadne, a man loses only his manhood, his reputation, his honour, and frequently his life, while with Maya he loses his only worthwhile possessions—ideals and ambition. Circe made boars out of men, but Maya makes steers out of them, to browse over her level pastures of convention forevermore in content—Oh Judas—content! Let me content myself with Evadne—

Better the serpent fangs of Evadne than the cloying and stultifying domesticity of Maya and her brood—for they are both daughters, after all, of the nameless goddess, though men call one Lilith and the other Eve. And Evadne is but an affair of the road, a wandering off the path, an unpleasant episode, which if it be unforgettable, may at least be concluded, whereas Maya, being utter illusion, can never be brought to an end, and means the permanent halting of the rider who goes down the long road to that utterly barren and arid goal of all dreamers which is the only thing worthwhile, which is worth more than any earthly kingdom—and which most men squander for a fat, sluggish life in the arms of a whining, waddling daughter of Maya.

Well, the Adversary be thanked, there is nothing about me to attract either a daughter of Eve or one of Lilith—so I will ride relentlessly down the long road to Antan and the doom that waits there, while the great majority of you, my sneering masculine readers, will be sitting under your chestnut trees with the scent of Maya's cooking in your nostrils, watching the antics of your brood through rose-coloured glasses.

—ROBERT E. HOWARD

E. H. VISIAK

Medusa

A young lad, William Harvell, accompanies an expedition to the Indian Ocean for the purpose of ransoming captives from pirates. The pirate ship is discovered empty but for a single madman, who directs the would-be rescuers towards destruction in the maw of an ancient and evil monstrosity. On its original publication, Medusa *was something of a failure, partially thanks to a ferocious review in* The Times *(somewhat too late, the paper referred to it as a 'tour-de-force' in the author's obituary). Visiak, not a prolific fantasist, lived long enough to see the novel back in print in the sixties and was encouraged by its renewed reputation to take up the pen again. Besides his three novels, he turned out several books of poetry,* Buccaneer Ballads *(1910) and* The Phantom Ship *(1912) among them, and a handful of fine short stories, including 'In the Mangrove Hall', 'The Cutting', 'Medusan Madness', and 'The Queen of Beauty'.*

I'm always a bit put off when someone asks me to name my favourite book of all time, or even the three best horror books. It's rather like asking one to name the best wine in the world or the finest dinner ever served. I'm sure that anyone who has read more than a dozen outstanding books—as you have, or you wouldn't be bothering with this—can sympathize with me in this problem. When pressed to give an answer, such selections inevitably become personal and quirky. It really would be easier and far more valid to list perhaps one hundred 'best' books. Oh, well . . .

A few years back I was asked by *The Twilight Zone Magazine* to generate three lists of thirteen books each of the best horror novels ever written. Even with that latitude, choices were of necessity eccentric. Only the Fates know how selection #39 pushed out selection #40. However, one of my selections was *Medusa* by E. H. Visiak. This novel is now among my Top Three selections, and if you asked me how closely it had nudged past David Lindsay's *Devil Tor*, I really couldn't say. Well, I'll try.

I believe that I once described *Medusa* as the probable outcome of Herman Melville having written *Treasure Island* while tripping on LSD. I can't add much to that, except to suggest that John Milton may have popped round on his way home from a week in an opium den to help him revise the final draft. We're talking heavy surreal here.

However. *Medusa* was indeed written by E. H. Visiak (born London, 20 July 1878; died Hove, Sussex, 30 August 1972). Despite living to the age of 94, Visiak left only three major novels: *The Haunted Island* (1910), *Medusa* (1929) and *The Shadow* (1936). These, in addition to a few short stories, poems, and critical studies of Milton (not surprisingly to one who has read his novels, Visiak was an authority on Milton) are about all he is remembered for today—and remembered by a few, at best. He was also a close friend of the afore-mentioned David Lindsay, another strange genius whose work has been similarly overlooked. Anyone who has read both writers' works will have readily noted comparisons.

All three of the above-listed novels read like drug-induced visionary interpretations of Robert Louis Stevenson's *Treasure Island*—a bit like Ingmar Bergman filming a William S. Burroughs screenplay of the book, with Richard O'Brien as Jim Hawkins. *Medusa* is the most successful of the three. It's a soul-eating Cthulhoid entity, not your common-garden-variety rubber-tentacled monster. It preys upon the human failings and spiritual evils that exist within every human being. We are all of us flawed creatures, flawed beyond the hope of redemption when confronted by genuine evil. Visiak suggests that such destroying evil comes from within ourselves. This is not a happy book.

If your horizons reach beyond knife-wielding zombies, check *Medusa* out. It might make you think, and then it might *really* scare you.

—KARL EDWARD WAGNER

37   [1933]

GUY ENDORE

The Werewolf of Paris

An overlapping series of accounts enables a modern American writer in Paris to piece together the story of Bertrand Caillet, the unfortunate offspring of a lecherous priest with an evil family history and a young peasant girl. Although raised by the kindly Aymar Galliez, Bertrand has a troubled childhood and is suspected of lycanthropy, cannibalism and incest. Galliez pursues Bertrand to Paris, but the werewolf's atrocities pale in comparison with the wholesale slaughter taking place in 1870 during the Paris Commune. The werewolf ends his days pathetically in an insane asylum. The Werewolf of Paris is the classic 20th-century treatment of the werewolf legend, unequalled until Robert

Stallman's The Book of the Beast *(1980–82). Endore was a commercial writer, who contributed to the screenplays of such classic horror films as* Mad Love *(1935),* Mark of the Vampire *(1935) and* The Devil Doll *(1936). The* Werewolf of Paris *was filmed, with the locale changed to Spain for budgetary reasons, by Hammer Films as* Curse of the Werewolf *(1961), directed by Terence Fisher and starring the young Oliver Reed as the afflicted protagonist.*

Though Guy Endore's *The Werewolf of Paris* boasts characters, settings and diction so convincingly Gallic that one instinctively glances at the title page for the translator's name, it is an English language classic that was first published in 1934, during that nightmarish period of twilight sleep between the two World Wars.

The Werewolf of Paris is a devastating dissection of the many masks of corruption, whether ethical, familial or governmental. Its hero is the pathetic lycanthrope, Bertrand Caillet; its villains are lascivious priests, bloodthirsty soldiers and inhuman authority figures, such as the doctors and orderlies at the insane asylum where Bertrand spends his last miserable days. Beginning with one of the most dreadful *conte cruelles* ever penned (the tale of Pitaval and Pitamont), Guy Endore tells a grisly and erotic story that masterfully offsets our sympathy for the titular protagonist with towering moral outrage for mankind's burgeoning savagery—an ironic stylistic device that prefigures the postwar disillusionment of such widely disparate works of fantasy as, say, Eugène Ionesco's absurdist drama, *Rhinoceros*, or Stephen King's popular vampire novel, *'Salem's Lot*, both of which, consciously or unconsciously, are thematically indebted to *The Werewolf of Paris*. Note, especially, this significant passage from Chapter Seventeen:

> The Commune shot fifty-seven from the prison of La Roquette. Versailles retaliated with nineteen hundred. To that comparison add this one. The whole famous Reign of Terror in fifteen months guillotined 2,596 aristos. The Versaillists executed 20,000 commoners before their firing squads in one week. Do these figures represent the comparative efficiency of guillotine and modern rifle or the comparative cruelty of upper and lower class mobs?
>
> Bertrand ... was but a mild case. What was a werewolf who had killed a few prostitutes, who had dug up a few corpses, compared with these bands of tigers slashing at each other with daily increasing ferocity! And ... future ages will kill millions. It will go on, the figures will rise and the process will accelerate! Hurrah for the race of werewolves!

The Werewolf of Paris is also reminiscent of Theodore Sturgeon's *Some of Your Blood*, a short novel about a sado-masochistic romance that attempts, not altogether successfully, to make the reader sympathize with its tormented hero. But Bertrand Caillet, in spite of the crimes of

87

passion he commits when 'the change' is on him, is the novel's ultimate victim. Even by today's jaded standards, Bertrand's bloody affair with the consenting, doomed Sophie de Blumenburg is deeply shocking, not because of its essential gruesomeness, but because Guy Endore treats his lovers with sensitivity and compassion, qualities too often lacking in contemporary horror literature.

—MARVIN KAYE

38   [1933]

MARJORIE BOWEN

The Last Bouquet: Some
Twilight Tales

Marjorie Bowen was one of the many pseudonyms used by Mrs Gabrielle Margaret Vere Long, authoress of a huge number of historical romances, biographies, history books, short stories and thrillers: most of Mrs Long's macabre output was published under the Bowen name (she should not be confused with her contemporary, Elizabeth Bowen). The Last Bouquet is devoted exclusively to ghost stories, typically involving either repressed but wealthy spinsters ('The Last Bouquet', 'The Crown Derby Plate') or horrid doings in a period setting ('The Avenging of Ann Leete', 'Kecksies'). Her novels of the macabre include Black Magic *(1909),* The Haunted Vintage *(1921) and* The Shadow on the Mockways *(1932), and she was also the editor of* Great Tales of Horror *(1933) and* More Great Tales of Horror *(1935).*

Among connoisseurs it is commonly heard that Marjorie Bowen is the première horror writer of our century. Yet she is under-represented in anthologies. Most of her books are so rare as to be known to the connoisseur and none other. The only modern edition, *Kecksies* (Arkham House, 1976) captures some of her best stories, but also some workman-like pieces, weakening the overall effect. Far more representative are *The Bishop of Hell* (1949) and especially *The Last Bouquet*.

As a prose stylist she was a throwback to the 1890s. Her reader can easily imagine Beardsley her illustrator, Leonard Smithers her publisher. She improves upon the aesthetic and decadent mode in that she is never actually florid, but stylish and moody, dramatic to the highest pitch. Best known in her day as an historical novelist, she had an output so enormous that the term 'hack' might appear apropos. Yet she achieved an average quality above the 'best' of more lionized writers, while her own best is untouchable by her contemporaries or our modern masters.

She certainly could write a trivial tale upon occasion, but none are to be found in *The Last Bouquet*. The low points are probably 'Raw Material' and 'The Prescription', this latter a retelling of too simple a ghost story previously told by Henry van Dyke as 'The Night Call'. One of her best-known stories, 'The Crown Derby Plate', has always struck me as pointless, yet this 'weak' piece is an anthology favorite. Finer is 'Kecksies', an anti-heroic fantasy, while the well-known 'Avenging of Ann Leete' is quintessentially Bowen in its sinister and romantic evocations; it represents the quality of the majority of these 14 stories. In Bowen's hands, ghost stories are transformed into parables of rage and passion both human and inhuman.

'The Fair Hair of Ambrosine', regarding precognition and murder, is a period tale of the grimmest sort. 'Florence Flannery' also has an historical setting and offers a tragic love affair; the suffering protagonist lives through her confused centuries of torment only to find herself, at last, in the arms of a demonic, avenging love. In tales like 'The Last Bouquet', 'The Lady Clodagh' and 'Madame Spitfire', we are treated to exceedingly refined portraits of passionate and insanely evil women, for whom Bowen seems to have had a niggling liking.

The famous tale of 'The Sign-painter and the Crystal Fishes'—one of her scant quarter-dozen tales commonly anthologized—is a break from her usual pattern in that sadness is evoked rather than anguish or hatred. It reveals Bowen's sensitive side to be as horrific as the dark passions.

Today's authors are more than ever intrigued by sexuality and horror. None achieves Bowen's heights of evil romance, her *sensuality* and horror. What in other hands is merely tacky or gross is, from Marjorie Bowen, a superior art, chilling and seductive.

—JESSICA AMANDA SALMONSON

39   [1934]

ALEXANDER LAING

The Cadaver of Gideon Wyck

Published 'as by a Medical Student', with Laing credited only as the editor, this novel purports to be an actual account of a murder case in which David

Saunders, the narrator, was a suspect. Gideon Wyck, a sinister and ill-liked member of the faculty of the Maine State College of Surgery, is involved in various bizarre experiments, which focus on the demented Mike Connell, a blood donor who has fits whenever anyone who has been given his blood dies, and on a series of abnormal births. When Wyck disappears, Saunders, his telephonist girlfriend Daisy and Dr Manfred Alling, the deformed head of the school, investigate and discover a variety of peculiar circumstances. Later, Wyck's corpse turns up, ineptly embalmed, in the school morgue, which has been sealed during the holidays. Further complications lead to several inquests and trials, during which various misdeeds are uncovered and a murderer (or two, or three) is exposed. An early example of the type of medical thriller latterly the province of Robin Cook, The Cadaver of Gideon Wyck *dabbles in mad science and demonology as it builds to its detective story finale. Laing also wrote* Dr Scarlett: A Narrative of His Mysterious Behaviour in the East *(1936) and its sequel,* The Methods of Dr Scarlett *(1937). His* The Motives of Nicholas Holtz *(1936, a.k.a.* The Glass Centipede*) was written in collaboration with Thomas Painter. The character of Dr Alling would seem to have impressed Robert Bloch enough to inspire a gruesome short story, 'The Mannikin', itself an influence on the film* Basket Case *(1982).*

I venture to say that few of the readers of this volume are familiar with *The Cadaver of Gideon Wyck*, or with its author, Alexander Laing. If this is the case, I'm not surprised, for the novel was published a half-century or more ago in a small hardcover edition, and I've been unable to ascertain if it was reprinted when paperbacks came into vogue. Moreover, 'Alexander Laing' was the pseudonym of a writer who didn't wish to risk his stature as a respectable author by attaching his real name to a horror story. Nonetheless, the book attained a small success in its initial publication—enough, apparently, to encourage an encore, entitled *The Motives of Nicholas Holtz*. The latter died a deserved death, and leads me to wonder if the 'Alexander Laing' byline had been used by another.

But the first book seemed to me, at the time, to be a genuine *tour de force*, dealing as it did with the then little-exploited phenomenon of teratology [the study of animal or vegetable monstrosities]. I base my esteem for the work on my initial encounter, and in all fairness, should probably re-read the book before giving it a place in this volume, thus ruling out such equally impressive efforts as Ramsey Campbell's *The Face That Must Die*, or work by Grant, Williamson, Straub, Somtow et al.

But first impressions are inclined to leave the deepest imprint, and I recall *The Cadaver of Gideon Wyck* as one of the most grisly and evocative readings of a misspent lifetime. I do wish I could unearth the volume and discover the real name of its author: both deserved better than this long languishment in obscurity. Strange, how so many worthwhile creations seem to be forever forgotten for lack of proper praise and attention upon first appearance. But for what it is worth, I recommend this chiller to your attention; if you track it down, I think you may share my opinion.

—ROBERT BLOCH

40 [1937]

SIR HUGH WALPOLE (Editor)

A Second Century of Creepy Stories

This huge collection, besides featuring short novels like J. Sheridan Le Fanu's 'Carmilla' and Henry James' The Turn of the Screw, includes many stories that have since become anthology perennials: Wilkie Collins' 'Mad Monkton', Ambrose Bierce's 'A Watcher By the Dead', Oliver Onions' 'The Beckoning Fair One', Guy De Maupassant's 'The Horla' and F. Marion Crawford's 'The Upper Berth'. Besides these Victorian and Edwardian classics, Walpole (who is himself represented by 'Tarnhelm') selects pieces from the leading ghost story writers of the day, Walter de la Mare, Algernon Blackwood, Marjorie Bowen, Margaret Irwin, and A. M. Burrage. Arthur Machen and M. R. James are included with comparatively unfamiliar stories, 'Change' and 'Mr Humphreys and His Inheritance'.

Simply the best anthology ever assembled; I've held this view for over thirty years.

Walpole edited the sequel to Hutchinson's *Century of Creepy Stories* in 1937, four years after the first volume. It was a vast improvement on the first as well, that book being merely several collections edited by Cynthia Asquith rather roughly cobbled together.

Despite having the appearance of a Walpole old pals' meeting (there is no denying it contains many of his literary chums), the contents alone make it unique. Find me another book that contains 'Carmilla', 'The Beckoning Fair One', 'The Horla' and *The Turn of the Screw*!

My interest in ghost stories began with this book (and the collected M. R. James) at a very tender age. I was a precocious reader and my parents' bookshelves contained many discoveries. These two were there, along with Eleanor Scott's *Randall's Round* and Robert W. Chambers' *Slayer of Souls*. I must have read them all by the age of ten, though I can't claim I understood much of them until later. Arthur Machen's 'Change', for example, made no sense at all until much later in my life, when I realized he was talking about the little people swapping one of their own for a human baby. In fact, Walpole still seems to be the only editor to have used the story.

The rarities include the Ex-Private X story from his impossibly rare collection *Someone in the Room*: an embittered rustic kills his daughter and her lover as the latter is a member of a rich family occupying his old home. The murdered pair return to avenge their death. It contains a line which made me shiver then and still does: *'There's company in the copse at night as you wouldn't like meeting. There's them that can't sleep because they lies hard and damp'*.

Other scenes firmly planted in my memory from the first readings of the book are: John Metcalfe's phantom boat chasing the owner's ex-wife; Le Fanu's description of the destruction of the vampire's body (floating in blood in its coffin!); Walpole's Uncle Robert who could change into a dog and smelt of caraway-seed (I still don't know what that smells like); Marjorie Bowen's ghost who said she lived generally in the garden and smelt of earth; the little-known but absolutely creepy Ann Bridge story where two dead climbers come and get two children—in my ten-year old mind, that struck home with a vengeance; and the pure terror (I can still feel it) of 'Browdean Farm', where a broken-necked ghost comes and taps at the window, and once—horrendously—starts towards the narrator when he looks out of the front door.

The production of such books is very much curtailed these days by economic considerations. The nearest we've seen to its 1023 pages in recent years has been the Mary Danby collections for Marks and Spencer. Even those, backed by a large retail chain, only dared go up to 700 pages. It's a pity.

No collection of ghost stories should be without Walpole's book. By size and quality of contributors alone, it is the best anthology I have ever seen. I do not think we will see anything like it again.

—HUGH LAMB

41   [c. 1938]

C. S. LEWIS

The Dark Tower

Orfieu, a Cambridge don, reveals to a company that includes the narrator, C. S. Lewis himself, and Ransom, the hero of the author's Perelandra *(1943)*

92

and That Hideous Strength *(1945), that he has constructed a chronoscope, a device which enables him to look into a parallel world. In this Othertime, they observe a horde constructing an exact replica of the Cambridge University Library and a worker caste subjected to a race of hive-mind components who are created by an overlord known as a Unicorn, who has a sting in his forehead. Scudamore, the youngest of the party, discovers that the current Unicorn is his double and is accidentally whisked away to live in his counterpart's body . . . This suggestive fragment, clearly influenced by H. G. Wells but in its parallel world theme also perhaps the dark side of Lewis' 'Narnia' books, was composed around 1938. The novel was either abandoned or has not survived complete. In this 1977 edition, with notes by Walter Hooper, it is accompanied by several uncollected science fiction stories and another fragment,* After Ten Years, *about the Trojan War.*

More years ago than I care to remember—probably about 1945/50—I was listening to an old Valentine Dyall *Man in Black* radio programme. It was the one about the man who was spending a jolly, mind-destroying evening observing a corpse in a glass-panelled coffin; only the corpse wasn't dead, and, when it tapped on the glass, the guy who was keeping his morbid vigil to win a bet apparently blew a fuse. Shortly afterwards the corpse-impersonator blew a fuse as well, and the result was as predictably cheerful as the last scene of *Hamlet.*

The point was that the hapless vigil-keeper was philosophizing about the hypothesis of fear: he said that fear consisted of the two words 'what if?' and that we entered the state we call fear only because of possibilities. Thinking about it intermittently over the past four decades, I believe there's some mileage in it. The most effective horror and the most spine-tingling fear are frequently centred on the unknown.

It follows, for me at any rate, that the extra edge of *unknownness* adds a certain piquancy to a horror story. We are familiar with what happens to Dracula and his minions when they get their xyloid cardiac implants; werewolves respond equally satisfactorily to silver blades or silver bullets; ghouls and poltergeists avoid Holy Water; and a good .44 magnum will put paid to mere physical monstrosities.

But how do we deal with unknown horror?

What if the author himself left the tale tantalizingly unfinished, and the reader's imagination has to supply the ending?

My choice of C. S. Lewis's *Dark Tower* depends not only upon its being a first class horror/mystery story in its own right as far as it goes (and we only have the first sixty-four pages of it) but upon this intriguing element of its missing ending.

I'm also fascinated by coincidences, or what we choose to call coincidences, and the real life coincidence attached to *The Dark Tower* is almost a story in itself. Lewis had a gardener named Fred Paxford, who saved the unfinished manuscript of *The Dark Tower* from the flames after Lewis died.

From all accounts, Mr Paxford was a great gardener, but very pessimistic. Predicting all manner of crop failures throughout the year, he nevertheless produced superb results each autumn. Upon him Lewis based the character of Puddleglum the Marshwiggle in *The Silver Chair*, part of the immortal 'Narnia' series for children. This Puddleglum was as pessimistic as the Apostle Thomas, and equally loyal and faithful when the chips were down. In the story he saves the other heroes by extinguishing the witch's fire and destroying her evil spell. That the real Fred Paxford saved many of Lewis's manuscripts from the bonfire after his death is an uncanny parallel with the action of his literary *alter ego* in *The Silver Chair*.

What makes *The Dark Tower* such an outstandingly good horror/ mystery story? Firstly, its intriguing, unknown ending; secondly, its very smooth transition from the ordinary to the horrific and weird: for my money, the best horror stories begin in the here and the now and almost imperceptibly remind us that the façade of everyday life, behind which we shelter from the Great Unknown, offers as much protection from the real universe as a chocolate fireguard. Thirdly, *The Dark Tower* incorporates one of my favourite horror story ingredients: an alternative universe. When the explorers get their chronoscope working, it dawns on them at last that they are looking neither at the past nor the future but a sinister, alternative *present*. Somehow that seems so much more threatening than a time that has passed or a time that is yet to be—there is always the danger of being sucked across into that horrendous *other now*.

Then, fourthly, there is the eternal conflict element in the story. In the Dark Tower of the title a battle is raging between good and evil: the same battle that vivifies Tolkien's *The Lord of the Rings*, or Lewis's *Ransom* trilogy. Perhaps it might be truer and more accurate to talk of *the* battle, or *the* war rather than a battle. Only this one great fight between Right and Wrong, Justice and Injustice, Order and Chaos, Truth and Lies— whatever names we choose to give the Contestants—is real. All other conflicts are merely symptoms and manifestations of it. This, too, is a major attraction of *The Dark Tower*: Lewis has no doubts about the eschatology. However hard the struggle, and however great the suffering before the final victory, Good will triumph.

The Dark Tower is not only a brilliant and fascinating ·unfinished masterpiece of mystery and horror: it is a worthwhile philosophical statement.

—LIONEL FANTHORPE

DALTON TRUMBO

Johnny Got His Gun

A young American soldier, hit by a shell on the last day of the First World War, lies in a hospital bed, a quadruple amputee who has lost his eyes, ears, mouth and nose. He remains conscious, and able to reason, and tries to communicate to his doctors his wish that he be put on show in a carnival as a demonstration of the horrors of war. Trumbo's impassioned novel—written in a pacifist fervour as the world geared up for another war—was one of the main causes of his later troubles with the House of Un-American Activities Commission. In 1971, the author returned to Johnny Got His Gun *and made his only film as a director, from his own screenplay. Despite Trumbo's obvious commitment to the material, and its universal timeliness, the film—which stars Timothy Bottoms, Jason Robards, Diane Varsi and Donald Sutherland as Jesus Christ—is an awkward work that adds little to the shattering brilliance of the original.*

This is the most powerful piece of fiction I know, and the most frightening. Like Andreyev's *The Seven Who Were Hanged* and Patchen's *The Journal of Albion Moonlight*, *Johnny Got His Gun* is a brilliant, all but unbearable *tour de force*, combining a high level of artistic technique with a fearless depth of human compassion to achieve a work that is not only breathtaking in its virtuosity but potentially life-changing for those who read it. Dalton Trumbo's novel certainly changed my life, and I suspect that it has altered irrevocably anyone daring enough to encounter it on its own fierce terms.

It is surely a story about the horrors of war. But to say that *Johnny Got His Gun* is a horror story would be tantamount to calling *Hamlet* a murder mystery: true enough as far as it goes, but a trivialization. This is difficult reading in the finest sense; its unflinching courage and passion demand a braver response than the rudimentary esthetic sense and readiness to be entertained that are required by most novels. As challenging as it is, its terrifying beauty has kept it in print for 50 years, and I suspect that it will outlive us all.

Since I have found it necessary to make my selection from outside the genre, I am moved to wonder why the best-known titles in dark fantasy, the very field that purports to deal most directly with matters of life and death, should compare less than favorably with a book by a man who was primarily a screenwriter (one of the blacklisted Hollywood Ten) and whose magnum opus remains unexamined, if not altogether unknown, by aficionados of horror. Perhaps the problem—the reason why such a question can even be raised—is inherent in the nature of genrefication.

It seems to me that to embrace the assumptions underlying such subdivision does a disservice to readers and writers alike. For favoritism, amusing and comforting though it seems to those receiving special treatment, may ultimately imply disrespect for oneself and for others, as does any indulgence. All injustices, arising as they do out of hierarchical thinking, have at their root the notion of dualism as a common factor. And just as slaves degrade their masters by co-operating with presumptions of superiority and inferiority, to accept the splitting of fiction into separate camps does violence to the medium itself as well as the individuals who comprise the body of world literature as a whole.

It finally occurs to Trumbo's Johnny that if guns are made they will be aimed, and if bullets are fired they may one day be directed at us.

> Already they were looking ahead they were figuring the future and somewhere in the future they saw war. To fight that war they would need men and if men saw the future they wouldn't fight ... The menace to our lives does not lie on the other side of a nomansland that was set apart without our consent it lies within our own boundaries here and now ...

I for one am willing to lay down my arms and forgo the false security of relaxed standards, the protectionism that can only prolong our adolescence and our vulnerability. How about you?

—DENNIS ETCHISON

43 [1939]

H. P. LOVECRAFT

The Outsider and Others

The Outsider *is one of the most important horror collections of the 20th century, in that it was both the first major book appearance by the already-dead Lovecraft and the first publication from Arkham House. The* Outsider *includes work from all periods of Lovecraft's writing career: his Dunsany-influenced dream stories ('The Cats of Ulthar', 'Celephais'), his extravagantly horrid horror tales ('The Rats in the Walls', 'Cool Air', 'Pickman's Model'), the key stories in what later became the 'Cthulhu*

Mythos' ('The Call of Cthulhu', 'The Dunwich Horror', 'The Whisperer in Darkness', 'The Shadow Over Innsmouth', 'The Shadow Out of Time'), and his rare attempts at pared-down science fiction-horror ('The Color Out of Space', the Poe-influenced 'At the Mountains of Madness'). The book also includes the essay 'Howard Phillips Lovecraft: Outsider' by August Derleth and Donald Wandrei, and Lovecraft's lengthy essay 'Supernatural Horror in Literature'.

I think of Howard Phillips Lovecraft as the Edgar Allan Poe of the 20th century. Both writers lived and wrote their tales in the early decades of their centuries—and their tales colored and set the patterns for the terror writers of their respective centuries. For Poe, the lingering horrors of the era before, of the beginnings of the scientific investigation of the hitherto unknown, of such things as Mesmerism and the Inquisition, of the coming into being of a new and uncertain world amid the rot and ruins of the old.

For Lovecraft, the terror of the newly discovered, the apparently infinite universe, the questioning of all established beliefs, the disintegration of the social structures cherished by those who had gone before and the confused kaleidoscope of things to come. *The Outsider and Others*, a collection of his most memorable stories, embodies therein his scariest tales and establishes his basic fears. These fears derived not from old legendry but from a new and even more frightening legendry that to him derived from the hints of what science was bringing forth in its most daring investigations of the universe all around us.

In a surprising, astute article by Paul Di Filippo in a recent fan journal (*Science Fiction Guide No. 11*) this author sets forth the basic paradigms by which one can identify the differences between science fiction, fantasy, and horror literature. Those for horror fit exactly the Lovecraft premises, as well as those of almost all similar horror writings. They embody three premises: 1. The physical universe is sentient and basically *unknowable*. 2. The physical universe is *malignant*. 3. Mankind is the persecuted object of the malignant universe's attentions.

Lovecraft himself claimed to be an atheist and denied that his stories were meant to be taken at their word. But taken seriously they were, for they fit the fears and suspicions of a world emerging into a universe far stranger than any envisioned in previous centuries or theologies. Basically, Lovecraft's tales were science-fictional rather than supernatural. The horrors he conjured up were subject to unknown laws of the vast and Creatorless universe. They were beings of substance no different from the innumerable species that exist on Earth, save that they were originated elsewhere with powers derived from laws inexplicable to humanity. This is what makes Lovecraft so effective in today's science-haunted world, for we recognize that we do not know as much as we had thought and that the 'laws' of science we believed we had discovered were but fragments and shadows of the real, uncaring, and possibly antagonistic universe.

His Old Ones and Elder Gods were but beings from other worlds somewhere Out There. His Cthulhu, a godlike being to us, was a hangover from an alien biology who could indeed wait and sleep for millennia to arise again some day. Beings from unsuspected worlds and cycles could and did own and dispute this Earth in which mankind was just another animal species to be treated as such and never as equals. Yuggoth was simply an outpost of these monsters, a planet undiscovered on the outskirts of our solar system ... and beyond Yuggoth were worlds outside any of our limited comprehensions.

He created the premise that much of these terrible truths could be detected by a few esoteric students and hinted at in secret books like the *Necronomicon*—a work which has been quoted and added to by many of Lovecraft's successors.

For the 20th-century mind with a knowledge of science's many unexplored boundaries, *The Outsider* plants the seeds of the horror paradigms. Indeed, it reinforces the conjectures of the outermost limits of man's ever-growing explorations. What new 'laws' are to be discovered? What new horrors shall come from laboratories controlled by investigators innocent of what may result from their pryings? We have new diseases and new disasters unparalleled, and in Lovecraft's tales there are shadowy outlines of such 'things to come'.

Lovecraft is science fiction horror that reaches the disbelievers. What is the color we cannot see? What are the natural orders of other worlds should they differ from our own? Where is the life on other planets and why should it be amicable? Are there dimensions we cannot probe or deal with? How much do we think we know that we are merely guessing at and revising steadily in those guesses?

This is what makes *The Outsider* and its tales a seedbed of horror thoughts for the most modern of readers. Lovecraft was the Columbus of the malignant universe—Stephen King and his contemporaries are but those who follow.

—DONALD A. WOLLHEIM

CLARK ASHTON SMITH

Out of Space and Time

Arkham House's second major collection assembles the varied and imagina-
tive work written for Weird Tales *by Smith, who was a Californian poet*
directed towards horror and science fiction by H. P. Lovecraft. Smith's stories
take place in an assortment of bizarre, imaginary locales: Zothique, a far
future continent with a vague Arabian Nights feel, very like Jack Vance's
later 'Dying Earth'; Averoigne, a lamia-haunted province of mediaeval
France modelled on James Branch Cabell's Poictesme; Hyperborea, an
imagined past that presumably neighbours Robert E. Howard's Hyboria, and
where worship of the toad God Tsathoggua (later appropriated by Lovecraft)
is common. The Arkham edition of Out of Space and Time *includes an*
introductory appreciation of Smith by August Derleth and Donald Wandrei.
Later Smith collections include Lost Worlds *(1944),* Genius Loci and Other
Tales *(1948) and* The Abominations of Yondo *(1960).*

He never wrote a complete novel, though a twelve thousand word
fragment of his intended full-length work, *The Infernal Star*—
begun and abandoned in February of 1933—lies unpublished in darkness, possibly in some dank subterranean crypt beneath stygian waters
and flooded ebon caverns through which crawl thick, white worms
whose semblances of countenance are the hideous, cilia-festooned simu-
lacra of the expressions of the human corpses on which they have fed. Or
maybe just in a safety deposit box in a San Francisco branch of The Bank
of America.

(One bite of the forbidden fruit of his lapidary prose, and I find myself
overwhelmed, engulfed, supersaturated; I find myself tipsy with language, uncharacteristically emulating; indulging in an unashamedly
baroque attack on the idea at hand in a syntax so rich and steaming with
visual evocations that it borders on logorrhea. A style so purple it sloshes
over into the ultraviolet. A writing style that would make Hemingway
break out in hives.)

He was a poet, a painter, a sculptor of the bizarre, and a recluse; and
though he wrote in excess of a hundred stories in a canon spread across
more than a dozen collections, he produced almost all of them in less
than a decade of furious activity, from the beginning of the Depression in
1929 till he inexplicably deserted fiction in 1938; and though his work is
solidly in the traditions of Poe, Bierce, Flaubert and Baudelaire, and

though he was one of the towering triumvirate that dominated *Weird Tales* in its most fecund period—the other two being Robert E. Howard and H. P. Lovecraft—he is virtually unknown today beyond the rarefied venue of those who love obscure horror stories.

Even his name, like those of his characters, seems to echo with intimations of Omar Khayyám and the silken opulence of ages beyond Time, of places beyond Space: Clark Ashton Smith. The magical lands he created bear in their syllables resonances with dreams of the faraway we have carried with us since the Flood: Zothique, Hyperborea, Poseidonis, Xiccarph, Averoigne, Phandiom and, of course, Atlantis. Now his stories, like silent songs in stone, are beyond the reach of modern readers condemned to the paperback illiteracies of a bumbling horde of 'horror' writers who have pilfered the cache of Smith's work, but who dash widdershins between their word-masticators and the Oxford Universal, forlornly and ineptly trying to unearth less-precise and commercially acceptable words for *ossuary* and *innominate* and *bitumen-colored cerements*. Purveyors of the recycled cliche and the *mot injuste* and language so inelegant it could stun a Visigoth.

And so, even as we have had our critical abilities systematically bastardized by motion pictures cut like rock videos, so that we cannot go fifteen minutes without a car crash, thus disabling us for the paced symmetry of a Kurosawa or Resnais, we have likewise been bludgeoned by decades of commercial writing below the level of Dr Seuss, on the theory that simple is best. (Einstein once pointed out: 'Everything should be made as simple as possible, but no simpler.') The stunned, the bastardized, and the bludgeoned cannot enjoy Clark Ashton Smith, more's the pity. His convolute style and sybaritic, depraved fantasies are to them as Vivaldi is to a teenager googly over Run DMC: it is merely white noise, at best impenetrable.

More's the pity, because Smith's was a voice singular and compelling. I have written elsewhere of the epiphany of my initial encounter with his remarkable fantasy, *The City of the Singing Flame*, an encounter that profoundly influenced my own writing, and palpably influenced my life. It was 1950, I was sixteen, and I found it in an August Derleth anthology in a school library in Cleveland, Ohio . . . and it was such a powerful icon that I stole the book, and own it to this day. As Frederic Prokosch's *Seven Who Fled* and Kafka's *The Trial* mercy-killed my innocence about what it took to be a writer worth reading, so Clark Ashton Smith's stories thrashed out of me my ignorance about the limits of language.

I would very likely not be writing films now, had I not learned lesson after lesson from Smith about writing visually. He has an eerie way of making mimetic in the mind even the most arcane scenes. (Oddly, however, there is very little aural and tactile freighting in his work. I can see it all, but in a disembodied, fingerless silence.)

Take, for instance, this snippet from 'The Last Hieroglyph'. An old, and not very talented astrologer has been commanded by the auguries to follow a terrifying guide, a mummy, through a 'region of stifling vaults and foul, dismal, nitrous corridors'. Overcome with fear, the astrologer breaks away from the mummy, and tries to retrace his steps, through the catacombs:

> Presently he came to the huge, browless skull of an uncouth creature, which reposed on the ground with upward-gazing orbits; and beyond the skull was the monster's moldy skeleton, wholly blocking the passage. Its ribs were cramped by the narrowing walls, as if it had crept there and had died in the darkness, unable to withdraw or go forward. White spiders, demon-headed and large as monkeys, had woven their webs in the hollow arches of the bones; and they swarmed out interminably as Nushain approached; and the skeleton seemed to stir and quiver as they seethed over it abhorrently and dropped to the ground before the astrologer. Behind them others poured in a count-less army . . .

Even those addicted to rap music and car crashes can *see* that horror in the dark passageway. Let Judith Krantz or Sidney Sheldon try to plow *that* field.

The passage above is from one of the twenty stories in *Out of Space and Time*, Smith's first major collection, published by the speciality house, Arkham, in 1942. Because of the rules of the game passim this book, I was allowed to pick only one title by Clark Ashton Smith. That's tough. It's representative, the one I selected, but by no means an adequate primer. I picked it because it contains 'The City of the Singing Flame'. One of my all-time favorite stories, as I babbled earlier. But that eliminates 'Genius Loci' and 'Lost Worlds' and 'The Abominations of Yondo' and a fistful more that delight and mystify. I go with *Out of Space and Time* because it remains with me, after more than thirty years since I first read it, as emblematic of what we mean when we say, 'It created worlds and feelings I never knew anywhere else.'

A pure wonder, especially in a time filled with white noise.

—HARLAN ELLISON

FRITZ LEIBER

Conjure Wife

Academic Norman Saylor is perturbed to discover that his wife Tansy has been advancing his career through the practice of white witchcraft. However, when he demands that she remove all her magical protections, he finds himself under attack from another faculty wife who is trying to use black magic to destroy the Saylors. Conjure Wife *has been filmed several times, as an* Inner Sanctum *mystery,* Weird Woman *(1944) with Lon Chaney and Evelyn Ankers, as a 1960 segment of the* Moment of Fear *TV show with Larry Blyden, and (unauthorized) as a sub-*Bewitched *skit* Witches' Brew *(1980) with Lana Turner, Richard Benjamin and Teri Garr. The classic adaption, however, is Sidney Hayers'* Night of the Eagle *(1962, a.k.a.* Burn, Witch, Burn!*)—written by Richard Matheson and Charles Beaumont— with Peter Wyngarde and Janet Blair. Leiber, best known for his short stories and science fiction, returned to the occult horror novel in triumphant form with* Our Lady of Darkness *(1977).*

It is hard to decide on a single word to describe Fritz Leiber; certainly 'technician' and 'professional' spring to mind. But so does 'versatile'. Even that seems a pallid description of what he has accomplished, writing hard science fiction, sociological sf, heroic fantasy, dark fantasy, satire, essays and criticism. Other writers have matched his range, but no other writer seems to have established himself as the best or near-best in so many areas.

Consider. In the early fifties he produced a number of stories ('Coming Attractions', 'The Night He Cried') that, in retrospect, seem to characterize the way sf changed in those volatile years. His 'Fafhrd and Gray Mouser' series is certainly the most critically successful writing in the heroic fantasy field. And probably no one did more to bring the art of M. R. James and Oliver Onions into the urban sprawl of this century's midsection than Leiber in stories such as 'Smoke Ghost', 'Black Gondolier', 'Four Ghosts in Hamlet', 'The Belsen Express' and, of course, *Conjure Wife*.

While John Campbell was changing science fiction from a principally romantic form of fiction to a principally realistic one in *Astounding*, he was attempting to do the same thing to fantasy in *Unknown*. It stressed a logical, extrapolative approach to the central themes of fantasy, which resulted in some of the strongest stories the field had yet produced. The magazine generated an excitement comparable, yet not identical, to that which *Astounding* was creating. It featured some of the best work by many of Campbell's best *ASF* writers, as well as fantasy writers such as Frank Belknap Long and Robert Bloch, and a number who never appeared in the field otherwise, such as Raymond Chandler. The magazine's success was based on two concepts: first, that fantasy is primary a source of good, grown-up fun; and, second, that the premise of a fantasy needs to be extrapolated with the same rigor as the premise of a science fiction story.

Conjure Wife, the first of Leiber's novels to see print, appeared in *Unknown* a month before *Gather Darkness!*, a novel that treated the same subject in science fictional terms, was serialized in *Astounding*. It was printed in its current version in the Twayne collection *Witches Three* in 1953 but its first solo publication was a paperback edition from the small but adventurous Lion Books, the following year.

Leiber's central idea is that all women practice witchcraft and men are unaware of it. Leiber's protagonist, Norman Saylor, innocently spies on his wife and discovers her secret, which he of course regards as superstitious and foolish. He proceeds to attack her supposed weakness until she agrees to abandon the practice and he smugly goes on with his life, or so he thinks. His life quickly begins to collapse about his ears.

We are told by Leiber that Saylor is not the sort of man who ordinarily spies on his wife, but he is certainly fond of busting icons. After he has forced his wife to give up her conjuring, we are treated to a classroom lecture where he demonstrates the primitive origins of fraternity practices to his students, especially one who happens to be the president of a fraternity. But already Leiber has begun the process of smashing some of Saylor's own icons. The way in which Saylor's life begins to crumble around him and he slowly finds himself accepting the possibility that his wife's beliefs may be justified is one of the main delights of the novel.

Although the novel breaks structurally into two parts, it is very well unified. In the first part (three-fifths of the book's wordage), the world Leiber postulates is depicted with the detail and love Jack Vance brings to his alien societies, and the brilliance Alfred Bester brings to his future ones. This build-up is so careful that when Leiber's concern turns from the story's concepts to the requirements of its plot, the reader is propelled along by the suspense in a way that is nothing but daunting to any lesser writer who's ever tried to do the same thing. And this was, remember, Leiber's first novel.

Leiber's main contribution as a horror novelist has been the skill and ease with which he has been able to express the traditional concerns of the classic horror writer using themes and settings contemporary to him. *Conjure Wife* takes place on the campus of a small, conservative university, a fairly common setting for popular novels (especially mysteries) in the early forties, possibly because the combination of small-town dynamics and urban sophistication represented the changes American society was undergoing at the time. Leiber combines the ability to find horror in commonplace things with a talent for writing intelligently and clearly, and it is this that has made him one of the best horror writers of the 20th century.

If there is one unresolved question about Leiber it is whether the secret of his talent lies in his sheer ability as a writing technician, or in the intelligence of his approach to his material. Both are aptly demonstrated in his horror stories, and both serve to explain why *Conjure Wife* is a triumph.

—GERALD W. PAGE

46 [1945]

CORNELL WOOLRICH

Night Has a Thousand Eyes

Tom Shawn, a detective, saves Jean Reid from suicide, and listens to the story of the strange events that have led her into despair. Harlan Reid, Jean's wealthy father, has been consulting Tompkins, a melancholy psychic, and is convinced that the man has genuine powers of prophecy. Tompkins has just predicted that Reid will be killed by a lion, and Reid has been reduced to a state of panic by the announcement. Shawn agrees to look into the affair, although no actual crime seems to have been committed, and sets his men on to the case from several angles, trying to find out how Tompkins has been making his predictions, whether anyone could be using the psychic as part of an extortion scheme, and if it's possible to prevent the prophecy from coming to pass. It seems as if a rational explanation is possible, but the brilliantly sustained finale plunges back into the supernatural as Shawn tries, on the preordained night, to keep Reid away from lions and is a helpless witness to the man's ironic fate. Many of Cornell Woolrich's masterly romans noirs contain horrific or fatalistic elements, but only Night Has a Thousand Eyes actually involves the supernatural. John Farrow's 1948 film, scripted by Barré Lyndon and Jonathan Latimer, is unfaithful to Woolrich's plot, but catches his mood successfully.

*N*ight Has a Thousand Eyes is surely the only horror classic to have inspired not only a movie but also a hit pop single (for Bobby Vee in 1963). But then, Cornell Woolrich's evocative, image-laden prose has inspired scores of adaptations in all media (film, TV, theatre, radio) because of the sheer power of its imagery.

Isaac Asimov called him 'THE Master of Suspense'; his biographer and literary executor Francis M. Nevins Jr described him as 'The Edgar Allan Poe of the 20th century'. Cornell Woolrich is indeed a unique writer whose approach to horror was never blatant. Not for him the hyperbolic monsters of Lovecraft or the Jungian archetypes of slime of so many other practitioners of the genre. Better known as a writer of crime stories and novels on the edge of darkness, Woolrich tackles horror through a relentless accumulation of despair, troubling coincidences and all-too-human characterization. The horror and fantasy element never becomes explicit, and gains in credible terror by confronting everyday people with whom the reader can easily identify. Indeed, what you only guess at, what you never see, is psychologically all the more frightening; a lesson that few horror film-makers since Val Lewton and Jacques Tourneur have learned well.

Written in 1945 under the byline George Hopley (Woolrich's two middle names), *Night Has a Thousand Eyes* was based on an earlier novelette, *Speak To Me of Death*, published in the February 1937 *Argosy*. It was seen as a breakthrough novel by his publishers, hoping for a larger audience following the first five of his brilliant 'Black' series (*The Bride Wore Black, The Black Curtain, Black Alibi, The Black Angel, The Black Path of Fear*). But, like all great writers who trawl the same wonderful obsessions from book to book, Woolrich, writing as himself, William Irish or Hopley, could only explore again in *Night Has a Thousand Eyes* with his customary intensity the genteel nobility of his cipher-like characters in uncommon distress. It all had a sense of existential *déjà vu*. Set in his familiar urban landscape of an unnamed city at night-time, in bleak anonymous diners and grey apartments, *Night*'s slow, claustrophobic first half sets up a simple but inevitable scenario which soon metamorphoses into a relentless chase against time and irrationality, a clockwork tension that never lets up as the hour of doom approaches.

And horror, *Night Has a Thousand Eyes* certainly reaches in its shocking conclusion. The worst has happened, despite the police's intervention and a set of simple explanations and coincidences that cancel out (or do they?) the need for supernatural explanations. Some of the main characters are inevitably dead, but the worse horror remains for the sad survivors, for whom love will now not be enough. They have discovered the sheer horror of inevitability, the fact they have no free will or choice.

The bleakness and despair of Woolrich's 'happy ends' was reflected in his own life and he mined this sad vein with consummate obstinacy in his prolific writing career. Time, or simple sentimentality, might, in some works, have taken its toll of his style, but his manipulation of suspense, the effective modern minimalism of his characters and the emotional impact of his tales remain as strong as ever. Ray Bradbury writes 'Cornell Woolrich deserves to be discovered and rediscovered by each generation'. I am not ready to contradict him.

—MAXIM JAKUBOWSKI

47 [1945]

H. P. LOVECRAFT AND AUGUST DERLETH
The Lurker at the Threshold

Ambrose Dewart inherits Billington House, a shunned old pile in the woods to the north of haunted Arkham, and learns of its evil history and reputation. He is cautioned by an ancient document to ensure that a river keeps flowing around an abandoned tower, and gradually realizes that the tower, the house, and a strange window of coloured glass are gateways to another dimension, in which fester indescribable monstrosities who lust to emerge into our world and cause chaos. The longest of August Derleth's posthumous 'collaborations' with H. P. Lovecraft, The Lurker at the Threshold *is, apart from two fragments totalling about 1200 words, wholly Derleth's work. Aside from pastiching his mentor's style, complete with italicized horrible bits, Derleth systematizes Lovecraft's collection of hints and references into what has become known as the Cthulhu Mythos, thus opening the way for many subsequent tales by other hands. Derleth proceeded to expand some more Lovecraft fragments into the stories collected in* The Shuttered Room *(1959), and made up out of whole cloth the Lovecraftian horrors of* The Mask of Cthulhu *(1958) and* The Trail of Cthulhu *(1962).*

Lovecraft's special talent was to create a world that was deeply unsettling in all its aspects. Even the *trees* flourished in Arkham 'centuries after time should have taken its toll of them'. Yes, we have taken the wrong fork again, folks, and we are back in the Massachusetts of gambreled roofs and retarded offspring and whippoorwhills in the hills.

The Lurker at the Threshold is a joy because it is so magnificently and unselfconsciously overwritten. The horror novels one reads these days are so often churned out in King-lish: which amounts to reams of unedited stream-of-word-processorese—pompous, self-regarding, and profane. Here, there is no concern for what the reader thinks of the writers: only an out-and-out devotion to being scary, expressed with a professionalism and a self-mocking elegance that today's horror writers would do well to study.

Beyond Dean's Corners, the benighted traveller still hastens by, urged on by a curious dislike for which he has no reasonable explanation; but which *we* know with a wonderful shudder of anticipation will be some of our favorite Frightful Things From Outside, especially Yog-Sothoth, *who still froths as primal slime somewhere beyond space and time!*

Apart from the hideous Great Old Ones, however, there are many other memorably disturbing devices in this book. The window of colored glass in the library at Billington's Wood, through which the terrifying world beyond can be glimpsed; the brilliantly faked-up documents and letters and diaries, recounting the raising of Daemons in No Human Shape. The sinister tower in the wood, which is the threshold at which the lurker lurks.

For personal reasons, however, my favorite creation in this novel is Misquamacus, the Indian Wonder-Worker, who became the Manitou in my very first horror novel, and whose ambiguity in his relationship with the Great Old Ones is one of the book's most frightening delights. Long may Yog-Sothoth froth.

—GRAHAM MASTERTON

48   [1946]

PAUL BAILEY

Deliver Me From Eva

Mark Allard, a respectable lawyer, marries Eva Craner after a whirlwind courtship, and is taken to Eva's palatial estate home, The Cradle of Light, where he is introduced to her peculiar family. Dr Craner, Eva's father, is an earless, legless genius who can increase intelligence through the manipulation of the plates of the skull. This treatment has turned Eva's brother Osman into a great concert pianist, and her sister Insa into an epileptic moron. Various atrocities and deaths ensue, culminating in the destruction of The Cradle of Light. A fast-moving, blatantly silly pulp novel, with touch of forties' 'steamy stuff' ('I bent her savagely to me'), Deliver Me From Eva has just enough jokes—quite apart from its punning title—to suggest that the author wasn't absolutely serious. Paul Bailey, author also of Sam Brennan and the California

Mormons *and* The Gay Saint, *presumably wrote his own jacket copy, which describes how 'restlessness and rebellion possessed his soul at an early age . . . He has tasted the bitterness of poverty. He has known that ghastly loneliness where city crowds are thickest. With eager eye, and hungry intellect, he has pried into the leaven of life.'*

Robert Bloch more than likely would have come up with this title if Paul Bailey hadn't thought of it first (1946). In fact, way back then he might even have written it.

It had been 40 years since I first read *Deliver Me From Eva*, so in order to write about it intelligently for this book I thought I had better re-read it to remind myself why, beyond *Dracula* or *Frankenstein* or *The Phantom of the Opera* or Guy Endore's *Werewolf of Paris* or Virginia Swain's *Hollow Skin*, it stuck in my memory across a gulf of eight lustrums as the book which I found the most horrifying.

The book's blurb describes it as 'a masterpiece of uninhibited, spine-chilling horror', from a writer of historical novels 'an event as rare and unexpected as angels in Hades'.

The hype and hyperbole continues: 'When the editor finished the last gripping line'—('God be thanked I'm a lawyer' is a gripping line?)—'his blood was running as cold as a lizard's belly, and for a week he dared not turn off his lights at night.' The Electric Co. must have loved him—and the author.

Finally: 'We swear it's the most gosh-awful, horrific spine-tingler imaginable. Like the weird and imaginative flights of Poe, Stevenson and James, *Deliver Me From Eva* will hold you entranced and glued to the chair.'

Well, now, in the sober light of day, four decades away from this horror novel, I see the comparison should not have been made with Poe *et al.* but Arthur J. Burks, Arthur Leo Zagat, Justin Case or one of the venerable old horror hacks who terrified legions of fans a couple of generations ago in the pulpy pages of *Terror Tales* and *Horror Stories* and *Dime Mystery*.

Yes, if legendary Ray Cummings, one of the maestros of the magazine macabre, had gone on from his novels *The Sea Girl* and *The Shadow Girl* and *The Snow Girl* and given us *The Slay Girl*, it would have read, I believe, very much like *Deliver Me From Eva*.

At the time I first read this novel it impressed me as ideal B-movie material. Johnny Eck, the half-boy of Tod Browning's *Freaks*, was born to portray the mad scientist half-man Dr Craner. (Name suggestive of cranial?—an appropriate name for a brain manipulator.) And after three years of persistence I sold it to Curtis (*Games/Queen of Blood/Who Slew Auntie Roo?*) Harrington. It has yet to be made but it is perfect fodder for a follow-up to *Re-Animator*. In fact, if *Deliver Me From Eva* had been made first, *Re-Animator* would have been a natural to follow in its bizarre and bloody footsteps, even if somewhat difficult to do, considering Dr Craner had no feet or legs.

In order to sell *Eva* to the movies as an agent, it was some, er, feat for me to track down the author, and by a trillion to one cosmic coincidence, where was he found to be living? In Horrorwood, Karloffornia, on . . . *Ackerman Drive!*

In 1988, as I approach my 72nd birthday, the old 'Ackerman drive' is still at work, keeping alive the memory of *Eva*. I hope some antiquarian bookseller can locate a copy for you. Or perhaps it's time for a book publisher to bring out a new edition. If you hear of it in advance, it might be profitable to buy stock in sleeping pills or electric bills.

Eva—Eva—I'm coming . . .

—FORREST J ACKERMAN

49 [1946]

BORIS KARLOFF (Editor)

And the Darkness Falls

One of the largest, most extensive anthologies of the forties, this volume of macabre stories and (unusually) poems includes contributions by ghost and horror perennials Oliver Onions, E. F. Benson, Guy De Maupassant, Lafcadio Hearn, Ambrose Bierce, Algernon Blackwood, August Derleth, H. R. Wakefield, Edgar Allan Poe, Arthur Conan Doyle, Elizabeth Bowen, John Collier, Clark Ashton Smith and H. P. Lovecraft, but also mainstream names like Paul Verlaine, Ivan Turgenev, Alfred Tennyson, John Galsworthy, Somerset Maugham, Algernon Swinburne, Robert Browning, W. B. Yeats, Charles Baudelaire, Stephen Crane, Jonathan Swift, Nikolai Gogol and Joseph Conrad, not to mention such then-popular figures as John Buchan, F. Tennyson Jesse, William Seabrook, L. P. Hartley, William Irish (Cornell Woolrich) and Dorothy L. Sayers. The pieces in And the Darkness Falls, *subtitled* Masterpieces of Horror and the Supernatural, *were selected by Karloff from a list of recommendations by Edmund Speare while the actor was touring with* Arsenic and Old Lace. *Karloff also put his name to* Tales of Terror *(1943) and* The Boris Karloff Horror Anthology *(1965).*

Rarely, if ever, has a marketing gimmick resulted in a better book. You can just imagine the chorus of enthusiasm from the salesmen at the idea of a big fat horror collection edited by Frankenstein himself!

And indeed, the taste and personality of one of the greatest actors of the century identified with horror informs this large and stimulating compendium. It was a successor to the critically acclaimed *Tales of Terror* (1943), which contained fewer, but longer, works. While it lacks the virtue of a long introductory essay (present in the earlier book), it more than compensates by the inclusion of informative and often quite extensive story notes by Karloff. Containing 72 stories and poems, it is one of the largest collections of horror fiction ever published.

The stories are selected for the most part from the first 40 years of this century, yet the occasional inclusion of excellent work by Gogol, Swift, and others, together with selections from 19th-century poetry by Poe, Baudelaire, Swinburne, Verlaine and others bestows on it the international and literary tone that the editors desired. Karloff's stated intention was to widen the field of consideration from the mere 14 selections of the earlier book to the rich and diverse materials herein, and thus broaden horror readers' taste. The book succeeds admirably in this, and it is the basis for its historic importance. Still, the whole does not entirely cohere, because certain selections break the tone and partially dispel the atmosphere of horror (the parodies by Swift and Onions, for instance). And while it is good to see a collection of a variety of material by unfamiliar writers, many of whom wrote little horror, the real strength of this book is in the stories by familiar names (and in the first inclusion ever in a horror book by Gogol's 'Viy', praised by Edmund Wilson as one of the greatest of all stories in the field). Never has 'star marketing' been used more effectively in the horror field, with ingenuity and broad-ranging taste: the result is a great anthology.

—DAVID G. HARTWELL

50   [1947]

AUGUST DERLETH (Editor)

The Sleeping and the Dead

Sub-titled 'Fifteen Uncanny Tales' The Sleeping and the Dead *includes work from both classic British ghost story writers (M. R. James' 'A View From a Hill', J. Sheridan Le Fanu's 'The Bully of Chapelizod', Lord Dunsany's 'The Postman of Otford', H. R. Wakefield's 'Farewell Performance' and the then-young masters of the American Weird Tales school (Derleth's own*

'Glory Hand', Ray Bradbury's 'The Jar', Frank Belknap Long's 'The Ocean Leech'). H. P. Lovecraft, a staple of Derleth's career as an anthologist, is represented by 'The Dreams in the Witch House' and by one of his re-write jobs, Hazel Heald's 'Out of the Eons'. Derleth's many other anthologies include Sleep No More (1944), Who Knocks? (1945), The Night Side (1946), Dark of the Moon (poetry, 1947), Night's Yawning Peal (1952), Dark Mind, Dark Heart (1962), Travellers by Night (1967) and Tales of the Cthulhu Mythos (1969).

E ver since I was a child I have loved bookshops, especially those that sell second-hand volumes and look as if they might yield the odd treasure or two to the patient searcher. It was back in the early fifties, when I was a teenager, that I came across a rather battered hardcover edition of August Derleth's anthology The Sleeping and the Dead in a shop in London's Charing Cross Road—the name of which I'm afraid I've long since forgotten. I'm not sure now whether it was the title or the unusual editor's name that caught my eye—it may even have been the rather strange publishers' names on the spine: Pellegrini & Cudahy Inc., who turned out to be American.

In any event, I leafed through to the contents page, which to someone just beginning to discover the horror genre promised a host of chilling reading. I'd actually been introduced to the world of macabre stories through—of all things—the television (then a small wooden box, with a tiny flickering, black-and-white screen that you watched in a room with the curtains drawn and the lights out). My parents, for reasons that still escape them—though their action has had a singular effect on *my* life—decided that the first adult programme I was going to be allowed to stay up and watch (it had been strictly *Children's Hour* until then) was a dramatization of Robert Louis Stevenson's horror classic *Dr Jekyll and Mr Hyde*. To say I sat watching it absolutely terrified would be putting it mildly—but I know it excited my imagination enough to want to know if there were any more stories like that to be found.

By the time I came across The Sleeping and the Dead, I had worked patiently through a good number of the classics like *Frankenstein* and *Dracula*. But it was the first anthology I had encountered (they were nowhere near as prolific then as they are today) and I ran through the names of the contributors with increasing interest: M. R. James (who I'd heard wrote ghost stories), Algernon Blackwood (wasn't he the man who read supernatural tales on the radio?), Lord Dunsany (who a school pal said told weird little stories about ancient gods), and a couple of Americans named H. P. Lovecraft and Ray Bradbury. Oh, and there was also a story by the editor himself.

I remember I devoured that collection in a weekend. Some of the stories, in particular M. R. James' 'A View from the Hill' and Ray Bradbury's 'The Jar' so impressed me I read them twice. I thought they were all excellent, and the book gave me for the first time an overview of the range and diversity of the short tale of horror. All the authors, I soon discovered, had produced other works, and I busied myself making a list for my next visit to the library—as well as one to keep with me for my bookshop browsing. *The Sleeping and the Dead* indeed became for a time the first volume in what is now a several-thousand strong library of horror and fantasy novels and collections in my Suffolk home.

I was interested, too, to read the biographical details about August Derleth—like me a fan of horror since his youth (and a published author at the tender age of 13, no less!) who had written and edited dozens of books of macabre stories as well as starting his own publishing company, Arkham House, which was busy resurrecting the work of H. P. Lovecraft and Clark Ashton Smith, and had published the first books of stories by Ray Bradbury and Robert Bloch (who were also to become favourites of mine). Out of admiration for *The Sleeping and the Dead*, I wrote a letter of congratulations to August Derleth—and initiated what became a friendly and instructive correspondence which continued until his sad death in 1971. August was always generous with his time and advice to this young fan across the Atlantic, and even passed judgement on some of the first selections of stories I was proposing to put together for British publishers. When I found a story difficult to obtain in England, he was almost invariably able to supply a copy of it from his own huge library.

August greatly encouraged me in the development of 'thematic' collections, which have become my speciality, and no matter what particular theme I wanted to explore, he could always be relied upon to have a few ideas for consideration. I miss his letters and his suggestions, and it is a pleasure to acknowledge my debt to him in these pages.

I'm also glad to be able to say that I showed my appreciation of his book in a more positive way while he was still alive. For when my career took me from journalism into publishing, before I finally became a full-time writer and anthologist, I had the great satisfaction of arranging the first publication in Great Britain of *The Sleeping and the Dead* in a paperback edition under the Four Square imprint of New English Library.

My only sadness was that it cost me that original copy of the book, for it never came back from the printers. If anyone could help replace it I'd be horrifically grateful . . .

—PETER HAINING

WALTER VAN TILBURG CLARK
Track of the Cat

A strangely Gothic Western, Track of the Cat *is a complex work which subliminally integrates the Death of King Arthur and a stern critique of the pioneer ethic into its snowbound family melodrama and neurotic outdoors adventuring. It was filmed by William Wellman—who had also adapted Van Tilburg Clark's best-known book in* The Ox-Bow Incident *(1943)—in 1954, with Robert Mitchum, Teresa Wright and Tab Hunter. In an attempt to match the book's bizarre, psychological feel, Wellman shot in CinemaScope and WarnerColor but restricted himself almost entirely to the use of blacks and whites.*

Mystic dreams. A half-mad, half-shaman Indian who carves portents of the future from bits of wood. Three brothers on a rite of passage that will see two of them dead and one the victor over an old, cunning evil. A snowstorm that tears at the soul, and a landscape of white mountains where crevasses lie hidden under smooth, deceptive powder. The land of the black painter, and blood on the snow.

A Western novel.

Right.

Walter Van Tilburg Clark, who wrote *The Track of the Cat*, is probably most famous for *The Ox-Bow Incident*, another Western-based novel that builds tautly to its conclusion in which a group of innocent men are mistakenly hanged for a murder that never happened. American high school students know *The Ox-Bow Incident* from Cliffs' Notes. Very few people know about *The Track of the Cat*, which is a horror novel dressed up in cowboy duds and riding a horse.

A panther has been attacking the livestock at an isolated ranch, and as a snowstorm gathers its fury the three Bridges brothers—the eldest Arthur, the hothead and 'manly' Curt, and the naïve, youngest Harold—go out into the mountains on the track of the cat. Arthur has had recurring dreams: the voice of a loved one, lost and searching in the storm. The dreams call him, and he must answer. Curt can hunt and shoot any animal; he's not afraid of any panther, no sir! Not even the spectral 'black painter' that their Indian ranch hand Joe Sam says cannot be killed. Harold, on the eve of his wedding, suffers under Curt's bullying weight, and he walks in the shadow of his older brothers.

Arthur is killed by his dreams; he is 'day-dreaming', a habit Curt warns him about, when the panther—not black after all, but an ordinary yellow cat—leaps upon him from a snowy ledge. From this portion of the novel, *The Track of the Cat* enters true nightmare country. Hunting the cat on his own in the mountains, Curt steadily roams farther from the ranch and familiar landmarks. He's so intent on bringing back the cat's hide—and impressing Harold's bride-to-be with his killing prowess—that he lets the hunt seduce him. A large part of the novel focuses on Curt, as the weather closes in and the snow falls and he begins to run out of matches. This is the center of *Track of the Cat*: the stalking enemy, the brutal and beautiful land, both murderous and seductive. Nothing is familiar to Curt; everything is white, dreamlike, and every shadow holds a panther. The mountains slowly break Curt down into a gibbering child who fires his rifle at darting, imaginary shapes and who feels weeping swell inside him when he loses all sense of direction. The mountains are cruel, and as Curt flees from the sound of snow slithering from a tree he steps into a crevasse and falls to his death.

Harold and Joe Sam find the panther and Harold shoots it, regretting that such a beautiful animal must die. He has found his harmony with the mountains, with the land that can so quickly turn monstrous. It's not a black panther after all, Harold says, as he looks at the carcass. And Joe Sam sweeps his hands in a circle that includes the sky and mountains, and he says, 'Black painter. All black painter.'

The Track of the Cat is a great horror novel because it takes a huge landscape and slowly narrows it until the reader is squeezed into a cramped cave with Curt Bridges, frantically talking to one of Joe Sam's carved cat figures as the meagre fire flickers and the storm roars outside. He is one match away from freezing to death, with the sense that the cat is now tracking him, and the hunt has turned into a struggle for survival. The Western setting gives *The Track of the Cat* a particularly American, folksy flavor, but underneath the cowboy's flesh beats a heart of true horror.

A great horror novel—but, first and foremost, a great novel.

—ROBERT R. McCAMMON

SARBAN

The Sound of His Horn

In a post-war clubroom, Alan Querdilion tells a tall story about his escape from a Second World War POW camp and temporary projection one hundred years into a future where Nazi Germany won the war and has established complete domination over a neo-feudalized Europe. Eschewing the science fictional/political speculations of most 'If Hitler Had Won' novels, Sarban (really John W. Wall) concentrates instead on a horrific vision of the Thousand Year Reich at play. Genetically-altered humans are hunted for sport, and Querdilion finds himself the quarry of Count von Hackelnberg, a bloated cross between Guy of Gisbourne, Count Zaroff and Hermann Goering. Sarban is also the author of two volumes of weird fantasy, Ringstones and Other Stories (1951) and The Doll Maker and Other Tales of the Uncanny (1953). The Sound of His Horn remains his best-known work, and has been an influence on such Nazi fantasies as Keith Roberts' 'Weihnachtsabend' and David Brin's 'Thor Meets Captain America'.

This short novel comprises a nightmare within a vision within a dream. The dream, of peaceful country life in post-Second-World-War Britain, contains in turn the vision of an alternative future in which advanced technology supports a carefully crafted, idealized version of an imaginary Aryan past. The estate of Hackelnberg is a theme park, a 'Naziland' which provides the illusion of a robust outdoor life of baronial pleasures to the fat, lazy functionaries of an urbanized modern tyranny.

But at the core of this amusement park is the Count, a fabulous, superhuman figure far more ferocious and horrifying than Hitler's heirs. The distance between this savage giant, Beowulf and Grendel rolled into one, and the Gauleiters whom he seems to serve out of whim, is one source of the resonance of the work.

The thought of Nazism victorious is horrible enough. But suppose these nauseating sadists have somehow conjured, by their attempt to restore some pure, hierarchical, morally unambiguous version of the past, a dreadful primordial spirit—the Master of the Wild Hunt.

The Count embodies the frightful truth behind all such reactionary longings. He treats everyone around him with the brutal contempt typical of the oldest, crudest deities, to whom human beings were merely slaves. That longed-for, perfect past is always mythical, and the world of myth reverberates with the wilful, utterly untrammeled ferocity of the early gods.

Their casual habit of turning men and women into animals surfaces here as the deliberate debasement of subject peoples, through science and art, to animal levels. Sarban dramatizes the link between the Count's archaic, macho ferocity and the modern urge to dehumanize all those perceived as weak—in the Nazi formulation, non-Aryans and, more particularly, women.

The women of the Count's domain are reduced to three basic western stereotypes: mindlessly predatory cat-women; game girls, fantastically costumed as exotic birds to become helpless prey fleeing the hunters; and gilded torch-bearers, who swerve beautifully but mutely. The shock of recognizing a heightened version of current sexist attitudes contributes strongly to the reader's unease.

In fact there are hardly any characters as such in *The Sound of His Horn*. It is filled with emblematic figures like creatures in a dream, with a dream's power to fascinate.

But the work has more amplitude and depth than its brevity suggests. Prodigies of economy are achieved with a deceptively artless style. The gradually accelerating narrative becomes not only an observer's tour of his own nightmare, but both a love story and a headlong adventure tale as well. The love affair is used not just as a breathing space in the form of a poignant idyll, but as an opportunity to give readers some chillingly realistic glimpses of the Nazified world beyond the estate fence.

The ostensibly distancing device of having the hero tell his story to a friend who then tells it to us serves rather to draw us easily into the heart of the tale, and by contrast sharpens the focus of the terror-filled final chase; and the book becomes a grim reflection upon the atavistic and sadistic aspects of all blood sport.

Above all, using a sure and delicate selection of sensory details the author evokes not only the horrors but the seductive beauties of Hackelnberg, and this ambiguity is the dark, dreamy heart of the book.

The bloodthirsty, joyous call of the Count's hunting horn, the gold and green livery of his foresters, the sunlit glades of his carefully manicured woods, the gabbling yammer of the maniacal cat-women— these flashes from a vision at once false and true, enchantingly beautiful and starkly hideous, sink indelibly into the mind. A lasting, eerie echo is the mark of Sarban's achievement in this brief, unforgettable book.

—SUZY McKEE CHARNAS

53   [1954]

WILLIAM GOLDING
Lord of the Flies

A vague crisis—perhaps a worldwide nuclear war—forces an aeroplane carrying a party of English schoolboys down on an isolated tropical island. The children, members of a public school choir, try to set up some form of adult civilization, but gradually revert to savagery. A decapitated wild boar becomes a sort of god and appears to speak to the children, influencing Jack, the bully, towards tyranny and—it is suggested—cannibalism. Piggy, a fat boy, becomes the tribe's ritual outcast and Ralph, the hero, is forced to make a stand against Jack's growing power. Golding's novel has survived being taught in schools, and stands as both a realist revision of R. M. Ballantyne's classic children's adventure The Coral Island *(1858) and an examination of the Jekyll-and-Hyde 'beast within' horror theme. Much of Golding's output, which includes the anthropological* The Inheritors *(1956) and the historical* The Spire *(1964), deals with fringe-horrific material.* Lord of the Flies *was starkly filmed in 1963 by Peter Brook.*

When William Golding won the Nobel Prize for Literature in 1983 there was an unsurprising amount of huffing and puffing, partly because he was considered a popular and even, horrors, accessible author (at least to those who haven't sought access to works like *Pincher Martin*)—but largely because his view of the human condition seems to be so unrelentingly negative. After all, Alfred Nobel wanted the award to go to 'the most distinguished literary work of an idealist tendency'. (So it's been given to such dewy-eyed optimists as André Gide, T. S. Eliot, Samuel Beckett, and William Faulkner.)

And he is indeed deliciously negative, probably never more so than in the grotesque fable *Lord of the Flies*. In fact, the repeatedly avowed dour purpose of the book was to 'attempt to trace the defects of society back to the defects of human nature', a misanthropic demonstration of our imperfectibility.

Whether the book seems to succeed in this goal, or in what way it fails, may be more a reflection of the reader's attitudes than of the writer's skill. I personally have no quarrel with the Nobel Committee's choice; I think Golding is a writer of remarkable virtuosity and power. Nevertheless, while I enjoyed *Lord of the Flies*, and was properly scared by it, the overall effect doesn't seem to argue strongly for his premise. The boys carry a great deal of obvious symbolic weight, the burden of representing

117

archetypes, which is wonderful for the atmosphere of the story, and has everything to do with its success as a horror classic. But I think that undermines its didactic power. Acting out their simplified stereotypical roles, the boys move inevitably towards disassociation and savagery. It's the inevitableness that gives the book its fearsome suspense, the reader worrying *not* 'will they change their behavior and save themselves?' but rather 'will an outside force save them from themselves before it's too late?'

Although in other aspects a comparison would be ludicrous, this pattern is the same plot dynamic that energizes most horror films, good or bad. A vampire or werewolf wouldn't be scary enough if its potential victims had any chance to vanquish it by simple application of intelligence and strength. There has to be the sense that inexorable Fate is in charge; they are only human, and human is not going to do the trick. God or Science has to intervene.

So we experience the delectable catharsis of being temporarily terrified, but then walk out of the theater into a real world where we know things are more complicated but at least are free of flesh-rending man-beasts or bloodsucking Eastern Europeans. I have a similar feeling of detachment after reading *Lord of the Flies* again. The book works beautifully on its own terms, but when I shut it, I don't accept those terms any more.

This may just go back to my initial premise, though. Golding and I are polar opposites when it comes to the central theme of the book. I believe human nature is improvable, if not perfectible; and that humans in ones and twos and even threes can be marvelously good, but in the diffusion of moral responsibility that 'society' brings, we gravitate toward the evil and ugly.

Of course I wouldn't want to discourage anyone from reading the book because of my quibble with its theme. It's an evening of good solid terror, and solid food for thought besides.

—JOE HALDEMAN

RICHARD MATHESON
I Am Legend

1976. Robert Neville, formerly a scientist, lives alone, besieged in his ordinary home by nocturnal creatures who used to be his neighbours. By day, he tries to find the lair in which the bulk of the vampires hide from the sunlight and destroys by staking those he can find. In flashback, we learn that he is the only immune human in a world blighted by an epidemic of vampirism. A rational, bacteriological explanation is presented for the ancient myth, and Neville is able to use some of the legendary trappings of the vampire hunter—garlic, the cross—against his enemy for medical or psychological reasons. Finally, he is hunted down not by the vampires he is seeking to destroy but by a new society of infected humans who have learned to live with the disease. In a world of vampires, the last human being becomes a monster. I am Legend, one of the first attempts to treat a traditional horror theme in a science-fictional manner, was an instant classic. It has been unsuccessfully filmed twice, as The Last Man on Earth *(1964) with Vincent Price and* The Omega Man *(1971) with Charlton Heston, but more importantly served as the inspiration for George A. Romero's seminal* Night of the Living Dead *(1968) and its sequels.*

B lood.
    Endless, red avenues of it, roaring in blackness.
    The body's ancient aqueducts splash its sleepless current; spreading life.
    Sometimes death.
    Like the famished death which the infected in *I am Legend* chaperone each night. Like the death which their sunset predation and thirst bring to Robert Neville. As the novel's crucified hero, his life hemorrhages before us. Rampant pain and loss pool around his existence; dark, inescapable. He is bleeding, somewhere deep; unseen. And the undead envoys who vulture and loiter septically outside his house each night want not only the red liquid inside him. They want the aching psyche which floats like a failing raft.
    Blood.
    Protected in our body vaults; royalty behind a walled city. Like Neville, barricaded within his battered house. He is blood; the wet voltage which runs within the book. Safe in his house, as blood in a body. His unrelenting flow is the kinetic stream which makes each chapter continue on, despite pestilent, viral assault from without.

Yet Neville, too, knows anemia.

It shifts within a wounded soul; an isolated dune, blown by empty routine. The liquor he is addicted to is only so much sweetened, civilized blood. The vampires who shriek obscene rage outside his house, as he drinks, simply crave a more horrid vintage and in Neville discover a warm, living vineyard.

Blood.

It drifts like thought and in *I am Legend* becomes the presence of evil itself; an unmerciful irrigation of post-war toxicity and dementia. The novel's layers are not unlike blood itself. Dense; intricate. Textured by a rich compositional weave. And in an era of AIDS, the global contagion which roves like some hideous vagabond, the ideas expressed in *I am Legend* are especially disturbing and prophetic.

The AIDS virus, too, hides amorally in human waterways. Waiting. Polluting the body's helpless Amazon torrents with death. It is impossible to stop; like the vampires Neville tries uselessly to slaughter.

Did my father have a vision which extended beyond merely a brilliant novel? Did he see what was coming?

I believe psychics exist. I believe we are all possessed of such ability. I therefore must, at least partially, support those visions which strike the psychically sensitive most powerfully; strike with most precise imagery and articulation.

And I find myself asking, what could be more specifically articulate than a detailed novel, the crux of which is a central image so exact, it's virtually the duplicate of AIDS; a blood holocaust.

I am Legend was set during a period between 1976 and 1979. The first, vague, unresponded-to reports about AIDS began to appear around 1980. It is, if nothing more, an evocative coincidence. Still, if Orwell's fictive predictions in the novel *1984* unsettle the nerves, what then should we make of what might be equally predictive, albeit equally fictive, visions contained within *I am Legend*?

Blood.

It is passed from father to son; a divine transfusion.

All life comes from it. Worships it.

Forfeits it in death.

It is essence.

And as we are all now grimly aware, it is the perfect messenger for horror.

Perhaps *I am Legend*, without my father's conscious awareness, might have been written not only to frighten us.

It might have been written to prepare us.

—RICHARD CHRISTIAN MATHESON

RAY BRADBURY

The October Country

The October Country is substantially a reprint of Dark Carnival (1947), an Arkham House collection of stories Bradbury originally published in Weird Tales and other magazine markets in the '40s. Dark Carnival was never widely available, and The October Country, which includes several tales original to the collection, stands as the definitive assembly of Bradbury's early horror fiction. As the title suggests, the mood is usually autumnal and sombre, as in 'The Scythe', where the protagonist becomes the Grim Reaper, chopping down wheatfields in the knowledge that every stalk represents a human life. However, there are also horrific tales along the lines of 'Skeleton', in which a hypochondriac becomes obsessed with the idea that his own bones have turned against him, and several stories ('Uncle Einar', 'The Homecoming') about a Charles Addamsish family of non-humans living in the Midwest. All these themes recur in the novel Something Wicked This Way Comes (1962).

*T*he October Country is a special place of dark magic where so many discriminating readers have ventured time and time again. It is a terrain where numerous writers and would-be-writers have also gone in search of a touch of Ray Bradbury's cool shadows, and sometimes those writers have enjoyed their visits so much, they have come back with souvenirs of his style and tone.

But that is understandable. This October Country is such a marvelous place, for all its fears, one hates to leave it.

The October Country is, to my mind, Bradbury's finest work. Certainly, it is his most magical. *Something Wicked This Way Comes* touches that dark magic now and again, but fails to sustain it. But here, in this volume of nineteen, perfectly honed stories, it is the status quo.

It is a shame and a surprise to me that his later science fiction tales, fine as they are (and it should be noted that Bradbury's so-called science fiction bears about as much relationship to that genre as a live pig does to pork) have overshadowed his ventures into the realm of horror, for it was in this realm that he was at his best. The stories have a feel of youthful enthusiasm, yet they are also the work of a mature artist coming into his own.

Fifteen of these tales originally made up his first collection, *Dark Carnival*, published by the justly famous Arkham House. These fifteen stories were reworked by Bradbury, sharpened, and grouped with four others to form *The October Country*, and from that point on, his poetry of shadows has defined the field of short story writing in the weird fiction category, and has had no minor influence on the literary world at large, though his influence here is probably less admitted due to his pulp origins.

His direct influence can be seen in the works of such writers as Richard Matheson, Charles Beaumont, William F. Nolan, and Chad Oliver, as well as more recent wordsmiths like Charles Grant, Dennis Etchison, Thomas Monteleone, Al Sarrantonio and Richard Christian Matheson.

Bradbury, like any writer of real literature, was writing about more in these stories than things that go bump in the night. More goes on in the scenes than just the scenes. After reading this collection and laying the book aside, attending to more mundane chores like polishing the woodwork, tying your kid's shoes or feeding the gerbil, the echo of these stories, of that peculiar October Country, continues to bounce inside your head, and its echo does not diminish with time.

Bradbury has the knack of making the commonplace mystical. It is as if everything in his stories is alive. The animate and the inanimate. After reading 'The Wind', who has not listened to the howling of the wind about the eaves and corners of the house and failed to think that it might not be a random force of nature, but might in fact have intent—dark intent?

And who cannot, when snug in their bed, half-drifting-off, with an infant down the hall, fail to think of 'The Small Assassin', and find themselves listening for the murderous slide of scooting baby knees on the carpet.

And what about the other things *The October Country* has forever redefined?

Hot Mexican nights and cisterns and the insides of strange men as viewed through a pane of stained-glass window; a man with a scythe; a man driving through the Tropic of Cancer, patting the empty car seat beside him; a dog bringing an unusual friend to see his sick master, and a dwarf in love with a funhouse mirror.

Bradbury is not without his faults as a writer. Sometimes his style is poetic for poetry's sake. Sometimes his dialogue is too precious. Sometimes his view of childhood too brightly nostalgic. Sometimes the point of his stories too trite. But these faults do not raise their heads in *The October Country*. When Bradbury wrote of shadows and dread, the disappointments and emptiness that all of us experience, his poetry was sharp, his dialogue lean, his visions of childhood bittersweet, his points as simple and effective as the sight of fresh blood on an infant's face.

We have many books by Ray Bradbury. Most of them collections of short stories. Novels like *Fahrenheit 451*, his best long work, and the flawed, but still marvelous, *Something Wicked This Way Comes*. But *The October Country* was, and is, his finest hour. Had he written only this

one volume of stories, his place in the archives library of the darkly
fantastic would have been assured. And his disciples no less numerous.

—JOE R. LANSDALE

56   [1958]

JOSEPH PAYNE BRENNAN

Nine Horrors and a Dream

*First published by Arkham House under the direction of August Derleth, this
collection consists chiefly of pieces written for* Weird Tales *in the early '50s.
Indeed, the book is dedicated to the memory of the magazine, and the best of
Brennan's stories typify the pulp imagination at its most concentrated.
Included here are the classic blob-of-hungry-ooze story 'Slime' and the highly
regarded tale of a cursed stretch of scrubland, 'Canavan's Back Yard',
together with such lesser but evocative tales as 'Death in Peru', 'On the
Elevator' and 'The Hunt'. One story, 'Levitation', has been adapted for the
TV series* Tales from the Darkside. *Despite the narrator's last words 'I have
never gone back since. And I never will', Brennan produced a sequel to
'Canavan's Back Yard'—'Canavan Calling'—twenty-five years later for
inclusion in* Night Visions 2: Dead Image *(1985). Brennan is also the author
of much poetry, the most macabre of which is collected in* Nightmare Need
*(1964) and has produced series of stories concerning Lucius Leffing, a
Holmesian psychic investigator, and Kerza, a lady barbarian.*

Fairytales apart, this was the first honest-to-God horror book that I
ever got my hands on to. I was about nine years old, certainly not
much more. It scared me stiff, gave me nightmares that actually shaded
into major-league hallucinations, probably warped me for life, and
certainly set me on target for what would eventually become a career. I
loved it, and still do. How much more can you ask of a book?

First let me tell you how I came to get hold of it. The collection had
originally been published in an Arkham House edition with a number of
the stories already having a *Weird Tales* pedigree, but the version that
reached me was a luridly-covered Ballantine reprint . . . and when I say
lurid I mean bright pinks, lime greens and purples, with the kind of
lettering that they used in the opening credits of *The Invaders* on TV. A
huge bulbous spider straddled the artwork from above, while down at

123

the bottom of the cover a tiny naked woman stood amongst Easter Island statues watching the sun rise—except that it wasn't the sun, but an immense and inhuman head with wide-staring eyes. Crude, but effective, as the villains used to say of their buzz-saws in the chapterplays.

I'm pretty sure it belonged to my uncle. He was an ex-Teddy Boy, ex-army conscript, ex-railway worker, then an employee on the Manchester docks. US paperback imports rarely made it into the shops in those days but a number of titles would make it over as ballast with other cargoes, as used to happen with comic books. Whether or not the Brennan was one of these, it's hard to be sure. It's only when I look back from here that I can appreciate how my uncle filled in some much-needed gaps in my early literary education; when they were making us read *Black Beauty* at school, he was the one who was telling me how the Frankenstein monster was put together. He provided my introduction to Edgar Rice Burroughs with a description of how the Leopard Men tenderized human flesh for consumption by breaking the limbs of their captives with clubs and then tethering them submerged up to their chins in a fast-flowing river. He told me who Doc Savage was.

And he lent me *Nine Horrors and a Dream*.

Ten stories don't exactly make for a doorstopper of a book. I read it quickly and in a state of awe. The one that I think impressed me most was 'The Calamander Chest'. It had many of the elements that I've come to think of as characteristic of the genre post-Lovecraft and pre-1970s, when tales of solitary young men and locked-up secrets gave way to a much broader sense of involvement that was more akin to soap opera. Each of the tales (with the possible exception of 'Slime', which at 32 pages was a more ambitious novella) was a similarly lean narrative built around a weird hook and calculated to leave the reader with that oddly satisfying sense of having taken a peek into forbidden territory from a place of safety.

Did I mention that I was staying the night at my grandmother's house when the book came into my hands? I'd better, because it has some bearing on what was to follow. My grandmother had a modest little place in a well-kept Salford backstreet (bulldozed, now, like everything of value in that city). It wasn't a spooky house at all, by any rational standard ... but to a child of my age, the gulf of time and taste was enough to make me feel ill-at-ease and a stranger in the home of any elderly relative. I read the last couple of stories in an unfamiliar bed with flannel sheets and heavy blankets—my own blanket at home had pictures of parachutes and jeeps on it—and when I finally switched off the bedside lamp, there was still a weak illumination in the room from a streetlight just outside the window. I could see the big, dark shapes of the furniture and, lit from the window like a little stage, I could see the top of the dressing-table.

On this dressing-table stood—or rather, knelt—two figurines. They were carved out of smooth black stone and they represented an African man and woman, both unclothed but tastefully featureless. Black nakedness somehow seemed to be considered apart from the taboos of the age, which would explain why *National Geographic* was never kept under the counter with all the skin magazines. I must have been lying there for about half an hour before anything happened.

So, what *did* happen?

What happened was that the male figurine got to its feet, and walked to the edge of the dressing-table and looked down. He seemed to move at double speed, with a flicker like an overcranked film. As he turned away from the edge, the female was standing up with the obvious intention of repeating the action. I tried to close my eyes and look away, but I couldn't. As the woman came forward the male was pacing back and forth behind her, as if trying to get the measure of this surface on which he found himself trapped. Neither of them made any sound. Every now and again they would dash back to their carved plinths for a few moments of rest and recharge.

I don't remember anything that ever scared me more. Not then, not since. I know exactly what was happening, of course. My body was on the brink of sleep and my mind was still racing, and the barriers between imagination and perception had dropped. I don't know how long I lay there, watching this bizarre show that my imagination was conjuring out of the available materials, but what I do know is that I believed in it without question.

I still do, in a way. You can add all of the later rationalizations that you want, but when you strip these away you're left with one simple certainty: you know what you saw.

I returned the book. Didn't see it again for twenty-five years, when I moved some paperbacks while browsing at a convention bookstall and found myself face-to-face with that same Ballantine edition. There had been other landmark books for me in the intervening time—Wells, Bierce, Levin, Farris, King, Straub—but this had been the first. I hesitated—there are few things more elusive and disappointing than past magic—and then I bought it. How could I do anything else? I felt as if I was welcoming it home.

The stories hold up. Styles and fashions have changed, but for me the line back in time stays unbroken. There's only one difficulty that I find myself unable to resolve.

I still can't work out which nine stories are the horrors, and which one the dream . . .

—STEPHEN GALLAGHER

ROBERT BLOCH

Psycho

Fairvale, California. The obese Norman Bates lives with his domineering mother and runs the isolated Bates Motel. Mary Crane, a young woman fleeing from a robbery she has committed on impulse, is beheaded in the shower by the insane Mrs Bates. Norman tries to cover up the crime, which is investigated by a private detective (who is also murdered by Norman's mother), and by the dead girl's sister and boyfriend. Finally, it develops that Mrs Bates has been dead for years, poisoned by her son, and that Norman is a schizophrenic who becomes homicidal when he takes on his mother's personality. Famously filmed by Alfred Hitchcock in 1960 from a screenplay by Joseph Stefano, with a definitive performance by Anthony Perkins, Psycho *has become the watchword for a certain kind of violent/suspense/psychological thriller. Bloch wrote a sequel,* Psycho 2 *(1982), which was* not *adapted into the 1983 film of the same name. Further sequels include the cinema's* Psycho III *(1986) and television's* Bates Motel *(1987).*

Never mind the movie. Mr Hitchcock did a masterful job on it, sure. And everyone on the planet who is interested in the horror genre must have seen the movie at least once by now. But Robert Bloch's novel was a masterpiece first. Mr Hitchcock didn't create Norman Bates and that spooky motel; Mr Bloch did. And not as any special project, either. Following on the heels of short stories, radio adaptations (of his own work) and at least four other novels, *Psycho* was just another product of Robert Bloch's wonderfully fertile and disciplined imagination.

Please note that qualifying word 'disciplined'. Because much of the strength of *Psycho* is in the writing.

From the beginning, Robert Bloch has written with clarity, using the language to communicate, not confuse. Too much of today's writing is intentionally obscure, deliberately aimed at having the reader ask himself on finishing a story, 'Now what was that all about?' Too many writers consider their work a contest between themselves and the reader, with, of course, the dice loaded in their favor and the reader bound to feel stupid for not 'getting it'.

Not Mr Bloch. His prose comes across like the clear, pure trumpet tone of a Bix Beiderbecke, not like a foghorn moan struggling to be heard through thick fog. So what he has to say is instantly understandable and hence all the more powerful.

What Bloch had to say in *Psycho* influenced the whole art of horror writing. Back onto dusty shelves went most of the vampires, the werewolves, and other such beasties of the Victorian novelists. To front and centre came a probing of people's minds and an awareness of the frightening things to be found lurking there. Never mind the crumbling old castle, the mad scientist, the ancient, horrid gods we wrote about in *Weird Tales* and other grand old magazines. Those were good stories for their time and will always be fun to re-read or collect; of course they will! But take a good, hard look now at your next-door neighbor who goes to an office every day or sells insurance or, in this case, runs a motel haunted by memories of an overpowering mother.

With this novel Robert Bloch took us from then to now in one big, scary leap, raising the hair of his readers while they eagerly turned the pages of what was scaring them, and showing writers how to handle a new kind of horror story.

Almost every present-day writer of horror has in one way or another been influenced by *Psycho*. Call it a milestone in horror fiction, written by one of the greats. That's what it is and what he is.

—HUGH B. CAVE

58   [1959]

NIGEL KNEALE

Quatermass and the Pit

While digging the foundations for an office block, London workmen discover a five-million-year-old spacecraft, complete with mummified Martians. Professor Bernard Quatermass, of the British Experimental Rocket Group, and archaeologist Dr Matthew Roney are among the boffins called in. Their investigations uncover a history of demonic manifestation and lead them to make some frightening conclusions about the nature of humanity. The third of Kneale's four Quatermass television serials was transmitted by the BBC in six episodes in 1959, with Andre Morrell in the lead role, first published as a book in 1960, and adapted for the cinema by Hammer Films in 1967 (US title: Five Million Years to Earth*), with Andrew Kier. In its various incarnations, it remains one of the most influential works of modern horror, leaving trace effects in movies like Tobe Hooper's* Lifeforce *and John Carpenter's* Prince of Darkness *and books like Stephen King's* The Tommyknockers*. The other Quatermass serials are* The Quatermass Experiment, *1953 (filmed 1955, US* *title:* The Creeping Unknown: *script published 1959)*, Quatermass II, *1955 (filmed 1957, US title:* Enemy from Space: *script published 1960) and* Quatermass, *1980 (theatrical title:* The Quatermass Conclusion: *novel published 1979).*

When is a book not a book? Answer: when it's a screenplay. More specifically, a television series in six parts entitled *Quatermass and The Pit*, written by Nigel Kneale and broadcast to genuinely alarmed and enthralled English viewers in 1959. When asked to cite a favourite or influential 'book', it may seem to be an anomaly to opt for a screenplay. But there are a number of reasons: ultimately the skill of Kneale's writing and his ability to play on subconscious dreads. Analysis of his writing nearly thirty years later still gives clues to any writer wishing to tap into the vein of 'supernatural terror' with any effect. As a seven-year-old back in 1959 I begged my father for the privilege of staying up late to watch *Quatermass and the Pit*. Under extreme pressure and with reservations, I was allowed to do so. Unfortunately, I was often despatched to bed after becoming too spooked. (Hell, even Trevor Duncan's background music was enough to make me hide behind the settee.) So my initial viewing was very fragmentary. Later, my childhood frustration at not really understanding why the series was so frightening drove me to the public library where I discovered to my delight that Penguin Books had published all of the *Quatermass* screenplays by Kneale. I devoured *The Pit*, reading it inside-out until the bizarre and fascinating premise—that the Martians were on Earth five million years ago and left their consciousness subconsciously implanted in mankind—was crystal clear.

Fantastic in the true sense of the word? Yes, of course. But written in such a down to earth way as to be extraordinarily convincing, with incident building upon incident, clue upon clue. The most original aspect of Kneale's story is the fact that the hobgoblin-like Martians of antiquity are in actuality the hobgoblins, and demons from the race memory of our mythical, superstitious past. As Quatermass says, 'Could it be that ghosts and the like were simply phenomena wrongly observed?' Quatermass' investigation ensues, resulting in the most effective build-up of unease and eeriness, until the climactic sequence where the Devil himself towers over the city in a glowing protoplasm of unearthly light. Only gradually does the full import of Kneale's title make its mark. *Quatermass and the Pit* not only refers to the clay pit in which the cylinder is found, but more specifically to The Pit of Hell itself.

One of the key elements behind the success of Kneale's premise is his depiction of a British no-nonsense sense of propriety. The characters themselves have difficulty in accepting the situation. But as traditional eerie goings-on are introduced into this modern (1959) situation and the characters are forced by the weight of evidence to accept the terrifying implications, so does the reader/viewer (subject to a slight mental wavelength adjustment from 1988 to 1959) accept them. Reader/viewer empathy with these realistic characters is strong, with a resultant 'suspension of disbelief'.

The Pit had a profound effect on me. The echo of its cosmic terror, I'm sure, was one of the reasons I strove to be a writer in the vein of terror fiction. As a screenplay, the story unfolds via dialogue and action. The mood is created by an escalation of gradual discovery and the growing suspicion that something long dormant and deeply disturbing is on the verge of reawakening. The more Quatermass investigates, the greater the underlying fear that his human probing and 'interference' in things perhaps better left alone will resurrect some terrifying threat from the past. By necessity, there is no lavish, descriptive prose; no long and detailed examination of the way people are thinking. This is, after all, a screenplay—not a novel. Everything stems from the realistic quality of dialogue, the character interaction and the fascinating investigative structure of the story. Reading the screenplay without direct recourse to the visuals makes one aware of just how much the reader's own imagination is being harnessed by Kneale's dark hints. This has been a useful benchmark for me in my own writing. Likewise, the need to establish a realistic setting with believable characters before introducing supernatural elements.

Another extremely important aspect to *The Pit* is the fact that it achieves its effects without any reliance on traditional horror motifs or blood'n'splatter (not that this would have been acceptable by the BBC in 1959 anyway). The keynote of Kneale's work here is 'terror' in its pure sense, a trademark which also applies to his writing for the *Beasts* TV series and *The Stone Tape* in the 1970s.

Quatermass and the Pit had a tremendous effect back in the '50s and it's easy to dismiss it now as a product of its time, dated and overtaken within the genre. But in a trend of ever increasingly visceral 'horror' in the 1980s, an examination of Kneale's writing and the way he achieves his effects gives some very valuable guidelines on how to weave a story so as to really frighten people. If Kneale's *The Quatermass Experiment* was 'man into monster' and *Quatermass II* was 'monster into man', then *Quatermass and the Pit* could be summarized as 'man was the monster all along'. And it's this latter theme which surfaces in some of the best horror fiction being written today. As Quatermass discovers, the worst demons are those which hide in the deepest recesses of the human mind.

—STEPHEN LAWS

H. P. LOVECRAFT

Cry Horror!

Previously published by Avon in 1947 as The Lurking Fear *and retitled for their 1958 reissue, this 1959 WDL edition was one of the first British paperback appearances of Lovecraft's work. Drawing substantially on the pick of the Arkham House collection* The Outsider and Others *('Cool Air', 'The Call of Cthulhu', 'The Color Out of Space'), with a few tales from other sources ('The Moon-Bog', 'The Unnamable', 'The Hound'),* Cry Horror! *introduced many British fans to the Sage of Providence. Later collections published as* The Lurking Fear *have slightly different contents.*

I first discovered Lovecraft's work around the age of 10 when I read a 1947 Avon anthology, *Terror by Night*. This had stories by Stoker, M. R. James, Blackwood and Machen, but it was Lovecraft's 'The Haunter of the Dark' that sent me scurrying out of the house in search of reassuring crowds. Though I eagerly scoured bookshops and libraries in search of more Lovecraft, it was not until a couple of years later that I came across a copy of *Cry Horror!*, the first HPL collection published in Britain so far as I know. I can still remember the elation of the discovery, and the satisfaction I felt as I read the stories and found them to be every bit as affecting as I had hoped. I've read thousands of horror stories since, but none have ever made quite the same impact as those first Lovecraft stories.

This collection, comprising of about one-sixth of HPL's output, offers a good sampling of his recurrent themes, and includes no less than seven of my favourite HPL stories: 'The Lurking Fear', 'The Color Out of Space', 'Pickman's Model', 'The Call of Cthulhu', 'Cool Air', 'The Hound' and 'The Shunned House'. 'The Lurking Fear', in which a Sawney Bean-like community of atavistic humans seeks cannibal nutrition in 'the terrible and thunder-crazed house of Martense' shows Lovecraft's talent for building a powerful, dense atmosphere of impending doom. So does 'The Color Out of Space', which includes some of HPL's finest visual imagery, shading from expressionism into surrealism. Lovecraft's strength as a writer was primarily in his descriptive power, and one can't help regretting that, unlike his friend Clark Ashton Smith, he was never tempted to extend his visual imagination into other avenues of expression. In 'Pickman's Model' he wrote: '. . . only a real artist knows the actual anatomy of the terrible or the physiology of fear—the exact sort of lines and proportions that connect up with latent instincts or hereditary memories of fear, and the proper colour contrasts and lighting effects to stir the dormant sense of strangeness . . .' An apt summation of Lovecraft's art.

'The Call of Cthulhu', written in persuasive documentary style, is the cornerstone of the Cthulhu Mythos, arguably HPL's greatest contribution to supernatural literature. Like all the best Mythos stories it has enough implications to fill six issues of the *Fortean Times*. The reason why Lovecraft towers over his contemporaries and imitators is surely that he writes with such *conviction*. Even today, rereading these stories, I catch myself thinking: 'what if he's *right*?'

Apparently I'm not alone. The British occultist Kenneth Grant has written several books in which he postulates that Lovecraft didn't invent the Elder Gods or the Great Old Ones—Cthulhu, Hastur, Yog-Soggoth and the rest—they're all *real*! Being hypersensitive, Lovecraft simply picked up on their vibrations and transcribed his dreams into works of art—just like that poor boob Henry Anthony Wilcox, the unfortunate sculptor in 'The Call of Cthulhu'.

This theory is either a tribute to the persuasive power of HPL's stories, or . . . No, the alternative is too lawful, too *Lovecraftian*, to contemplate.

Writing about the artists he admired, HPL wrote: 'There's something these fellows catch—beyond life—that they're able to make us catch for a second.' That's a talent Lovecraft himself possessed to perfection, as these stories more than adequately demonstrate.

—MICHEL PARRY

60 [1959]

SHIRLEY JACKSON

The Haunting of Hill House

Eleanor Vance, a lonely spinster racked with guilt over the recent death of her tyrannical mother, is asked by Dr John Montague to take part in his investigation of the supposedly haunted Hill House. Joining Eleanor and Montague in the house, which has a long and evil history, are Theodora, an ambiguous young psychic, and Luke, a cynical young man who hopes eventually to inherit the property. Eleanor, who has been selected by

Montague because she was as a child the focus of poltergeist phenomena, becomes the target (or the source) of a series of manifestations. She comes to believe that the house wants her, and is finally driven to become one of the ghosts (or perhaps the only ghost) of Hill House. The Haunting of Hill House is perhaps the most critically respected genre novel of the last fifty years, and has been widely influential. *There are shadows of Hill House in books as different in approach as Robert Marasco's* Burnt Offerings *(1973), Richard Matheson's* Hell House *(1971), Anne Rivers Siddons'* The House Next Door *(1978), Lisa Tuttle's* Familiar Spirit *(1983) and Stephen King's* The Shining *(1977).*

It was Shirley Jackson's achievement to write *the* great modern novel of supernatural horror.

In general, I think, supernatural horror is most successful at shorter lengths. While it is possible to build and sustain a feeling of horror throughout the length of a novel, horror that is specifically supernatural places an additional demand on the modern unbelieving reader. A short story leaves no room for argument; it gets by on style and atmosphere, overwhelming rationality, forcing the reader (if it succeeds) to accept its view of the world in one, shuddering gulp. A novel is a more leisurely affair, and the reader's trust in the writer is crucial. When the author is writing about things we (ostensibly) don't believe in, like vampires and ghosts, the reader agrees to accept a different reality, and to believe in it, for the duration of the novel. This willing suspension of disbelief allows the novel to be enjoyed, but it also blocks a certain intensity of experience: in a sense, we are pretending to believe, and so we are only pretending to be scared.

Although she was writing a novel which treats of the supernatural in the modern world, writing for sophisticated, 'mainstream' readers in the late 1950s, Shirley Jackson demanded no special suspension of disbelief; no more than that required by any realistic, psychological novel of the day. She postulated no vampires, no ghosts, no hierarchy of malevolent spirits, but only the existence of *something* besides our tangible, material world, and the experience of such psychic phenomena as have actually been reported. She was writing a realistic novel of character—actually, about the disintegration of character, as the protagonist, Eleanor Vance, goes through an intolerably stressful situation. And yet, this is not 'merely' a psychological novel; the fact that it takes place in a haunted house is absolutely essential. The supernatural elements cannot be interpreted as misperceptions or evidence of madness on the part of some 'unreliable narrator'—*The Haunting of Hill House* is narrated coolly, elegantly, and utterly sanely in the third person, and the setting is an archetypal evil place, a house which, from the very first paragraph, is attributed a personality, and given the status of antagonist.

The idea for the novel came, Jackson said, from her chance reading of a book about the experiences of a group of nineteenth-century ghost-hunters: 'I found it so exciting that I wanted more than anything else to set up my own haunted house, and put my own people in it, and see what I could make happen.' I know the feeling, having tried it myself; Jackson's starting point strikes me as more suggestive than Jane Austen's favourite '3 or 4 Families in a Country Village', and even more dependent on the author's genius to make of it something worth reading.

Reading *The Haunting of Hill House* first in my teens, I found it genuinely don't-turn-out-the-lights frightening, and it went immediately into my pantheon of the 'really scary' along with certain short stories by M. R. James, Walter de la Mare and L. P. Hartley. Like those other writers, Jackson invokes terror less by what she says than by what she doesn't say; by suggestion rather than explanation; and, rather startlingly, by a noticeable lack of description. Unlike the others named, Jackson was a contemporary writer; there are no Victorian frills or *fin-de-siècle* flourishes to her prose. Re-reading it recently, I was particularly, and favourably, struck by the absence of description, and considered it as an example of what Willa Cather called the 'unfurnished novel'. Cather thought that the writer who was an artist should renounce cataloguing, explaining and minute descriptions; whatever 'furniture' was included should be chosen for its emotional charge and because it was necessary to the story being told. Cather's prescription came at about the same time as the revolt by Hemingway, Stein and other modernist writers against the overstuffed novels of an earlier generation. My increased admiration for Jackson's writing may have something to do with a surfeit of modern blockbusters insisting on a tediously detailed 'reality' before allowing their even more lavishly described horrors to intrude. I happen to believe, with Henry James, that the imagination is more terrified by unseen terrors than by anything a writer can describe, and Shirley Jackson's *The Haunting of Hill House* is the best argument I can think of for this point of view. This book is a work of art. And it is still one of the scariest stories I've ever read.

—LISA TUTTLE

PHILIP K. DICK

The Three Stigmata of Palmer Eldritch

In the 21st century, life is only bearable for the fed-up colonists on Mars if they take Can-D, a drug that allows them to enter a saccharine fantasy world populated by dolls. Palmer Eldritch—a tycoon who may be possessed by an alien demon—returns from a protracted trip to Proxima Centauri with alien lichens that produce a new drug to rival Can-D. Marketed as Chew-Z, Eldritch's drug can transport its consumers forever into a world of illusion. In the sixties, Dick moved away from the more-or-less conventional science fiction of his early novels and concentrated on bizarre, surreal, often drug-related, visions of frightening or disorienting alternative realities. The Cosmic Puppets (1957) is his sole attempt at using supernatural horror to deal with his themes, but more interesting than this competent, minor novel are the mind-twisting weirdness of The Man in the High Castle *(1962),* Martian Time-Slip *(1964),* Do Androids Dream of Electric Sheep? *(1968),* A Maze of Death *(1970) and* A Scanner Darkly *(1977).*

I suppose there are people to whom a book like *The Three Stigmata of Palmer Eldritch* might not seem horrifying, at least in the traditional sense. It contains almost none of the conventions of the horror genre; in fact, I can remember only one scene in the entire book that takes place at night. It is also *very* science-fictionish: people go jetting about in shuttle rockets, and much of the action takes place on moon-colonies, or in robot-driven taxicabs.

Nevertheless, Dick had firm hold of something that seems to exceed the grasp of many writers who have made a career out of horror fiction, namely: there is *nothing* so frightening as the naked vulnerability of the human mind.

Perhaps Philip K. Dick speaks most strongly to those who have some first-hand experience of madness, either inherent or chemically induced. The labyrinth within the skull is deeper, darker, and more desperate than any Usher, deadlier than any pendulum-pit or other worldly construction. One's own mind can inflict tortures that would leave the canny professionals of the Inquisition gaping in reluctant admiration. And as many of us have come to learn, even those who are stout-minded by nature can experience such bottomless depths with the aid of certain recreational or religious chemicals.

This is not an anti-drug screed, mind you, although Dick himself certainly seemed to rue his association with the drug scene. While the psychedelic experience was ultimately a bitter one for him—as it was for many people—it also opened his fiction in a way that will keep it a subject of serious discussion when the work of other, more 'popular' writers has long faded from notice.

In a way, I could have picked any of several books by Dick that address the frailty of the rational human mind: time and time again his characters find the seemingly firm foundation of reality almost literally rotting away around them. Still, although many of Dick's books travel in this realm, there is a scene in *Palmer Eldritch* that stuck a sliver of ice into the base of my skull the first time I read it—a sliver that, for me, has never quite melted—and which seems to well represent the literary turf on which Dick staked out his largely uncontested claim.

Leo Bulero, a smart and self-righteous man, finds himself up against something he cannot understand: the transmutation of his rival, Palmer Eldritch. When Eldritch forces the drug Chew-Z on Bulero, Leo finds himself in a bizarre and desolate fantasy world that is entirely permeated and manipulated by the mind of Eldritch. Through force of will, Bulero escapes from this induced nightmare, back to his business office on Earth. He summons his associates to tell them what he has learned.

It is only after he notices a hideous, unearthly *thing* under his desk that he realizes he has never left the drugged dream at all—that in fact he has only wandered into a more familiar-looking room within the larger maze of his hallucination. The 'actual' world has become an unretrievable idea. He bemusedly dismisses his unreal associates, and surrenders himself up to Eldritch's control.

This is the true nightside, and it is also where Dick cuts across the grain of most other writers who traffic in horror. *There is no way to tell what is real.* There is no talisman, no silver bullet, no sword of cold iron to separate holy from unholy. The human mind can only guess—but, as Dick shows so well, when trying to bring rational order to the infinite vistas of both the internal as well as external universe, the mind is out of its league.

The dark shadow cast by the psychedelic era's sunshine is the fragility of sanity. It is a lesson many of us cannot forget, and it was a spectre that Philip K. Dick could not exorcise, no matter how many times he wrote about it.

In the latter stages of *Three Stigmata*, as the line between hallucination and reality becomes increasingly blurred, and as the characters wander in and out of both time and space in a most disturbing way, Palmer Eldritch—who may or may not be: an alien; a transmogrified human; or even God—manifests himself everywhere. The stigmata of the title— Eldritch's slitted electronic eyes, steel teeth, and mechanical hand—begin to appear on innocent bystanders, on friends and associates, and even on the protagonists themselves. Eldritch himself seems to be ubiquitous at all the levels of reality, sometimes merely speaking through the body of one of the characters, sometimes supplanting that character entirely. There is no safe haven; there is no fortified place in the mind or elsewhere where anyone can feel protected from intrusion. They cannot ever *know* beyond doubt that they are back in the 'real world'. A crack in reality has opened, and Palmer Eldritch is what has oozed through; his presence spreads like a disease.

Perhaps it is wrong to suggest that those who have experienced some type of madness will best understand and appreciate Philip K. Dick's work. Maybe everyone, even the most placid, stable sorts, need to travel across that line of safety every now and then, to be reminded that ultimately we are all living in our own dark and solitary universes, looking desperately outward for the distant lights of other lives.

The only problem is, once you have crossed that protective barrier— even if only through literary means—and have spun purchaseless into the void, nothing ever feels quite comfortable again.

—TAD WILLIAMS

62   [1965]

JERZY KOSINSKI

The Painted Bird

In 1939, a six-year-old boy from a bourgeois city family in Eastern Europe is sent to a distant village to escape the war. In the turmoil of the German invasion, the boy's parents lose contact with the man into whose care they have entrusted their child, and the boy suffers the loss of the woman who was to be his foster mother. Left to wander aimlessly through the region for the next four years, the child narrator takes shelter where and with whom he can and is exposed to every breed of human cruelty and misery imaginable. In a calm, even tone of voice, he describes the ancient superstitions of the peasants among whom he lives and the repeated atrocities to which he is a mute witness. He falls in with criminals, Nazis, prostitutes, communists, savage Kamluks and liberating troops before being returned, a silent ten-year-old, to his family. The Painted Bird—which in its approach is something of a precursor to J. G. Ballard's Empire of the Sun (1985)—is an example of a realistic novel that deals with events so awful and awesome that it reads like a catalogue of surrealist horror.

S ome books are read; others seem to become part of our own, private experience.

Perhaps it's a function of youth, just as the music we hear during adolescence and early adulthood remains part of our intensely evocative experience. Yet I find something like that still happening: even now certain books become my own. Perhaps art enables us to overcome the ennui and cynicism of 'maturity' and suspend our disbelief. Thus, we become innocents once again, opening ourselves to life.

The Painted Bird still burns in my memory, perhaps more brightly than any of the others. It is still an experienced nightmare, a waking dream, after fifteen years. I discovered the book when I began to write fiction, when I was crossing that bridge from being reader to writer. The initial horror I remember experiencing when I first read the book has transformed itself over the years into a sensation of numinal perfection, of something magical and yet terrible, something so incandescently pure and frightening as to be insidious.

So when asked to recommend my favorite novel of horror, I went back to my library to re-read *The Painted Bird*.

It is a devastatingly realistic novel about the mythic journey of an eleven-year-old boy through the peasant villages of an unnamed war-torn country, most likely Hungary.

What struck me upon my second reading was that the horrifying events—the continual and almost pornographic depiction of violence and cruelty—filtered through the mind of a boy, acquired the same magical reality as legend and fable. In fact, that is exactly what makes the book so horrifying: the real events are too terrible, too palpably real, to be interpreted realistically.

Fantasy takes on the same valence as reality.

Suspecting a young plowboy of a dalliance with his wife, a miller invites the plowboy to his home for dinner. After dinner, he attacks the plowboy and plunges a spoon into his eyes. The protagonist watches as the eyeballs roll down the miller's hand to the floor, where housecats play with them as if they are marbles.

> Now it seemed that the eyes were staring at me from every corner of the room, as though they had acquired a new life and motion of their own.
>
> I watched them with fascination. If the miller had not been there I myself would have taken them. Surely they could still see. I would keep them in my pocket and take them out when needed, placing them over my own. Then I would see twice as much, maybe even more. Perhaps I could attach them to the back of my head and they would tell me, though I was not quite certain how, what went on behind me. Better still, I could leave the eyes somewhere and they would tell me later what happened during my absence.
>
> Maybe the eyes had no intention of serving anyone. They could

easily escape from the cats and roll out of the door. They could wander over the fields, lakes, and woods, viewing everything about them, free as birds released from a trap. They would no longer die, since they were free, and being small they could easily hide in various places and watch people in secret. Excited, I decided to close the door quietly and capture the eyes.

The miller, evidently annoyed by the cats' play, kicked the animals away and squashed the eyeballs with his heavy boots. Something popped under his thick sole. A marvelous mirror, which could reflect the whole world, was broken. There remained on the floor only a crushed bit of jelly. I felt a terrible sense of loss.

The horror of this scene, and the many other scenes which carry the same weight as this one in the book, is generated by the objective reality—what is observed to be 'out there'. The attending fantastic element is generated by the need to make sense of that which can be observed but not believed or understood.

The protagonist is later taken to the home of the peasant Gabros for safe haven. Gabros, however, has a known history of sadism. He beats and tortures the boy constantly. Trying to defend himself from these unprovoked and irrational attacks, the protagonist concludes that the peasant's fits of rage must be caused by something subtle and mysterious.

Once or twice I thought I had detected a clue. On two consecutive occasions I was beaten immediately after scratching my head. Who knows, perhaps there was some connection between the lice on my head, which were undoubtedly disturbed in their normal routine by my searching fingers, and Gabros's behavior. I immediately stopped scratching, even though the itching was unbearable. After two days of leaving the lice alone I was beaten again. I had to speculate anew.

After overhearing a priest explaining the concept of indulgences, the boy believes he has deciphered the ruling pattern of world. The defense against Gabros's sadistic attacks is simple and obvious:

One had only to recite prayers, concentrating on the ones carrying the greatest number of days of indulgence. Then one of God's aides would immediately note the new member of the faithful and allocate to him a place in which his days of indulgence would start accumulating like sacks of wheat piled up at harvest time.

Although he prays continuously for indulgences, he is still beaten and forced to hold on to hooks in the ceiling while Gabros's dog snaps at his feet and waits for him to weaken and fall to the floor. But this kind of fantastical religious reasoning is a precursor to the boys eventual understanding of 'the real rules of this world':

A man who had sold out to the Evil Ones would remain in their power all his life. From time to time he would have to demonstrate an increasing number of misdeeds. But they were not rated equally by his superiors. An action harming one person was obviously worth less than one affecting many ... Thus, simply beating up an innocent man was worth less than inciting him to hate others. But hatred of large groups of people must have been the most valuable of all ...

The boy whose family has sent him away from the 'civilization' of Nazi Germany in hopes that he might survive in the country becomes a witness not only to the cruelty of the uneducated peasants, who are contrasted to the smooth, neatly groomed, larger-than-life German soldiers and commanders, but to the human condition itself.

After peering into the mirrors of human depravity, the boy concludes that his only course is to join those who have sold out to the Evil Ones. It is then that his psychic pain disappears, then that he feels new strength and confidence.

> Cold sweat drained over me in the dark hutch. I myself hated many people. How many times had I dreamed of the time when I would be strong enough to return, set their settlements on fire, poison their children and cattle, lure them into deadly swamps. In a sense I had already been recruited by the powers of Evil and had made a pact with them.

But even that, perhaps terrible, revelation gives way to numbing objectivity and distancing when he witnesses a Kamluk raid.

In a sense the protagonist, as silent witness to Kosinski's diorama of horrors, is emblematic of the reader ... or perhaps just this reader. The shock of his experience as a wanderer, outsider, and evil-eyed 'gypsy', leaves him mute, only able to watch, no longer disbelieving, unable, in the final analysis, even to rationalize. As he watches the Kamluks destroy a village, raping and looting and murdering in every disgusting manner possible (and the author in his introduction to the book emphasized that 'Every village of Eastern Europe knew of such events, and hundreds of settlements had suffered similar fates'), he becomes a camera for us, a neutral eye, since the marvelous eye, the mirror that could reflect the whole world, is indeed broken.

Unlike most genre horror novels and stories (and this is not to denigrate those forms in any way), the shocking element is that of reality. In the genre, the horror element is the supernatural, which is often symptomatic or symbolic of our fears and frustration. But Kosinski's *The Painted Bird* cuts to the bone because the experience itself is not easily digested, and we—like Kosinski's protagonist—are left frightened and perplexed after this brush with the dark, perverse antinomies of human nature.

My own writing has, to some extent, been a reaction to this book. From my horror story 'Camps' to *The Economy of Light*, a novel-in-progress about the possibility of moral transformation, I have felt the obligation to 'testify', to try to become 'a marvelous mirror' and perhaps transfuse a bit of our past into our present. It may well be a superstitious hope that if we can only remember our past, we won't repeat it; and fiction, which John Gardner called 'a waking dream', is one way of experiencing and remembering.

But as Kosinski has shown us, sometimes superstition is our only defense.

—JACK DANN

63   [1966]

J. G. BALLARD

The Crystal World

Dr Edward Sanders travels to West Africa to investigate reports of a strange phenomenon. He discovers that a growing expanse of the jungle has been turning crystalline, fusing the flora and fauna into a glittering mineral formation. Finally, Sanders is compelled to travel into the abstract sculpture jungle himself, hoping to merge with the landscape. The Crystal World follows Ballard's The Wind from Nowhere (1962), The Drowned World (1962) and The Burning World (1964) (a.k.a. The Drought), and forms the final part of a loose quartet of disaster novels dealing with the four elements. While the first book in the sequence was conventional sf in the John Wyndham vein, the later books are increasingly bizarre, surreal and unclassifiable.

Disaster is a proud tradition in fantastic literature, from H. G. Wells' Martian invasion to such modern-day bestsellers as *Swan Song* and *War Day*. The fifties and the early sixties were a particularly fertile time for disaster novels, what with new awareness of atomic bombs and ecology, producing such end-of-the-world (or end-of-humanity) classics as John Wyndham's *Day of the Triffids* and Richard Matheson's *I am Legend*. It is in this tradition that J. G. Ballard began writing his book-length fiction, culminating in his fourth novel, *The Crystal World*.

The central disaster in Ballard's book is quite simple. Something is happening in remote tropical sections of the world. The landscape is transforming, changing from lush, humid vegetation, to cold, arid crystals. But how Ballard handles this disaster is quite atypical. Instead of fighting the disaster with non-stop action or the latest scientific marvels, his characters act almost as if the change wasn't even taking place, and in a way that is most certainly secondary to their immediate emotional concerns.

Death and decay are everywhere in *The Crystal World*. The opening image in the book is one of rotting vegetation along black river water. The protagonist, Dr Sanders, a specialist in leprosy, searches for a former lover who has, herself, contracted the disease. In the book's most dramatic sub-plot, two men fight violently over a woman who is dying of some wasting illness.

And, moving slowly but unstoppably, is the crystalization of the jungle and the world. Ballard describes this transformed jungle as a place of great beauty—the crystals pulse with a light of their own—but it is a place without heat, and a place of total silence. Everything, vegetation, water, birds, animals, humans, perhaps even air, is being turned to crystal and frozen in place.

Ballard sets up the universe of *The Crystal World* as a place of opposites, foremost among them the living/rotting jungle versus the dead/magnificent crystals. The protagonist has two loves: Suzanne, who contracts leprosy and is drawn to the crystal world, and Louise, a journalist investigating the phenomenon, who wants to return to the unaffected outside world with Sanders. But Sanders cannot resolve either of his love affairs, and all the opposites in the book seem equally unresolvable. Life goes on, for the most part passively, as the crystals approach. The only moment of true passion in the book occurs when a character, rescued by Sanders from a crystal shell and returned to bleeding, aching flesh, demands to be taken back, to be frozen again in crystal.

In the end, Sanders decides to return to the crystals, to be frozen forever. In fact, none of the characters leave, not even Louise. Perhaps no one can leave. It is the end of change. The world, the sun, the universe, everything will turn to crystal. And this end of change, Ballard implies, is what all of us desire. It is this unique combination of the psychological and the physical that makes *The Crystal World* a very quiet, yet very effective, work of horror fiction.

—CRAIG SHAW GARDNER

ROBERT AICKMAN
Sub Rosa

Sub Rosa *is an original collection of ghost stories—or 'strange stories', to use the author's preferred term—concentrating on ambiguity, unease and stark terror. It consists of eight novella-length tales: 'Ravissante', 'The Inner Room', Never Visit Venice', 'The Unsettled Dust', 'The Houses of the Russians', 'No Stronger Than a Flower', 'The Cicerones' and 'Into the Wood'. Aickman's other collections, all of a similarly high standard, are* Dark Entries *(1964),* Powers of Darkness *(1966),* Cold Hand in Mine *(1975),* Tales of Love and Death *(1977) and* Painted Devils *(1979).*

At the beginning of 'Ravissante' our anonymous narrator recalls meeting a married couple at a party. The man told him he had given up painting for easier and more lucrative employment editing coffee-table books. His wife the narrator describes as a 'nearly invisible woman'. She did not speak. 'I remark on this,' says the narrator, 'simply as a fact. I do not imply that she was bored. She might indeed have been enthralled. Silence can, after all, mean either thing. In her case, I never found out which it meant.'

The Latin tag *sub rosa* means 'secretly; in strict confidence'. The estimable E. Cobham Brewer explains that 'Cupid gave Harpocrates (the god of silence) a rose, to bribe him not to betray the amours of Venus. Hence the flower became the emblem of silence.' Robert Aickman tells us secrets, secrets we would generally rather not know; secrets so bizarre we do not know how to take them; secrets so private we may doubt whether he has told us anything at all.

He has. He has shown us views of the domain of Harpocrates: told us something of the nature of the silence.

In the silence there may be anything. Most often it is sex or death, or, for Curtis in 'No Stronger Than a Flower' as for Coleridge's Ancient Mariner, one wearing the mask of the other. We long for silence as we long for sleep; as we long for one another. We do not know the face of what we long for; but when we see it, we know it, and with that we are extinguished.

The editor of coffee-table books leaves an account of the horrid experience that induced him to give up painting. In a foreign country, in a house he did not know, the squat, ugly widow of an artist he much admired subjected him to a sexually degrading ritual before a canvas he immediately recognized as his own work, but which he knew he had never painted. It was to keep out of this region of terror and humiliation that the man gave up his art and married a woman who would efface herself for him; or perhaps because he had been there already.

'The Inner Room' tells how a woman shelters from a storm in a house that resembles entirely the macabre doll's house she owned briefly as a child, but could never open. The musty, embittered inhabitants show her a photograph of herself when young, pierced with a rusty needle. Robert Aickman's 'strange tales' enter into secret limbos and private hells where the outer world has come to resemble the inner. Coded out of gestures, urges, and hesitations, their landscapes are no more comprehensible and no less compelling than the scenarios of dreams. 'These areas,' says Aickman in 'Into the Wood', 'are not uncommon if you know how (or are compelled) to look for them.'

Trant, the central character of 'The Cicerones', comes with ease among the tombs of the bishops of St Bavon. 'The gate had every appearance of being locked, but in fact it opened at once.' In this story it is Christianity itself, with its mechanisms of martyrdom and election, that generates horror. At the last it is not clear whether Trant has been saved or damned, only that he has been removed from the world of guidebooks and wristwatches.

Aickman's characters are tourists and travellers, solitaries abroad. Nugent Oxenhope, in 'The Unsettled Dust', is an official forced to put up at a dreary stately home, the barely tenanted husk of a former grandeur. Aickman thought this a suitable image for Britain in the twentieth century. In 'Never Visit Venice' and 'Into the Wood', as in 'Ravissante' and 'The Cicerones', Britons carry their disappointment and loneliness into Europe, where different forms of paralysis await them. In 'The Houses of the Russians' a British surveyor's clerk on business in Finland is given a gratuitous vision of an Orthodox heaven and hell, and a protective talisman. Harpocrates too can be kind.

Aickman's was not a malign universe, or even a retributive tragic order that automatically punished transgressions and oversights. Rather he maintained, in the stories of his eight collections (one collaborative, one posthumous), that human existence is a narrow path through the absolute unknown; and we occasionally, inevitably, stray. Introducing the ex-painter's manuscript, the narrator of 'Ravissante' says: 'The sheer oddity of life seems to me of more and more importance, because more and more the pretence is that life is charted, predictable, and controllable.'

In the house of the dead artist, so the manuscript records, the writer suddenly noticed a small black poodle in the room. 'It seemed to me, as I looked at it, to have very big eyes and very long legs, perhaps more like a spider than a poodle.' He lost track of it, and mentioned it to the widow.

She had not seen it. 'If it's not yours,' he told her, 'it must have got in from the darkness outside.'

—COLIN GREENLAND

65

KINGSLEY AMIS

The Green Man

Maurice Allington, owner of a pub in Fareham, Hertfordshire, called The Green Man— which numbers Brian W. Aldiss among its patrons—begins to see ghosts. A heavy drinker and a womanizer, Allington is at first more preoccupied with his complicated day-to-day life, specifically his attempts to get his wife Joyce and mistress Diana to join him in a bout of troilist sex, than the supernatural visitations. However, the sinister presence of Dr Thomas Underhill, a dead magician, soon persuades him to take an interest. It develops that Underhill has plans to return from the beyond; plans which involve Maurice and his young daughter Amy, not to mention the imposing folklore figure after which the pub is named. A witty, scary combination of typical Amis social/sexual comedy and the M. R. James tradition, The Green Man includes several fine digressions on the natures of death, ghostliness and the ghost story itself. Although Amis has tried his hand several times at science fiction, this remains his only major venture into the horror field.

*T*he Oxford English Dictionary gives as its definition of Horror, 'A painful emotion compounded of loathing and fear'. *The Green Man* provides plenty of fear and loathing, as well as painful emotion in its own right.

Unlike some novels, which take a while before introducing their frisson, *The Green Man* begins briskly: a ghost arrives on page four of the text. This relatively harmless—that is, merely disconcerting—female apparition serves as a prelude to a series of malevolent figures, some more substantial than others, all capable of raising the fear and loathing level. We meet an old man, a young man, an unpleasant bird, and the particularly unsettling creature of the title.

This might sound like gilding the lily, but not in Kingsley Amis' hands. An acclaimed novelist makes his horrors telling by staging them in the prosaic setting of a public house, The Green Man, eight miles off the

M1 in Hertfordshire. The owner of the pub is Maurice Allington, a man with a drink problem and several other problems of a personal nature which lead to the disaffection of his second wife and the alienation of his young daughter. *The Green Man* works as a novel, rather than just as a horror tale, its strengths being the rough-edged character of Allington and the lucidity with which his pub and its working life are described. A reader soon feels that he could find his way round the premises alone at night, from the bedrooms to the bar.

Not that this would be the most desirable of activities. For The Green Man is home to the evil shade of a 17th-century practitioner of the black arts, Dr Thomas Underhill. Allington comes up against him in what is now the pub dining-room, once Underhill's study.

> In leisurely fashion, but without delay, the head turned and the eyes met mine. They were dark brown eyes with deeply creased lids, thick lower lashes, and arching brows. I also saw a pale, indoors complexion scattered with broken veins to what seemed an incongruous degree, a broad forehead, a long, skewed nose, and a mouth that, in another's face, I might have called humorous, with very clearly defined lips. Then, or rather at once, Dr Underhill recognised me. Then he smiled. It was the kind of smile with which a bully might greet an inferior person prepared to join with him in the persecution of some helpless third party.

Amis never piles on the agony, using words with his customary care. This coolness also characterizes much of Allington's behaviour, whereas his old father dies of shock when confronted by one of the apparitions.

If Underhill was once human, the bird which flies through Allington's hand—to his terror—manifestly is not. The green monster, which Underhill once controlled, is even further from human, though it takes on an approximately human shape. It is a destructive force arising from nature, not entirely unlike Theodore Sturgeon's *It*. Last in the apparition queue, most far from humanity, is 'the young man'. The young man, appearing in the upstairs dining-room when the whole world is struck by temporal paralysis, is God himself. However many times I read the novel, these passages, with the universe stopping and this pallid apparition sitting in a chair, strike me with deep and genuine dismay. Allington's conversation with the young man touches profound depths of ontological discomfort: the Almighty is a petty creature.

In all, *The Green Man* is one of Amis's most agreeably rancid novels, packed with disconcerting moments, both human and inhuman, and ending on a memorable note of *Angst*. It's genuinely and enduringly chilling, the real McCoy, and no tomato sauce.

—BRIAN W. ALDISS

ANTHONY BOUCHER

The Compleat Werewolf, and Other Stories of Fantasy and SF

This collection assembles the best of Anthony Boucher's short fiction. A major influence on the field as founder and editor of The Magazine of Fantasy and Science Fiction, *Boucher (the pseudonym of William Anthony Parker White) wrote these stories between 1941 and 1945, mainly for John W. Campbell's* Unknown. *The title story is a classic mix of lycanthropy, private eyes, fiendish Nazi agents and wisecracking humour. In a similar vein, the book also includes such witty variations on old horror themes as 'Snulbug', about a deal with a demon, 'Mr Lupescu', about an imaginary friend, 'The Ghost of Me', a doppelgänger with a twist, and 'We Print the Truth', about a newspaper editor given the power to change the world. 'They Bite', a rare straight horror tale about desert-dwelling mutants (perhaps an influence on* The Hills Have Eyes) *is one of the most often-anthologized and praised '40s horror stories. Boucher's other work includes fine, traditional detective novels like* The Case of the Seven of Calvary *(1937),* The Case of the Crumpled Knave *(1939),* Nine Times Nine *(1940),* The Case of the Baker Street Irregulars *(1940) and* Rocket to the Morgue *(1942).*

I saw one of the most distressing newspaper headlines of my life last month; someone was reading *The Sun* at Haywards Heath railway station, and the headline blared out from the cover and it made my heart sink and my fingers cross. 'Oh *no*,' I thought. 'They *haven't!*'

The Headline read: *Werewolf Captured in Southend.*

The concept was terrifying. If there really were werewolves—and Southend did seem the kind of place they'd find one—then werewolves would be reduced to reality, be codified and counted, make TV appearances, be explained away. No longer could shapechanging lycan-thropes stalk the darkness outside the circle of firelight that fits into everyday experience and dry textbooks; no longer would they be fair game for any writer with a yen to set someone howling at a full moon. Instead they'd be case histories and oddities and half of the fun would vanish as we learned the facts. Make that all of the fun.

Luckily, like much else in the tabloid press, the headline bore no relation to the actual state of affairs at all. The disgruntled gentleman in Southend wasn't actually a werewolf. But it had been a close call.

I think I would feel the same way if any of the creatures of Dark Myth actually turned up and became quantifiable: if a Unicorn was caged in Bognor, or a Zombie in Blackpool, or if Count Dracula landed at Grimsby and was detained by Immigration. If they existed then we could no longer invent them, and the world would be poorer by a myth or three.

It was Ogden Nash who said that 'where there's a monster there's a miracle', but I'd discovered that for myself at the age of ten, when I read *The Compleat Werewolf* by Anthony Boucher.

At first glance the book might not seem a prime candidate for a *Best Horror* selection it's a short-story collection, of which less than half the ten stories could be categorized as strict horror, and three are simply good-natured *Astounding*-type sf. But it contains at least two stories worth their weight in chilled blood, and the title story, which, for me, is special.

'They Bite' is one of the blood chillers. On re-reading it I realized that I had forgotten the plot, what there is of it, that I had in memory stripped the tale down to a leaner framework. But the central motif (of the Carkers—emaciated, brown, desert-dwellers who live in the corner of your vision, moving faster than the eye can follow; cannibals, and they bite) had always stayed with me, as had the final scene, of Tallant, the protagonist, trapped in the adobe hut the Carkers have made their home, blood pouring from his severed wrist, waiting for the returning female Carker to come and finish him off.

'We Print the Truth' tells of the town of Grover. The Editor of the local paper, MacVeagh, wishes that his paper will always print the truth; his wish is granted. Whatever is printed in the paper is the truth—in Grover. The opportunity to play God becomes too much for MacVeagh; he ends the Second World War, marries the girl of his dreams, tries to make a perfect world. But fairytale wishes always have catches, and this has worse catches than most. His wife is unhappy, commits adultery with the man she would have married, eventually attempts suicide by drinking iodine. MacVeagh 'fixes' this with a newspaper article but the results are even more unpleasant than he expected. And outside Grover things are even worse; after all, outside the paper's sphere of influence, the war continues. That things resolve eventually, according to the rules, doesn't subtract from the overall feeling that one is watching MacVeagh dig himself further and further into a pit from which there really is no escape—like the bartender given a wish by the same old wish-granting god (Wayland Smith) who wishes for an inexhaustible beer pitcher, and drinks himself to death. The post-coital moment at which MacVeagh realizes that his wife can never possibly love him is true horror indeed.

'Mr Lupescu' is an elegant variation on a theme, which recalls to mind John Collier's superior short story, 'Thus We Refute Beelzy'. Both stories involve fathers murdered by 'imaginary friends'. In the Boucher tale the imaginary friend is more real than might initially be imagined;

and the imaginary friend has an imaginary fiend . . .

'The Pink Caterpillar' is a time-travel black magic detective story about a man and a skeleton; 'The Ghost of Me' is a doppelgänger variant, about a man whose ghost turns up to haunt the spot where he was killed, but slightly too early.

And then there's the story that changed the way I saw things.

'The Compleat Werewolf' isn't a horror story. But it's a story that affects how you perceive the icons of horror—especially if exposed to it early enough. It affects whose side you are on from then on out; I'm on the side of the werewolf, have been ever since.

Wolfe Wolf is a professor of old German, hopelessly in love with Gloria, a feckless film starlet. When, during the course of a drunken night, Wolfe discovers from Ozymandias the Great (a real magician who no longer practises, because people want fakes) that he is a werewolf, that he can change into a wolf simply by saying 'Absarka', he sees glory ahead, a chance to impress and win Gloria. But there are disadvantages— like the fact that in wolf form it is impossible to say Absarka and change back again, or the trouble one has with one's lack of clothes on changing from wolf into human form in front of a classroom of students.

He converses with cats, listens to Ozymandias' endless anecdotes of magic in Madagascar, and unfinished tales of Darjeeling, rescues small children, and even begins to understand how people could snack on them . . .

Again the plot—chock-full of fifth columnists, spies, Germans, film people, FBI men and Fergus O'Breen (red-headed Irish private eye)— matters hardly at all. It's the werewolf. Compleatly the werewolf.

And you could ask me why I picked this book, rather than any one of well over a hundred other possibilities, many of them written by authors for whom I have more respect or affection, or books which are more deserving masterworks of outstanding literary or artistic or horrific achievement . . .

I suppose it's because they didn't catch a werewolf in Southend last month, and, Fate willing, they never will.

—NEIL GAIMAN

JOHN GARDNER

Grendel

The story of Beowolf, *told from the point of view of Grendel, the monster who terrorizes the meadhall of King Hrothgar until the mighty hero— nameless here—slays him in combat. Unlike Michael Crichton's* Eaters of the Dead *(1976), which retells the same myth but rationalizes Grendel and his mother as the last surviving Neanderthals, Gardner's novel accepts the fantastic elements of the original story—monsters, dragons, heroes—and re-uses them as part of a meditation upon the nature of humanity, the indifference of God, and the interdependence of heroism and monstrousness in legend and song. John Gardner, an American academic, was also the author of* The Resurrection *(1966),* The Wreckage of Agathon *(1970),* The Sunlight Dialogues *(1972) and other novels.* Grendel *was filmed a little too whimsically as an animated feature in Australia, entitled* Grendel, Grendel, Grendel *(1980), directed by Alexander Stitt, with Peter Ustinov as the voice of the monster.*

At first literary glance there seems little enough reason to include John Gardner's *Grendel* in a listing of Horror's 100 Best: the short novel contains none of the disturbing *frissons* common to successful dark fantasy, offers no hint of the dark-night-of-the-soul distortion of Lovecraft's twisted lens, and certainly exhibits no sign of the disquieting promise of biological horror which so many of our contemporaries bring to the genre. A critic might say that Gardner's *Grendel* has no place on this list. John Gardner might well agree. Both would be wrong.

John Gardner's *Grendel* is a brilliant reversal of the Beowulf tale in which the reader identifies not with the warriors boasting of victory in their mead hall, but with the adolescent monster, his arm torn from its socket by the humorless 'hero', dying alone in his cold cave of forest and night. It is fitting that Gardner has reached back to English's oldest epic tale to give us what may be fiction's most sympathetic depiction of *monster*, for it is this very exploration of the reductive inevitability of monster-in-man which has served as a major theme in the best horror fiction.

Like Mary Shelley's creature in *Frankenstein* or Thomas Harris's fiend in *The Red Dragon*, Gardner's Grendel is a watcher who waits. Gardner's creature describes himself clearly: 'Pointless, ridiculous monster crouched in the shadows, stinking of dead men, murdered children, martyred cows'. Grendel's observation of mankind is equally clear; he sees a rapacious horde of murderers and earth-destroyers, hiding their ultimate disharmony behind songs of glory, cloaks of religion, and other hypocrisies. Occasionally the thanes will eject a too-obvious murderer into the night, but even among these fellow outcasts the waiting monster can find no fit company: 'At times I would try to defend the exile,' says Grendel, 'at other times I would try to ignore him, but they were too treacherous. In the end, I had to eat them.'

When Gardner's Grendel falls through time and space to visit the old dragon, we are confronted with one of the great cameo appearances in all of fantastic literature. As old as time and twice as cranky, capable of seeing the far future as easily as the past, Grendel's fearsome mentor is a masterpiece of fibre-breathing cynicism, a scaled, Sartre-ish nightmare of nihilism.

Gardner commented in a 1978 interview: 'As a medievalist, one knows there are two great dragons in medieval art. There's Christ the dragon, and there's Satan the dragon. There's always a war between these two great dragons.' Grendel is caught in the middle of this war as surely as he is torn between his conviction that he is a cog in a mechanistic universe and his grudging admiration of the glorious feats of free will exalted in the minstrel Shaper's meadhall songs. For a while the monster protects his precarious philosophical balance by refusing to kill Wealtheow, Hrothgar's lovely queen, thus postponing his own 'ultimate act of nihilism'. But when the time comes, Grendel's adolescent, romantic ideals prove as fragile as the queen herself: 'I would kill her, yes! I would squeeze out her feces between my fists. So much for meaning as quality of life! I would kill her and teach them reality. Grendel the truth teacher, phantasm-tester!' But in the end, of course, it is Grendel who dies, seeing in his unnamed nemesis (Beowulf) overtones of the dragon as well as hints of something even less human.

John Gardner's prose throughout *Grendel* is knife-sharp, painfully honest, and faithful to the word beauty of the great poem it celebrates. It is a wonderful book.

It should be mentioned that Gardner himself might not have appreciated being listed among horror's luminaries. In his many writings on writing, he relentlessly equated genre fiction with inferior fiction, going so far as to urge young writers to forestall their initial publication rather than succumb to the sirens of '... bad fiction (pornography, horror novels, and so forth)'. Once, to illustrate contemporary bad writing, he quoted an out-of-context extract from the work of perhaps the finest fantasist North America has yet produced.

All of this detracts or adds nothing to the inestimable worth of John Gardner's *Grendel*, but it is oddly fitting that the man's masterpiece lies firmly imbedded in the tradition of dark fantasy. It is equally fitting that when Grendel approaches the dragon with some thoughts of abandoning his career of terrifying humans, the dragon's reproach may apply not only to Grendel but to all doubting practitioners of horror's craft:

'You stimulate them! You make them think and scheme. You drive them to poetry, science, religion, all that makes them what they are for as long as they last. You are, so to speak, the brute existent by which they learn to define themselves. The exile, captivity, death they shrink from—the blunt facts of their mortality, their abandonment—that's what you make them recognize, embrace! You *are* mankind, or man's condition: inseparable as the mountain-climber and the mountain. If you withdraw, you'll instantly be replaced. Brute existents, you know, are a dime a dozen. No sentimental trash, then. If man's the irrelevance that interests you, stick with him! Scare him to glory!'

—DAN SIMMONS

68 [1971]

WILLIAM PETER BLATTY

The Exorcist

Georgetown, Washington. Eleven-year-old Regan MacNeil starts exhibiting bizarre psychological and physiological symptoms. She hears funny noises, develops a skin condition, becomes strangely malicious and foul-mouthed, and appears to have a personality split. After the medical and psychological experts consulted have failed, Regan's mother calls in the church. Father Damien Karras, a doubting priest, investigates and gradually becomes convinced that Regan is an authentic case of possession. He summons Father Lankester Merrin, an experienced exorcist, who recognizes the demon in Regan as Pazuzu, an Assyrian spirit he once bested in a similar case. The two priests administer the sacrament of exorcism and drive Pazuzu out of Regan, but at the cost of their own lives. Along with Ira Levin's Rosemary's Baby, The Exorcist *took the horror genre out of the specialist category and into the bestseller racks. It was famously filmed by William Friedkin in 1973 and spawned a host of imitative 'possessed/evil child' books and films.*

Mention *The Exorcist* and what comes to most people's minds? The movie, of course: rotating heads and pea-soup vomit. The visual excesses may have been necessary to convey the horrors of demonic

151

possession, but they blunted the moral content of the story, and they have completely obscured the spirituality of the source novel.

Over the years it has become fashionable in certain circles to interpret *The Exorcist* as a paradigm of adolescence. (Right. Just as *The Shining* is an impassioned plea for tougher hotel security.) This meretricious view cheapens and trivializes a deeply felt religious novel, strips it completely of its numinous power, and has been kept in vogue by a small pharisaic cadre of writers and critics who dismiss as junk any novel wherein evil has an extrinsic source.

Ignore them. Here's the real dope.

Ego talking? I don't think so. This novel speaks to me as have few others. I've never met Williams Peter Blatty, but I feel I know him. Like him, I had a Catholic upbringing and a Jesuit education—four years each at Xavier High School in Manhattan and Georgetown University, the site of the novel. Does that, along with my status as a fallen-away Catholic, leave me particularly vulnerable to the tale Blatty tells? Perhaps. But I prefer to think that it makes me more sensitive to the finer nuances of *The Exorcist*.

And there are so many nuances that can easily slip by someone not raised in the Church.

I remember my first night with *The Exorcist*. I was a third-year medical student. I hadn't been able to afford the hardcover but I snapped up the paperback the moment it hit the stands. At 2 a.m. I was the only one awake in the apartment. My wife and infant daughter were sound asleep. I had early pediatric rounds in the morning but I couldn't put the damn book down.

Until that snake scene.

That's when the mother watches her little girl, Regan, glide along the floor on her belly, hissing softly, her tongue flicking in and out as she winds about the room.

A chilling scene even if you're Hassidic. But when you've been raised in the Church and have spent endless hours sitting before statues depicting the Blessed Mother crushing the serpent, that timeless symbol of Satan, under her foot, and now you're reading of little Regan's body becoming serpentine and gliding free and unhindered through the house, the effect is devastating. Up to now, the novel has given you a few bumps in the night (clever!) and some strange goings on, all of which could have rational explanations. Up to now. In those of us who share Blatty's past, the snake scene leaves no doubt that something unspeakable has invaded the MacNeil house and usurped the body of an innocent child.

Our apartment was suddenly too dark and too chilly to bear alone. I confess I slammed the book closed and hightailed it for bed.

In a broader sense, *The Exorcist*, published in 1971, is a fitting book to cap the sixties.

We all lost something in the sixties. Sure, we still play the music and at times look back fondly on edited memories of the sunniest of those days, but it was not a kind decade. Some of us lost men we looked up to as leaders, some lost faith in government, faith in the political process, faith in God. Some of us lost our minds. We all lost our innocence.

In *The Exorcist*, Father Damien Karras, a Jesuit priest who is also a psychiatrist, is struggling to hang on to his faith. He has already lost much of his faith in Man and, worse yet, feels his faith in God slipping from his grasp.

> ... In the world there was evil. And much of the evil resulted from doubt; from an honest confusion among men of good will. Would a reasonable God refuse to end it? Not reveal himself? Not speak?
> *'Lord, give us a sign ...'*
> The raising of Lazarus was dim in the distant past. No one now living had heard his laughter.
> *Why not a sign?*
> *... Ah, my God, let me see You! Let me know!*
> The yearning consumed him.

This is one of the few areas in the novel in which Blatty is unambiguous. And with good reason. Fr Karras' crisis of faith is crucial to the novel. He is yearning to know God, to find an answer to the evil in the world around him. Then comes the poor, stricken child, Regan MacNeil. Her doctors are baffled. All her tests are negative, so they offer lame ideas about hysteria. The child *believes* she is possessed, therefore she *acts* possessed. Maybe an exorcism will reverse the autosuggestion that is making a hell on earth out of her life and her mother's.

And so finally Damien Karras comes up against something that goes beyond rational experience. Fr Merrin, an old priest who has performed the rite of exorcism before, is called out of retirement. The demon knows Merrin. They have met before. It tells the priest, 'This time you will lose.'

The exorcism occupies only the last forty pages of the novel, but it draws together all the threads that have been woven through the story thus far. Within the crucible of the rite, a crescendo of horror, Damien's faith in Man is restored by Fr Merrin's simple, unwavering courage.

And his faith in God?

When Fr Merrin's heart gives out and he dies at the foot of the bed, Karras challenges the demon:

> 'You're very good with children! ... Little girls! ... Come on, loser! Try *me!* Leave the girl and take me!'

We aren't shown what happens next. We are shifted downstairs to the point of view of Regan's mother, who hears the final shouts and the shattering glass. But as Karras lies dying on the stone steps below the bedroom window, we are permitted to look into his eyes, which seem 'to glow with elation'.

That final scene is one of the many ambiguities that make this novel endlessly fascinating, fit for multiple readings.

Other ambiguities? Well, to whom does the title refer? Merrin or Karras? Merrin has performed exorcism in the past, but it is Karras who succeeds here. Also, we are told that the possessed is never the target of the demon, but rather those around the afflicted one. Who is the real target here? Merrin or Karras?

As for that ambiguous climax: I believe I know what Karras is feeling as he's dying. His intent in taunting the demon to 'take me' was perhaps not totally altruistic. If he could *know*, if he could experience first hand the hideous purity of supernatural evil, then surely he could once again believe in the Ultimate Good. Before he went through the window, he had that experience. Thus the elation in his eyes. Damien Karras has finally resolved his crisis of faith, finally found his answer.

The rest of us go on searching.

—F. PAUL WILSON

69   [1972]

JOHN BRUNNER

The Sheep Look Up

In the 1980s, the world is choking on its own excrement. Austin Train, a scientist who has spoken out on matters ecological, has been forced by the repressive US government to go underground, and 'Trainites' are either committing acts of terrorism in his name or living on would-be self-sufficient communes. A mysteriously poisoned shipment of food sent as an aid package to an African nation causes an outbreak of homicidal psychosis and much home-grown controversy. Colorado, where many of the novel's large cast of characters live, is racked by avalanches, earthquakes, pollution, disease, anarchy, mutant worms and other perils directly related to man's abuse of his environment. America slides closer to martial law as resistance to the murder of the planet grows. The last in a rough trilogy of dystopian visions—the others are Stand on Zanzibar *(1968) and* The Jagged Orbit *(1969)—* The Sheep Look Up *is one of the most frightening, plausible and angry of the many science fictional forecasts of a hellish future.*

The hungry sheep look up, and are not fed.
But swoln with wind, and the rank mist they draw,
Rot inwardly, and foul contagion spread.

—Milton: *Lycidas*

154

For those you love—for *all* you love—I ask you to picture this.

Above: a sky of pale and lifeless blue. No clouds. No birds. No motion.

Below: a scorched and lifeless plane that stretches on forever. Sand baked to slats, flat brown and brittle. No motion. No hope of motion.

No hope.

All that's left of the Earth.

In the foreground, he stands: a dead man, all but naked, his body transparent, the slats bleeding through. He holds in his hand a sun-bleached skull. The skull of a sheep, in grinning profile: black socket staring, the joke long gone. Some flowers, too: the green stems bowed, red petals withered. So much for beauty.

The dead man has no face. A gas mask, only. Robotic. Horrific. The gaping holes where the eyes should be are neatly bisected by the flat horizon, where lifeless earth meets lifeless sky on the far side of that lifeless apparition . . .

I've just described the cover of the Del Ray paperback edition of *The Sheep Look Up*, John Brunner's ultimate nightmare vision. It is without question the most horrifying novel that I have ever read.

I'd like to tell you why.

Let's face it. Here at the sputtering tail-end of the 20th century, we've got a lot to be frightened about. On top of the same ol' primordial dreads that we dragged up out of the slime with us—fear of death, and disease, and disfigurement; uncertainty as to where we stand, from moment to moment, on the food chain; fear for the fate of the soul/spark/self when the bag of meat gives up its ghost—on *top* of all that, the plugged-in contemporary *Homo sapiens* now has the Big Picture to contend with.

And a pretty goddam scary picture it is, boys and girls (as if you didn't know). The word has come in from McLuhan's global sanitarium, and it ain't entirely encouraging. *Particularly* for those of us who grew up on systems theory, the Whole Earth catalogues, and an integrative world-view that sees all things as connected to everything else: viewed in that light, it looks like hard times a-comin' for the bright blue ball of spinning mud on which we live.

It is precisely that kind of holistic overview that Brunner brings to bear, with excruciating focus, in *The Sheep Look Up*. As in *Stand on Zanzibar*, the novel that netted him the Hugo award, the main character is not so much an individual human as *the world itself*, viewed from a thousand individual human perspectives.

Many of those perspectives are predictably uninspiring: you've got your bureaucratic dullards and corporate greedheads, your booming bigots and shrill subversives, your hell-bent nihilists and quavering faithful festooning the ever-increasing ranks of bleating do-what-you're tolders. You've even got a character named Prexy who, I swear to God, is a crystal-clear crystal-ball vision of Ronald Reagan's presidency, written some eight years earlier (and you thought this wasn't a horror novel!).

But a surprising, even *alarming* number of the characters are compassionate, wilful, wise, intelligent and (*heavens!*) even noble in their vision.

In the end, none of that matters.

Each one, like the earth, is utterly doomed.

And therein lies the ultimate horror at the heart of *The Sheep Look Up*. It's the feeling of utter powerlessness that Brunner conjures up: the feeling that, once we've let it go too far, nothing we do in retrospect will make a goddam bit of difference.

Take, for example, Austin Train: the ostensible hero of the story. He's a brilliant man who's taken the time to articulate the extent of our predicament: the poisoned water, the poisoned air, the poison we feed to our cattle and crops which, in turn, are fed back into us; the implements our governments have developed for chemical, biological, and nuclear warfare; in short, the anatomical fine points of the machines dragging us towards annihilation.

A major *faux pas*, it would seem. Train's just desserts? He's driven underground, hunted by the government that has dubbed him traitor and by the movement that has sprung up around his name. Because, yes indeed, the Trainites are here: a million strong, and madder than hell. Their motto is, STOP! YOU'RE KILLING ME!; and they spend their time running around, sabotaging factories, destroying cars, and basically getting their last bitter eco-licks in before the machine can grind them all into burger.

Swell plan. Too bad it's too late. In Brunner's book, it's all over but the screaming, and his people are caught up in the last turns of the wheel. Those last turns are meticulously, painfully detailed; for all of the novel's vast staggering scope, each individual tragedy is treated with heart-shredding intimacy.

And this is where Brunner's sf epic steps neatly into the horror domain, despite the absence of supernatural Good vs. Evil fisticuffs: in the extent to which we fear for and care about the people. Indeed, this is where the novel's impact goes well beyond most genre fare.

Because *The Sheep Look Up* doesn't give us an out. The good guys are as guilty as the bad guys in the end, for sitting around with their thumbs up their asses, Monday morning quarterbacking us over the brink. No Dread Shape from Beyond the Pale to blame it on; no benevolent bearded Father On High to swoop in with an eleventh-hour reprieve. Solly, Cholly. The hot, the cold, and the luke-warm alike have to suck on the Big One before this baby's through.

In *The Sheep Look Up*, we are the monsters, replete with our cowardice, greed, and stultifying dirth of vision. We, and the machines that we built in our own image.

Just like real life.

Nice story, huh?

Allow me to take the gloves off for a moment and just say it: this book fucking pisses me off and scares me half to death. As well it should. Brunner's fear and rage and pain are amply displayed and enormously contagious, overshadowed only by his brilliant grasp of the minutiae comprising his macro-analysis.

Here at the tail-end of the 20th century, we're close enough to taste a Better Tomorrow. We could feed, clothe, shelter and educate the world. We could move out into space. We could activate all that dormant gray matter, enjoy quantum leaps in human awareness and potential. We could awaken as a species and shuffle *off* this goddam veil of tears without having to ditch the mortal coil with which it has seemed inseparable.

(We might even learn how to get along with our relatives, although that's pushing it a bit. What the hell. It's worth a try.)

But to paraphrase David F. Friedman, king of the exploitation film, 'We're sitting here with the goose that lays the golden eggs, and instead of just patting it every night we've done everything but strangle it and run our hands up its ass to try to grab another egg.'

If we're really too stupid to survive as a species, I just hope somebody thinks to carve that on our global tombstone.

Along with a copy of *The Sheep Look Up*.

It's a cautionary tale. We could use a good cautionary tale right now. The only thing between us and the tar pits is the kind of dangerous knowledge that Brunner has so painstakingly provided here. If this book has been allowed to go out of print, the people responsible should be lined up and shot.

If not, go get a copy. Read it. Weep.

And then tell me it's not a horror novel.

—JOHN SKIPP

70   [1973]

MANLY WADE WELLMAN
Worse Things Waiting

Worse Things Waiting *was the first book from the North Carolina imprint Carcosa. Established immediately after the death of August Derleth (when it* was wrongly assumed that there would be no further Arkham House volumes), publishers Karl Edward Wagner, Jim Groce and David Drake decided to produce the kind of book they as collectors would like to own. The result was a beautifully-designed, 367-page hardcover that collects together two poems and 28 of Wellman's best stories, selected from Weird Tales, Strange Stories, Unknown and The Magazine of Fantasy and Science Fiction. It includes The Terrible Parchment—Wellman's tongue-in-cheek salute to H. P. Lovecraft and the Weird Tales circle, two previously uncollected John the Balladeer stories, such classic chillers as 'Up Under the Roof', 'The Kelpie', 'Dhoh', and a pair of novellas: 'Fearful Rock' and 'Coven'. 'Larroes Catch Meddlers' and 'School for the Unspeakable' were produced on the Light Out television series, 'The Valley Was Still' appeared as one of the most effective Twilight Zone episodes, and 'The Devil Is Not Mocked' was adapted for Rod Serling's Night Gallery show. The book is illustrated with more than thirty original illustrations by Weird Tales artist Lee Brown Coye.

Choosing a favourite book is next to impossible. What is your favourite piece of music? Food? Friend? All impossible. There are too many to choose from. However, Worse Things Waiting is my choice in this instance for several reasons. First, it is an overview of the man's great writing talent. Next, it shows his extensive knowledge of Civil War history, of folklore and his love of the American Indian, to mention only a few subjects. His earliest stories about John the Balladeer, which led to his classic collection Who Fears the Devil? (1963), appear here. And the book was chosen Best Book by a Single Author at the World Fantasy Convention in 1975. In giving the award, Gahan Wilson said, 'Mr Wellman always knows how to give you a good scare.'

The book opens with 'Up Under the Roof', which is based on a real-life experience Wellman had as a very small boy. It frightened one of the editors so badly that he finished reading it from a corner where he had a good view of his surroundings. Wellman said that the experience had cured him of fearing anything for the rest of his life.

Although Wellman was born in Africa and retained many sentimental feelings about the place, it only appears in a few of his stories. One of the best is in this volume, 'Song of the Slaves', which has also been produced on television.

Wellman was a recognized scholar of the Civil War, which he preferred to call The War Between the States. One of my favourite stories about this period is 'The Valley Was Still', which is in this book. This is another story which has seen television production, with many re-runs.

The two John the Balladeer stories are 'Frogfather' and 'Sin's Doorway'. Both are based on mountain folklore—the weird custom of eating a dead person's skin in order to save him from Hell is a fascinating story.

It is interesting to look at the critics' comments from this distance: The WSFA Journal said, 'The quality of writing is evenly superb in the twenty-eight stories and novelettes. It presents the dark side of America so loved by Sinclair Lewis, Carl Sandburg and Stephen Vincent Benet. It merges the reality of city and farm, of mountains, peace, of woodland with the other reality of the beings, both friendly and inimical, that coexist with men.'

Several of the stories reflect Wellman's love of the mountains and the mountain folk, and they established him as a top folklorist in America. They made him a citizen of the mountains and a welcome guest in the mountain homes. This is one of the aspects of Wellman's stories that I like the most.

In sum, all that I can say is that my love of the book comes from the fact that it is a good representation of the man and his work.

—FRANCES GARFIELD

71   [1973]

ROBERT MARASCO

Burnt Offerings

Ben and Marian Rolfe try to escape from New York for the summer by renting a spacious but dilapidated country house from the Allardyces, a peculiar brother-and-sister couple. The Rolfes, with their son David and Aunt Elizabeth, move in, and settle down for some peace and quiet. The catch is that the Allardyces are only charging such a reasonable rent because they want the Rolfes to look after their aged mother, who never leaves her room on the top floor. As summer progresses, the house strangely repairs itself, the Rolfes suffer a series of puzzling accidents, and the old lady upstairs stays out of sight. Marasco's novel has many of the same ingredients as Stephen King's The Shining, *but is a quieter work, though no less chilling.* Burnt Offerings *was filmed by Dan Curtis in 1976 from a screenplay by William F. Nolan with Oliver Reed, Karen Black and Bette Davis.*

Shirley Jackson's *The Haunting of Hill House* has cast such a long shadow over the body of post-war supernatural fiction that it comes naturally to the fore whenever the subject of 'haunted house novels' arises. It's easy to think of it as the only such novel that matters, and that's not true. It is the best, without question, but there are other novels on the subject which are extremely fine: *Hell House*, by Richard

159

Matheson, *The Doll Who Ate Its Mother*, by Ramsey Campbell, and William Sloane's *The Edge of Running Water* all come immediately to mind. But my nominee for the runner-up in the category—and a damned close runner-up at that—is *Burnt Offerings*, by Roberto Marasco.

Briefly, *Burnt Offerings* is the story of one family's hellacious—and ultimately fatal—summer holiday in the country. The family of four—father, mother, boy-child, and ageing-but-sprightly aunt—rent the dilapidated summer home of Roz and Brother Allardyce for the amazingly low price of $900 ... not per month, but for the whole summer season. The only catch (other than the fact that the large estate seems to be sinking into a state of terminal neglect and ruin) is the fact that Roz and Brother's mother will be staying in the house. 'Our dear one,' Brother rhapsodizes, 'our darling.' She will be no trouble, Roz and Brother assure the Rolfe family; in fact, she will probably never leave her small upstairs suite. Their only responsibility is to leave a tray of food outside her bedroom door three times a day.

Ben Rolfe has misgivings, but they are swept away by his wife Marian's nearly obsessive enthusiasm for the place ... and the Rolfes make the deadly mistake of moving in, bag and baggage.

What follows is a memorable and remarkable descent into terror. The Allardyce house begins to regenerate itself. This process is slow at first—dying flowers which return to full bloom, seemingly of their own accord, cracked walls and ceilings which seem to heal themselves—but as the summer goes on, the process begins to accelerate.

The Rolfe family, pleasant and rather average (as average as any New York City cliff-dwellers can be, anyway), begins falling to pieces. Tirelessly cheerful Aunt Elizabeth finally begins to show her age. Marian becomes more and more obsessed with the house and with the Allardyce's mother, 'our darling'. She sits in the old lady's little parlor for hours on end, looking at the hundreds—or is it thousands?—of pictures on the tables and walls ... and some of the subjects of these photographs seem to be in a state of stupefied terror. Worst of all, Ben Rolfe comes chillingly close to drowning his son, David, when some ordinary father–son horseplay in the newly regenerated pool turns deadly serious. The house is, in fact, a living entity, a psychic vampire, and it is sucking the Rolfe family dry, as it has untold families before it.

What elevates Marasco's novel of terror to a plateau of near brilliance is his answer to this question: why in the hell don't the Rolfes *get out* once they have sensed what is happening to the house, and their role in it? The house is able to make flight difficult ... but not, Marasco is careful to point out, actually impossible. His answer is so simple it's chilling. Because, he tells us, they can't.

And neither can we. We only *think* we own the things we want; the truth is, our possessions actually own us. We can all lay claim to a little piece of 17 Shore Road, and we have all jumped, completely of our own accord, into the hell of stewardship.

Horror stories are waking nightmares, and the best of them are whispering of very real fears at the same time they are screaming of ghosts and demons and werewolves. It is the sound of these two intertwined voices speaking together, one at top volume, the other very softly, that gives the good tale of horror its dreamlike power, I think. But writers of horror very rarely attempt out-and-out allegory, and the novels of this sort which come immediately to mind are not generally considered horror stories at all: *Lord of the Flies*, for instance, or George Orwell's political fable *Animal Farm*.

Marasco's haunted house tale *is* such a novel, and it lends the tale a richness and resonance even really good horror stories rarely achieve. It is a cautionary and disturbing tale, and one which comes highly recommended not just to fans of the genre but to the general reader.

—STEPHEN KING

72   [1975]

STEPHEN KING

'Salem's Lot

Jerusalem's Lot, Maine. Antique dealer Richard Straker moves into the ill-famed Old Marsten House, and sets up a business in town, promising the imminent arrival of his partner, Kurt Barlow. Ben Mears, a local writer traumatized at an early age by an experience with Old Marsten House, is suspicious. Children start to disappear, and it becomes clear that Barlow is a King Vampire intent on spreading his plague throughout 'Salem's Lot. Mears and a group of Fearless Vampire Hunters—which includes his girlfriend, Susan, her doctor father, the local priest and young Mark Petrie—try to resist the vampire take-over. Stephen King's second novel is a transposition of the basic plot of Dracula *into a small town setting patterned on Grace Metalious'* Peyton Place *(1957), and fruitfully plays its sources off against each other. It was made into a two-part TV mini-series by Tobe Hooper in 1979, but Larry Cohen's 1987 film* A Return to 'Salem's Lot *is a sequel in name only.*

I t certainly might seem odd calling a vampire novel published in 1975 a seminal work, but that's just what I'm calling *'Salem's Lot*.
I suppose I should find out what I'm saying.

I've looked up the word seminal, and besides describing a tribe of American Indians it also means other things. Webster's gives its number 1 definition as 'of or containing seed or semen'. As far as I can remember, none of that stuff was in my copy of 'Salem's Lot when I read it—heck, as far as I can remember (not very far, these days, I'm afraid) I wasn't even wearing my trench coat and dark glasses when I bought the book!

And so, on to Webster's number 2 definition: 'of reproduction [*seminal* power]'. Though, as you can see, Webster even gives an example here, it still sounds like sex to me.

Finally, when we reach beyond Webster's smutty mind, we find that definition number 3 says seminal is 'like seed in being a source or in having a potential for development; germinal; originative.' Ah.

I don't know why I just said 'Ah', but I do think I've finally found what I'm looking for. A *metaphor*. You see, writers are lost without metaphors, and Webster seems finally to have figured that out and (grudgingly, given the lingering sexuality of the earlier entries) decided to give writers, the only ones except perverts to use dictionaries, something to work with. (More likely he's figured out, as you already know, that writers *are* perverts, and, in his infinite wisdom and kindness, decided to feed the groin before the mind.)

Anyway, what I really want to say is that 'Salem's Lot is certainly *like* seed, because, though it is arguably a mirror of Bram Stoker's *seminal* 1897 novel *Dracula* (which, of course, owed allegiance to John William Polidori's *seminal The Vampyre* of 1819), it, like the books which preceded it, gave birth not only to gaggles of vampire stories (Anthony Boucher, for one, cites *The Vampyre* as the spark of a 'vampire craze' culminating twenty-eight years later in *Varney the Vampire*—which, sadly, was not followed by *Wally the Werewolf*) but also all kinds of creepy works in general. While *Rosemary's Baby* and *The Exorcist* mined supernatural niches in the bestseller list, I would argue that 'Salem's Lot, because of its genuineness, its verve, its originality, its willingness to reflect, expand and *celebrate* its sources, and, most importantly, its establishment of Stephen King, after the sincere but *un*seminal *Carrie*, not as an interloper but as a pioneer in a field ripe for re-invention, was *germinal* and *originative* of the entire boom in horror fiction we find ourselves in the middle of—with no culmination in sight.

As soon as I put on my trench coat and dark glasses and look up *germinal* and *originative*, I may even know what I'm talking about.

—AL SARRANTONIO

HARLAN ELLISON

Deathbird Stories

Subtitled (in some editions) 'A Pantheon of Modern Gods' and with an introduction titled in the Ellison manner 'Oblations at Alien Altars', Death-bird Stories consists mainly of stories written in the sixties and early seventies, woven into some kind of a tapestry by brief linking passages in which Ellison, in his Rod Serling persona, adds pithy messages and pauses for thought. If H. P. Lovecraft drew on myth and lore and his own nightmares when creating his monster gods, Ellison is inspired by 20th-century obsessions, appalling news items and the sixties' counterculture ethos. Included are pieces on the Kitty Genovese incident ('The Whimper of Whipped Dogs'), drugs ('Shattered Like a Glass Goblin'), Vietnam ('Basilisk'), car culture ('Along the Scenic Route'), a twist on the Twilight Zone *possessed one-armed bandit theme ('Pretty Maggie Moneyeyes'), a Genesis re-write ('The Deathbird'), the bankruptcy of modern religion ('Bleeding Stones') and the self-explanatory 'Paingod', 'Ernest and the Machine God' and 'Rock God'. The Hugo-award-winning 'Adrift Just Off the Islets of Langerhans: Latitude 38° 54'N, Longitude 77° 00' 13"W' is, almost subliminally, a sequel to the 1941 film* The Wolf Man.*

For sheer ferocity and general fearlessness of both language and vision, few writers can compare to Harlan Ellison. And strangely enough—for Harlan has a long-standing loathing to genrification—few writers have done more to blaze the trail for modern horror. The original splatterpunk, a good twenty years before the advent of that ostensible phenomenon, his work has punched holes in the body of Literature that may never fully heal.

With a career as prolific and multifarious as Ellison's, it becomes difficult to try and peg it all down to one book. No analysis of his impact on the contemporary condition of mortal dread is complete without mentioning titles like 'I Have No Mouth, and I Must Scream', 'In the Fourth Year of the War', 'Try a Dull Knife', 'The Beast That Shouted Love at the Heart of the World', 'All the Birds Come Home to Roost', 'Knox', 'Croatoan', 'Hitler Painted Roses', 'Grail', 'The Cheese Stands Alone', 'All the Faces of Fear', 'Mona at Her Windows', and 'The Prowler in the City at the Edge of the World'.

But *Deathbird Stories*, Harlan Ellison's book of gods, a collection written during the decade that began with the hopefulness of *Camelot* and ended with the hardline of *Kent State*, stands out as a definitive must-read. This book, with its presaging *caveat* ('Please do not attempt to read the book in one sitting ...') is not fucking around. The author means what he says. And he means to take large bites out of the reader's coziest assumptions: about life, and death; about hope, and despair. About gods.

And devils.

It begins with 'The Whimper of Whipped Dogs': a story so strong and so mythically precise that it earns the book admission to the *100 Best* on its merits alone. From its initial Kitty Genovese-style killing to its innocence-slaying finale, the story is a masterpiece of grim admission and the price of denial. If you haven't read it, go. Read. Now. It will kick your ass clear down to Hell's lowest level.

From there, you're on your own: from the sexual betrayal of 'Pretty Maggie Moneyeyes', 'The Face of Helen Borneau', and 'Ernest and the Machine God', through the tortured patriotic psychosis of 'Basilisk' and god-abandonment of 'Neon', the manically kinetic mayhem of 'Along the Scenic Route' and the absolute full-tilt slaughter of 'Bleeding Stones' (a blitzkrieg splatterfesto years ahead of its time, and yes, a very funny story), it's a long crawl back.

And only then, at the very end of the journey, will you find the namesake story of the collection, 'The Deathbird': a transformative piece of fiction that takes radical stances in both its narrative structure and concept. 'The Deathbird' remains one of my all-time favorite Ellison stories. I first encountered it over twelve years ago, under circumstances so different that it's sometimes tough to fully gauge its impact. But one thing is for sure: it changed me. It was the first story in my experience to suggest, plain as day, that maybe we'd been set up and suckered the whole time—that God was lying, and the serpent was a victim of bad hype.

There's no overestimating the implicit subversiveness, or the importance of that subversion on the modern mind. And Ellison's gift is in articulating the dark side of the higher self, laying waste to the notion that blind subservience to a popular 'moral' code is in any way the One True Path to wisdom or compassion. 'The Deathbird' stands out: as hauntingly brutal love story, and as allegory for a dangerous age.

And it ages well, to boot; Harlan rode the cutting edge of fiction when most of today's new crop of writers were still fresh from cutting teeth, and the ultra-hip of twenty years past sometimes falls on the current palette like a vintage wine that doesn't quite know whether to turn to vinegar. And true, some of the stories in this collection fall prey to one degree or another of the dreaded AHS: ageing hipness syndrome, that peculiar neurological dysfunction that can make you wince at pictures of yourself wearing a nehru jacket and bell-bottomed hip huggers—or a spiked purple mohawk and safety-pins, for that matter.

But this is not a big problem, at least not to the extent that it so much detracts from the work as underscores the time in which it was written (thus supplying the reader with a wealth of handy historical subtext). And regardless, the stories in this collection stand unfazed by Time's relentless onward trudge. 'The Whimper of Whipped Dogs' is, in my humble opinion, a classic. And 'The Deathbird' remains timeless, ageless, elegant, evocative; a chilling, bittersweet coda that taught me a lot about how we can touch nerves through as simple a thing as words on paper. How the right words, the right *story*, can permanently change the way we see the world. *Deathbird Stories* did that for me, way back when I was too young and hungry and lost in America.

And you know what? I still am. It still does. And I think it always will. Thanks, Harlan.

—CRAIG SPECTOR

74   [1977]

HUGH B. CAVE

Murgunstrumm and Others

Published by the North Carolina imprint, Carcosa, Murgunstrumm and Others is almost 500 pages long and collects together 26 tales of horror—the best of Hugh B. Cave's hundreds of published stories, covering forty years of writing. Rarely reprinted since their original appearances in the pulp magazines Weird Tales, Strange Tales, Ghost Stories, Argosy, *etc., this line-up of lurid chillers includes 'The Isle of Dark Magic' and 'The Death Watch', Cave's only two contributions to H. P. Lovecraft's Cthulhu Mythos; 'Horror in Wax', a grisly tale of vengeance from the single issue of* Thrilling Mysteries; *'The Affair of the Clutching Hand' and 'The Strange Case of No. 7', two early tales of Cave's occult investigator, Dr Ronald Hale; 'The Whisperers', 'The Strange Death of Ivan Gromleigh', 'Prey of the Nightborn', 'Purr of a Cat' and 'The Caverns of Time', all written under Cave's jokey pseudonym, 'Justin Case' for* Spicy Mystery Stories; *and 'Murgunstrumm' itself—a 30,000 word short novel about the cursed Gray Toad Inn and its vampiric inhabitants. The book is gruesomely illustrated with more than thirty-five original drawings by* Weird Tales *artist Lee Brown Coye. Winner of the 1978 World Fantasy Award for Best Collection.*

I started reading the *really* weird stuff in my early teens. By then I'd already explored all I could of Haggard, Wells, and some Poe—Poe was a little more difficult. Mainly I loved adventure stories, and the stranger the adventures the better. Then I got lucky: I gained access to a second-hand book market littered with piles of old American pulps. *Weird Tales* may well have been the 'unique' magazine, but it was only one of many, many pulps. Back in 1950–51 I could buy 15- to 20-year-old copies of *Strange Tales*, *Ghost Stories*, *Black Book Detective*, *Argosy*, and many other titles for as little as sixpence (2½p to you—or maybe four cents to *you*) per copy!

Certain names would recur in the contents pages: names like Robert Bloch, Henry Kuttner, Robert E. Howard, until I got to remember them and started to look for them, just as in a few more years I'd be hunting for Lovecraft, C. L. Moore, Clark Ashton Smith. The reason I looked for them was because I'd learned they wouldn't let me down—or rarely. Oh, these were only 'pulp' stories, no doubt about it, but their authors had something; and someone who had an awful lot of it was one Hugh B. Cave. I'd had some bad old times with *that* bloke!

The years intervened. Times changed. Titles I remembered had been extinct even *before* I had read them! Long before! All of those magazines were collectors' items by the time I became a soldier. And I stayed a soldier until December 1980. But in 1977 Karl Edward Wagner's Carcosa Press had published this book called *Murgunstrumm and Others*—by one Hugh B. Cave—and I had sworn to buy a copy. Actually meeting Cave at Worldcon in Providence, October 1986, galvanized me into action—at long last. We spoke only briefly but . . . Hugh was *so* nice and easy to talk to! You had to like him. He had what his stories had.

And that was why I bought the book: to see if it was still there, that certain something which had kept me turning over those piles of old pulps which (God help me for a cretin!) I really should have bought up and kept, each and every copy, by means of which I'd now be half-way to rich. That certain something was still there in Lovecraft, I knew, and in Bloch and Moore. But was it there in Cave? I needn't have worried. Yes it was still there: treasure. A treasure 'Cave'. A veritable Aladdin's 'Cave'!

I didn't remember all of the titles but I certainly remembered some of the stories. 'The Watcher in the Green Room' and 'The Crawling Curse' were both from *Weird Tales*, and 'Boomerang' from *Argosy*.

But . . . talk about a *book!* Pushing five hundred pages of book! And 43 wide lines to the page. And illustrated (profusely simply does *not* do it justice) by the entirely alien and yet superbly earthy Lee Brown Coye. He was from *Weird Tales* too. With a book like this . . . I mean, which story do you read first? And what wonderfully grotesque illo do you study? 'Murgunstrumm', the title story, is itself a short novel—and after that there are twenty-five more stories!

But describe them? Hint at their contents? Not here, friend! No way—no room—and anyway, how to start? The best I can do is steal a line from a Karl Wagner letter to Cave, which goes: 'For sheer unrestricted horror, I don't think there's ever been anything like it'. And about Coye's artwork: 'Turning Coye loose on something like this is like giving a straight razor to a psychopath.' And about the pair of them together: 'You (Cave) and Coye ought to flood the coronary care units all across the country!' Now I know Karl personally and he's said a few true words in his time, but none truer than these.

So here's me stuck for space, just a few more words, and not having said anything very much about my subject. Some things are like that: too *big* to allow room for trivial observation. *So* big that even detailed observation might appear trivial.

But if I had to choose my favourite book again next year, it would still be this one. That is, unless someone had been damn busy between times!

Hugh B. Cave is still alive—is he ever alive! His latest weird story (or one of them), 'No Flowers for Henry', can be found in *Whispers* for October '87. It's polished—an example of Cave's art perfected. On the other hand many of the stories in *Murgunstrumm* have rough edges too. These are the ones that tore my imagination and put splinters in it back when I was a kid. And reading them anew . . . why, the scars start itching all over again!

—BRIAN LUMLEY

75 [1977]

BERNARD TAYLOR

Sweetheart, Sweetheart

David Warwick returns to England from New York because he instinctively feels that his twin brother, Colin, has died. In Hillingham, the village where Colin lived, David begins to gather the full extent of a series of tragedies which have recently claimed the lives of Colin and his wife, Helen. Moving into Garrard's Hill Cottage—which has a history of unhappy owners meeting violent ends—David begins to suspect that murder has been done. When David's American girlfriend, Shelagh, joins him, the girl becomes the focus of a series of attacks David at first thinks are the work of Jean Timpson, a local woman who helps out at the cottage. Gradually, he learns that the place is home to a malevolent, jealous female spirit who has notched up many victims over the years. Taylor's second novel, which follows his The Godsend *(1976), has been called by Douglas Winter 'one of the finest ghost stories ever written'. Subsequently, Taylor has written* The Reaping *(1980),* The Moorstone Sickness *(1982),* Mother's Boys *(1988) and* Wild Card *(1989), and a study of British crime,* Cruelly Murdered *(1979).*

167

Ghosts were a reliable staple of dark fantasy long before they were ever shrouded in fiction and put to paper. And because of their longevity, and their evident tenacity, there is by now little new about them. We know what they are, what they represent, what they portend—usually before the author gets around to his own explanation. Yet, whether these ghosts are pranksters or tragic figures or something in between, they persist in our literature. Perhaps as reminders of our own mortality, or as promises of life after death, or as warnings that life after death isn't what we hope or pray it will be. The viewpoint depends on the writer, and the reader, and just as often does not really matter.

Just as often, a ghost is a ghost is a ghost, no further explanation necessary.

The author who attempts such a story must be aware that he's walking on well-trod ground, and his tread has no recourse but to be different if the story is to be notable, and lasting. That difference does not have to be drastic, nor need it be even visible at first glance. But to add substance to the canon requires *something* that has not been done, or done well, before.

Sweetheart, Sweetheart, by Bernard Taylor, is then the best ghost story (in novel form) I have ever read, and am ever likely to read. Nothing on either side of the Atlantic has thus far even come close.

Any number of elements make this novel special: that it is a true novel, and not some spawn of a television generation noted primarily for its minuscule attention span, marks it out as distinctive; that its elegant use of language demonstrates no condescension signals a respect for the reader's intelligence far too often lacking in contemporary fiction of any stripe; and that it achieves its effects without artifice speaks volumes about the care and caring that went into its writing.

A ghost story ought to have a certain unease, an anxiety, an air near palpable tension that is played upon by the writer to summon and engage as much of his reader's imagination as possible, in what amounts to active collaboration. Through this, the fact that we already know this is a ghost story means nothing. What are important are the lives of the characters, the *people*, who are involved, and how they deal with the real and preternatural forces which oppose them.

Or lure them.

And rather than opt to pile explicit horror upon gruesome horror, throw one body atop another, toss one cliché after another into the pot, to satisfy what such a story is 'supposed to be', Taylor has successfully created both a world and a population we can reach and understand with all our senses, and all their attendant, honest, emotions.

In dark fantasy, to give one an honest chill through a story that holds and entertains us is a mark of success; to multiply those chills without dissipating them, to entertain without pretense, and at the same time conclude an already emotionally draining story with a wrench that is at once heartbreaking and horrifying, is the mark of a potential classic. *Sweetheart, Sweetheart* is precisely that.

—CHARLES L. GRANT

76   [1977]

JOHN FARRIS

All Heads Turn When the Hunt Goes By

In 1942, Clipper Bradwin, a promising young army officer from a wealthy family, plans to marry a socially prominent heiress. The lavish ceremony, which takes place at an exclusive Southern Military Academy, is disrupted by the mysterious ringing of a silent bell, an apparent earthquake, and the bridegroom's sudden attack of sabre-wielding homicidal mania. Although Clipper, his bride, and his demagogue father are killed, his brother Champ and young mother-in-law Nhora survive. Two years later, Champ returns shattered from the War in the Pacific to Dasharoons, the huge family plantation, accompanied by Jackson Holley, a mysterious English doctor. The tragic events that follow are traced back to unpleasant experiences Jackson and Nhora had while younger at the hands of an obscure African tribe, and a race riot-cum-massacre in which Champ's father was dishonourably involved. Farris weaves a powerful and complicated story, and delivers the best modern treatment of the lamia and voodoo themes in horror literature. The novel reflects the author's interests in Africa, the military, social history and America's power elite, as also examined in his Catacombs *(1982),* Son of the Endless Night *(1985) and* Wildwood *(1987).*

No frills: *All Heads Turn When the Hunt Goes By* is a unique horror novel; the strongest single work yet produced by the field's most powerful individual voice.

The title countermands the phony melodramatics of drippy gerunds or the exhausted syllabary of horror's titular clichés: *dark* or *blood* or *night* this or that.

'This house was built on the bodies and blood of Africans,' notes the half-breed prophet of the resurgent goddess Ai-da Wédo—'a ravishing serpent woman who waxed and grew powerful as a consequence

169

of—sexual desire.' *This house* is Dasharoons, wellspring of three generations of Bradwins, a sprawling Southern estate still going strong at the
close of America's age of slavery. Farris' strongest theme is cultural
collision, represented in the collaboration of pedigree that is Little
Judge—half Bradwin, half high priest of ancient African sorcery. Farris'
juxtaposition of a partially sunken Mississippi riverboat with a voodoo
temple (secreted in the swamplands that are slowly swallowing the
vessel) is the fulcrum image of this complex saga of deadly erotic
obsession and racial karma debt repaid.

Far from 'feel good' horror that restores order to the world by the final
chapter, Farris prefers to concentrate on the evils people wreak upon
themselves. The restoration of balance is not always a good or pretty
thing, and the ultimately poisonous mingling of disparate cultures in *All
Heads Turn* offers not even temporary respite—regardless of allegiance,
all the characters are doomed. Apart from being a rare *racial* horror
novel, the fatal magnetism of the Ai-da Wédo and of Nhora Bradwin for
Jackson Holley and the cursed Bradwin clan make *All Heads Turn* the
finest modern sexual horror novel yet written.

Most fiction employing Haitian or African magic boils down to
elementary vengeance-via-voodoo, or a procedural 'how to' story about
little more than its own occult research. The novel's plot is a finely
tangled viper's nest of incident into which Farris has not only deftly
braided the voodoo, but dovetailed two fascinating bloodlines united by
a common past. The horror elements and character narrative are inextric-
ably interdependent (a similar structure, minus the supernatural, is seen
in *Shatter* [1981]).

The succinct prose artfully forms instantaneous brain pictures for the
reader. Clipper's aborted wedding turns hallucinogenic as the stuffy
formalities skew into a surgically dispassionate slaughter. Farris never
wallows in artificially inflated detail or masturbatory excess, yet his
writing is always unflinching, specific, precise. He is not terrified of good
sex between adults, or confused by it, as most of his contemporaries seem
to be. The veracity of his erotic passages serves well this book's unusual
story, which redefines love and shows us a compelling aberrancy as pure
as a genetic mutation. The closing scenes, symmetrically recapitulating
the wedding which opens the book, are surreal and hypnotic. The web
pulls taut and knots tight. The end is unforgettable, the blackest of
fade-outs, a conclusion whose potency does not pale with repeated
reading.

Farris claims that he 'hated every page' of *All Heads Turn* while it was
in-work, and that 'up until the last night [of writing], I had no idea how it
was going to end'. That night, ironically, preceded his marriage to his
second wife, and today he notes the book as his personal favorite among
his own novels. 'There's nothing that I've seen or heard about that's
remotely like it,' he says.

Likewise, when John Farris is on high-burn, no one can match the skill with which he puts words together. *All Heads Turn When the Hunt Goes By* is conclusive proof. Period.

—DAVID J. SCHOW

77   [1977]

STEPHEN KING

The Shining

Jack Torrance, a would-be writer, takes a job as winter caretaker at the Overlook Hotel, a vast resort—snowbound from October till April—in Colorado. Alone with him in the place, which has a history of violence and evil, are his wife Wendy and his slightly psychic son, Danny. Jack tries to get to work, but falls increasingly under the malign influence of the Overlook, while Danny starts seeing the ghosts of the hotel's previous victims. Finally, Jack becomes completely absorbed in the Overlook and attempts to repeat the crime of an early caretaker who murdered his wife and children in the place. Only Danny's psychic link with Dick Hallorann, a black cook who works in the hotel in the summer, can help him and his mother escape from the transformed Jack. The Shining works many of King's favourite themes—the child with paranormal powers, the pressures that turn a basically decent man bad, a horror that threatens to destroy an average American family, the extremely haunted house. The novel was controversially filmed by Stanley Kubrick in 1980, with Jack Nicholson and Shelley Duvall as rather more grotesque versions of Jack and Wendy than King intended. It is Kubrick's Jack, however, who reappears as a character in David Thomson's mosaic novel Suspects (1985).

I'm not sure that *The Shining* has ever been properly understood or appreciated—it has been imitated (even its *title* has been imitated), filmed, and analyzed, all badly; by now it is an early element in a large and varied body of work, the merits of which tend to be taken for granted; its extraordinary special merits, not quite taken in at the time of its publication except perhaps by other writers, have become less visible as its author followed it with novel after novel and became not only a fixture on the best-seller list but also something like a personification of the best-seller list. The reasons why that should have happened to

171

Stephen King are all present in full strength in *The Shining*, but at the time conventional wisdom declared that he was (only!) a phenomenal paperback success, read by young audiences—his subject matter inspired a certain degree of condescension among people who should have known better. The fact is that *The Shining* is a masterwork, a bold product of an original vision, a novel of astonishing passion, urgency, tenderness, understanding, and invention.

I think its most significant characteristic is its rich and generous inclusiveness, which is the inclusiveness of a powerful talent discovering its full capacities. *The Shining*'s themes encompass alcoholism, child abuse, imagination, madness, responsibility and loyalty, historical crime—a very Jamesian history—art, and giftedness, and the novel effortlessly locates all this material within a narrative frame that glides with great assurance towards its many, carefully nuanced, expertly judged and *placed* climaxes.

The first time I read it I was moved by the beauty of its ornamentation, which was as florid and precise as the pattern in a Persian carpet: Jack Torrance's childhood is as fully ornamented as the Overlook Hotel: for it was that sort of instinctive detailing that made the terror *ache* throughout the book and in which the lyric terror accumulated. I remember also being stunned by the book's style. This was not exactly literary, but much better than a conventional literary style, being a fresh freewheeling unrestrained representation of the way his characters' minds actually moved. It was quick and lively, as responsive to mood as music. This way of writing became more familiar as Steve adapted it to the requirements of books that followed *The Shining*, but it was never done better than here.

The first time I finished reading *The Shining*, I turned right back to the beginning of the book and started it again. I can't think of another book in the field of horror that affected me as strongly, and of only very few outside it. In its uniting of an almost bruising literary power, a deep sensitivity to individual experience, and its operatic convictions, it is a very significant work of art.

—PETER STRAUB

WILLIAM HJORTSBERG

Falling Angel

New York, 1959. Harry Angel, a Chandleresque private eye, is engaged by the mysterious Louis Cyphre to track down Johnny Favorite, formerly a successful crooner, who is believed to have been institutionalized since the Second World War. Angel soon learns that some kind of switch has been made and that Johnny has dropped completely out of sight. He also finds out that the various witnesses he visits have a tendency to turn up gruesomely murdered soon after. The police also make the connection, and Angel finds himself suspected of mass murder. He also learns about a voodoo cult who meet in an abandoned cavern beneath the New York subway, and begins an affair with Epiphany Proudfoot, their high priestess and Johnny's daughter. Angel realises that Cyphre is Lucifer himself and that he is after Johnny because the singer has been trying to welsh on a deal involving his soul. It seems that Johnny has cheated the Devil by taking on another identity through a magic ritual, but Angel finally deduces—unhappily for all concerned—who his quarry really is. A crackling combination of hard-boiled detective story and Faustian horror novel, Falling Angel *borrows a plot element or two from the film* Black Angel *for its slightly guessable twist ending. It was filmed in 1987 by Alan Parker as* Angel Heart, *starring Mickey Rourke and Robert de Niro.*

In 1978 I was browsing a Los Angeles bookstore when a particular title caught my eye, a Harcourt Brace Jovanovich hardcover. The dust jacket was arresting: a winged angel, gun in hand, prowling above the multiple towers of Manhattan, pursued by an evil-smiling, horned Satan, knife in hand, cloven hoof extending between skyscrapers. All this under a gold-foil sky.

I read the inside flap copy. Here were the likes of Stephen King, Robin Moore, and Thomas McGuane showering the novel with all-out raves: 'brilliant . . .', 'compelling . . .', 'terrific . . .', 'breathless . . .', 'spellbinding . . .'. And when I found out that the plot involved a tough private detective named Harry Angel versus the occult world of voodoo and witchcraft in New York I was hooked. I paid $8.95, plus tax, and *Falling Angel* was mine.

I read the book that same evening—with the hair standing up on the back of my neck. This week, a full decade later, I read it again. My opinion has not changed: it's one of the top horror novels of the century. It is also one of the century's finest examples of hard-boiled detective fiction, a novel fully deserving to be shelved next to Philip Marlowe and Sam Spade.

What Raymond Chandler did for Los Angeles in the 1940s William Hjortsberg does for New York in the late 1950s. He paints a grim and poetic portrait of New York's mean streets in 1959, bringing the Big Apple to raw life. There's a haunting sense of desolation in his sequence at Coney Island in the off-season, and his portrayal of life inside the plush, high finance office suites of Manhattan is equally convincing.

Harry Angel, in dangerous and desperate pursuit of an elusive shadow-self, is a man fated to lose—the ultimate, cynical, hard-headed private eye forced into a nightmarish descent into the netherworld of evil. As he tells his story in classic first-person style, we are with Angel in his doomed quest, graphically experiencing a voodoo ceremony in late night Central Park, then a murder in which the victim's heart has been ripped from her body, and finally a truly chilling Black Mass conducted in an abandoned subway station during which a squalling baby is sacrificed to Satan.

A brutal fight to the death on the underground subway tracks between Angel and a member of the cult is Hammett-tough:

> I left the shipping millionaire lying on the tracks to be dismembered by the next train through. The rats would feast tonight.

The book's prime figure of evil, Louis Cyphre, is drawn in brimstone and Black Magic, a character who bedevils the dreams of Harry Angel and whose power is absolute.

Hjortsberg's heroine bears a name worthy of a James Bond thriller, Epiphany Proudfoot, an expert practitioner of voodoo and erotic sex. But even this strong woman cannot save Harry Angel from his self-created fall.

A superb *tour de force*, *Falling Angel* achieves the impact of a .45 slug to the chest. You'll keep your lights on at night after reading this one.

—WILLIAM F. NOLAN

WHITLEY STRIEBER

The Wolfen

Brooklyn homicide cops George Wilson and Becky Neff investigate the gruesome murder of two patrolmen, and discover the existence of a pack of wolflike superintelligent urban animals. The Wolfen, who have survived down the centuries preying on the unwanted and outcast, realize that they have been exposed and set out to silence Wilson and Neff. Strieber's first novel gives the werewolf myth a radical rethink, much as his later books would, less successfully, reinterpret the vampirism (The Hunger, 1981) and black magic (The Night Church, 1984) themes. The Wolfen remains his best-written, best-plotted solo novel. It was filmed with the 'The' dropped from the title in 1981 by Mike Wadleigh, with Albert Finney as an unlikely New York cop, but Wadleigh's issue-heavy two-and-a-half hour cut had to be trimmed and rearranged by an uncredited John Hancock into a slick thriller only tinged with pretension.

In the mid-seventies, Whitley Strieber lived near New York City's Central Park. There he enjoyed the quiet of late night strolls until the night he was in the Literary Walk, going toward Bethesda Fountains, and noticed something in the trees nearby that appeared to be following him, pacing him step for step. The movement proved to be of canine origin—but it wasn't simply one dog, loose in the park that night. Rather it was a pack of some eight or ten feral dogs of various sizes.

Strieber beat a hasty retreat, but the thought of those creatures stayed with him—'The wildness of these animals in the middle of the city', was how he later described it. Eventually that incident became the spring-board for his first novel, *The Wolfen*, and an ongoing theme that can be found in his work, in various guises, up to the present day.

With hindsight, it's easy to look back on his career to study this theme of alien beings coexisting for millennia with the human race. It also became Strieber's method of redefining hoary aspects of the genre in which he began his career.

The Wolfen examined the possibility of werewolves existing on the fringes of society and also postulated an intriguing origin of the vampire myth—a question he went on to address in an entirely different manner with his next book, *The Hunger*. Subsequent novels investigated secret societies (*Black Magic* and *The Night Church*) and faeries (*Catmagic*), and while he strayed from that theme for his next few books, which dealt with environmental concerns, he has returned to it once again with his latest book, *Communion*.

The difference with *Communion* is that, with it, Strieber no longer considers his present work fiction. The imaginary parasitic aliens of his earlier novels have been replaced with mysterious *others* that, Streiber assures us, really do exist.

But whatever one's feelings on Strieber's current projects, nothing can diminish the power and originality of his earlier work. *The Wolfen* in its day, and upon re-reading at the present time, retains all of its strengths.

Foremost of these is the care with which Strieber revealed the novel's preternatural element. The presence of the Wolfen is with us from the first page until the last, but the reader comes to understand their nature only at the same time as the principal protagonists. At that point, the storyline occasionally switches perspectives to the Wolfen's points of view, where Strieber does an admirable job of conveying their alienness—though not so much so that the creatures lose their impact through becoming indecipherable.

They are presented as a race of carnivorous hunters—not noble savages as they were portrayed in the film version of the book, but more in the manner we've come to understand from documentation of other carnivorous creatures, such as Serengeti lions and the like. Because of this, the Wolfen remain believable in the context of the work, a very real menace with which the characters must deal.

The novel's other strong point is Strieber's understanding of how, if one wishes the preternatural to be effective, the natural world must be conveyed to the reader in clear, unaffected terms. Because of this *The Wolfen* reads almost like a police procedural as we follow the workings of the NYPD's investigation into the escalating horror of the Wolfen's presence in their city.

The characters are fully drawn, with concerns that operate beyond the confines of the storyline. The novel's background and action were conveyed with just the correct amount of detail and power to effectively tell the story. And while Strieber's prose became more assured in later books, *The Wolfen* remains far more than merely a competently told first novel.

To this day it stands up as one of the classic works of fiction to emerge from the horror genre, a book that will undoubtably be read and re-read by enthusiasts in the field for many years to come.

—CHARLES DE LINT

DAVID MORRELL

The Totem

Nathan Slaughter, a small-town police chief in Wyoming, is confronted with a series of strange incidents. A corpse apparently revives and frightens a coroner to death, animals turn savage overnight, children go mad, and outbreaks of irrational violence disrupt the smooth running of the community. It develops that a strange strain of rabies has originated in a hippie commune degenerating up in the wilderness, and soon the town is under siege. Following his brutal and horrific thrillers First Blood *(1972) and* Testament *(1975) and the ambitious Western* Last Reveille, *David Morrell in* The Totem *turns to more explicit horror, mixing in supernatural elements and a scientifically-rationalized form of vampirism/zombiehood/lycanthropy. Recently, with* Blood Oath *(1982) and the Trilogy commencing with* The Brotherhood of the Rose *(1984), he has revitalized the international espionage genre with a heavy dose of Gothic complication. Plot similarities between* The Totem *and the film* I Drink Your Blood *(1971) are probably coincidental, but the book might be one of the inspirations for Shaun Hutson's* Erebus *(1983).*

The door crashed open and he hurtled through it, slamming it behind him, breath coming in gasps.

The door to the sitting-room was open and he blundered through, vaulting the coffee table, landing with a crash on the sofa.

The beginning of *The Totem* . . . ? Is it hell! That was me coming back from the bookshop after I'd bought it. Having read Morrell's earlier novels (*First Blood* and *Testament*) his third book looked like a bit of a departure for him, but it is written with the same breathless speed of its predecessors. *The Totem* is one of the few novels I've ever read in a day—usually I'm lucky if I get through two chapters in a week. But once I'd started reading it, the rest of the world could have disappeared in a ball of flame for all I cared. Immersed in it? God, if I'd been any more involved I'd have drowned . . . I chopped the dog's legs off so it wouldn't want walking, nailed my fiancée to the front door to keep visitors away and ploughed into Morrell's book.

It's like the literary equivalent of an aerobics work-out. By the time you've finished you can hardly breathe. You can reel out all the clichés you like for Morrell's superb handling of a horror story that is constructed like a thriller and which, if you analyse it (I'm not going to but *you* can), is occasionally an extension of some themes he explored in

First Blood (the scene where Rambo crawls through the cave full of bats being the one which immediately springs to mind). As I say, the clichés to describe *The Totem* are endless but I mean it when I say that this novel moves at such a pace it makes the bullet train look liks a shunter. If it was a car its number plate would be 'Turbo Speedburst Maniac'. When I say it moves, it moves. I'm getting tired just thinking about it . . .

At times you feel as though you should be hanging on to your seat in case you fly off. The thing about the book which also makes it so admirable is that the speed never overshadows the characters. I mean, the central character's name is Slaughter, for Christ's sake . . . With a name like that you can't go wrong. Quite appropriate too, especially in the scene where . . . No, why should I? Read it for yourselves.

There is of course the other tiny detail which I've so far neglected to mention and that is that *The Totem* is one hell of a frightening novel. Well, I counted at least two changes of underwear and that was just reading the blurb! The set pieces are beautifully constructed, the short chapters accentuating the speed of the novel.

In fact, now I come to think about it I hate David Morrell: With *The Totem*, he's written a book which set a standard few authors could ever come close to in the horror/thriller genre. Yeah, I hate him. He's a genius.

Buy it, borrow it, steal it. But for God's sake read it. *The Totem* isn't a rollercoaster ride, it's a high-speed journey on a Harley Davison, straight towards a brick wall. Living dangerously? Damn right. Only problem is, the brakes don't work . . .

—SHAUN HUTSON

81   [1979]

PETER STRAUB

Ghost Story

Milburn, New York. A group of old men who call themselves The Chowder Society, linked by their long-ago involvement in the drowning of the strange Eva Galli, meet regularly to tell each other ghost stories. Don Wanderley, a writer of occult novels, returns home to Milburn after his involvement with Alma Mobley, the latest incarnation of shape-shifting Eva, which has led to the death of his brother. During the siege of a vicious winter, Don and the

Chowder Society have to face up to the ancient and deadly monster woman. Straub's third novel, patterned in its use of the background community on Stephen King's Salem's Lot, is a conscious attempt to evoke the shades of the classic ghost stories of M. R. and Henry James, Hawthorne, Poe and others, within the framework of a complex and multifaceted modern Gothic plot. Its success established him as second only to King as the leading figure in contemporary horror. The 1982 film, directed by John Irvin, is a travesty of the material, despite a strong cast of veterans and the very creepy Alice Krige as the many faces of Eva.

It's obvious from *Ghost Story* that Peter Straub loves genre horror fiction, and indeed he has many times professed great admiration for Stephen King, with whom he was later to collaborate. But on the evidence of this, his best book, Straub is most entertaining when he is not consciously working within the genre, just flirting with it.

Ghost Story is a serious work of *mainstream* fiction which takes as its subject a writer of horror fiction ('A nice exercise in genre writing. More literary than most.') who transforms real-life horrors into art, or so it seems at first. Later it seems as if the real-life horrors may in fact *be* his art, as if he somehow dreamed them into existence.

The title of the book is a very careful choice; it is a ghost story and it is about a ghost story, and within it are many ghost stories, including those told by four men almost old enough to be ghosts. The word 'ghost' flickers wittily into and out of its pages. At the very end, as Don the ghostwriter chops up what may be a wasp and may be something female and infinitely more dangerous, a passing observer remarks 'That thing ain't *ever* gonna give up the ghost.'

I don't want to sound pretentious, but I think *Ghost Story* is partly a book about how we create within our own minds the things that most frighten us. On the surface it seems that the terrible woman whose initials are A.M. (Alma Mobley, Anna Mostyn *et al.*) has a solid, external reality: that she is a manifestation of some ancient shape-shifting nature spirit, now feeding vampire-like on the imaginations of the humans she destroys. But the subtext seems to be that she is in some sense *created* by human imagination. (I think therefore I A.M.)

It is no accident that she is both destroyed and most vividly brought to life by a writer. (Even the elderly lawyers have the names of the two writers, Hawthorne and James, who between them created in the real world a kind of consensus image of the New England guilt, which is partly what this story is about.)

The theory that A.M. was dreamed up by Don also explains the mysterious exchange between man and creature that is returned to throughout the story. At the beginning, narrator to little girl: '"What are you?" She smiled all through her amazing response. "I am you."' Or near the very end, dead brother to narrator: '"You invented these fantastic beautiful creatures, and then you 'wrote' yourself into the story as their enemy. But nothing like that could ever be defeated."'

If Alma is a beautiful poem, as the book suggests—'Could you defeat a cloud, a dream, a poem?'—Don is her author. (But then, how real are Don and even Straub, whose surrogate Don is? The uncertainty runs deep, for at the key moment when allure turns to horror, when Alma, sexual athlete and monster, turns round in the darkness, we get this, though it takes us most of the book to find out: '"You are a ghost." You, Donald. You. It was the unhappy perception at the center of every ghost story.')

We will always as humans write such monstrous, lovely poems the book suggests. Somehow we need them, and feed on them just as they feed on us. The moral outrage we feel at the vanity and cruelty of A.M. and her disciples is outrage at something dirty and attractive in the corner of our own minds.

And that dirtiness, of course, is the other great attraction of *Ghost Story*. I refer to its central metaphor, which is especially forceful for any male Australian of my age who grew up in a puritanical and sexually repressive society. A.M. is fundamentally a *female* horror. What is it that peeping Toms see through her window, what is it that she shows foolish old men in bedrooms, something so horrible that it drives them mad, their faces locked in a rictus of fear?

The real answer is surely *vagina dentata*. This novel is fundamentally about repressed men appalled at the sexuality of woman, their strength, their darkness; the wetness, the cavernousness, the dangerousness of their sexual parts.

Peter Straub's amusingly bitter insight into this question might usefully be extended to all horror fiction, where the succubus, the lamia, so often makes her vilely seductive lair. 'The horror! The horror!' as Kurtz said when he reached the Heart of Darkness up that long, Freudian, dank yet somehow tranquil river that Conrad so beautifully describes in another, related, classic.

—PETER NICHOLLS

JONATHAN CARROLL

The Land of Laughs

Thomas Abbey, the son of a famous film star, is obsessionally interested in the works of Marshall France, a mysterious children's writer whose classic books include The Land of Laughs, Pool of Stars, Peach Shadows *and* The Green Dog's Shadow. *Spurred by Saxony Gardner, his girlfriend, Abbey decides to attempt a biography of his hero, who chose to live a reclusive life in Galen, Missouri, and whose estate is jealously guarded by his daughter, Anna. Abbey and Saxony travel to Galen, and after some teasing the author's heiress agrees to let Abbey attempt the biography. However, it soon develops that Galen isn't quite the middle American idyll it seems to be: tragedies are shrugged off by the population, some of the local dogs can speak, and a weird kind of predestination appears to rule everyday life. The author has not subsequently been prolific, but he has added to his bizarre reputation with* The Voice of Our Shadow *(1983) and* Bones of the Moon *(1987).*

The best novels resist easy categorization, and there's a point in *The Land of Laughs* where the protagonist, Thomas Abbey, says that he hates horror books and novels—sentiments which we suspect Jonathan Carroll himself shares. Nevertheless, Carroll is writing a horror story of a sort, and he understands that the best moments of terror are mental rather than physical and lie in the collision between the mundane and the extraordinary, the sudden juxtaposition of the familiar with the bizarre.

The Land of Laughs has several moments of high terror, the more effective because they do not come until the reader is well into the book. We are lulled by plenty of realistic narrative while at the same time kept uneasy by the macabre overtones of the writing itself. This is perfectly illustrated very early on when Abbey enters a bookstore and comes upon a rare edition of a book by his beloved author, Marshall France. 'I staggered over to the desk,' Carroll has Abbey tell us, 'and, after wiping my hands on my pants, picked it up reverently. I noticed a troll who looked as if he had been dipped in talcum powder watching me from the corner of the store.'

This is an arresting image, and even though we swiftly discover that the troll is simply an ordinary storekeeper, we have a presentiment that darker things lie in store for Thomas Abbey. Carroll continues to tease us with hints of the grotesque or aberrant: Abbey's girlfriend collects marionettes; Abbey himself collects masks and lives in the psychological shadow of his famous movie-star father, now dead; the character of France's daughter is ambiguous to say the least.

Carroll sustains the tension masterfully. Ensconced in France's midwestern hometown, Abbey starts work on France's biography. But deceit and manipulation lie everywhere, not least in Abbey's secret affair with France's daughter. More than ever, we know he's courting disaster. One of the women in the town is serving dinner when Abbey momentarily sees her as 'Krang coming out of the kitchen [with] the wide empty eyes that betray the joy in the mouth's full, happy smile'. Krang is a character from one of France's books. Soon afterwards Abbey arrives home to find the friendly household dog asleep on his bed. It's talking in its sleep. Now the terror of the place begins to take hold as Abbey discovers that the townsfolk are literally the creation of Marshall France and that he must complete the biography in order to keep them alive. This is no Ray Bradbury small-town America. 'You finish that fucking book, Abbey!' one of the inhabitants tells him. 'You finish it or I'll cut your fucking balls off!'

The Land of Laughs is in part a meditation on the seductions of creativity (one of the impressive things about the book is the way in which Carroll makes the reader believe that France's books really exist) and in part the study of a slide into madness. The three-page epilogue has Abbey hiding in Europe after having escaped France's hometown. He's begun the biography of his father and has brought him back to life as a result. Or, to read it another way, his madness is now total and all the bizarre happenings in the book are seen to be a product of the narrator's mind. Strongly characterized and beautifully paced, *The Land of Laughs* combines elements of fantasy and horror into a piece of modern American Gothic which is ultimately *sui generis*.

—CHRISTOPHER EVANS

83 [1980]

RICHARD LAYMON
The Cellar

Malcasa Point, California. The Beast House is a local tourist attraction, the site of at least eleven gruesome murders between 1903 and 1977. To Malcasa Point come Donna Hayes and her daughter Sandy, fleeing from Donna's recently released homicidal maniac/child molestor husband, Roy. Judgement Rucker, a mercenary, has been hired by Larry Mayhew—who once survived an encounter with the beast of the house—to kill the creature. Donna and Jud fall in love at first sight, and resolve to deal with both Roy and the beast. However, the creature that lurks inside the old house turns out to be only one of a whole brood of human and inhuman monsters and destroying them isn't as easy as it seems. Richard Laymon's first novel is a violent, face-paced, cynical chiller modelled on contemporary horror movies like The Hills Have Eyes *(1977) and* Friday the 13th *(1980). Laymon returned to Malcasa Point in* The Beast House *(1981) and has subsequently turned out many similar entertainments in the splattery vein of* The Woods Are Dark *(1981),* Out Are the Lights *(1982) and* All Hallows' Eve *(1985).*

In an era where horror novels are sold by weight, Richard Laymon slices away all the surplus fat and cuts down to the bone. Down to the bone and beyond.

The Cellar is fast moving and written in a very cinematic style, using the minimum of detail and description. Even the violent episodes are told in the same sparse manner, with no more emphasis than the rest of the book. (Scenes chosen for the back covers of some of Laymon's later NEL paperbacks, for example, had to be expanded with more graphic detail by the blurb writers in order to appeal to the potential purchaser.)

Laymon never chooses the easy route by revelling in gory mutilation. The literal documentation of slaughter takes no great skill, only access to a textbook on surgery. (Not that this stops several alleged horror authors and their crude accounts of pre-mortem autopsies.)

Although he has chosen to aim at the less cerebral end of the horror spectrum, Laymon writes with a style and flair which sets him far ahead of his pulp rivals. In this context, perhaps his most significant achievement is the creation of his characters. They do what real people do: they talk. Much of the action is carried forward via dialogue.

Every word counts, and every character is there for the same purpose: to move the plot onwards. They are not created as mere prey, thrown in at random to fill a few pages so that the author can simply kill them off. The shock of their deaths comes because we have grown to know them, not because they have been disposed of as bloodily as possible.

For example: one chapter ends with a woman about to be tortured, but we never discover her ultimate fate until much later, when Laymon makes casual reference to her tormentor having lit *three good fires in one day*. Laymons' subtle technique leaves far more to the readers, who are free to add their own vivid details to the scenes which he has outlined. The only limit is their own imagination.

It seems that Roy is the villain in *The Cellar*. He has just been freed from jail, having served time for raping his own six-year-old daughter. In his quest for revenge, he slays and steals, brutalizes and burns; he tries to run down a dog and sexually abuses another juvenile girl.

Laymon gradually draws the diverse threads of his novel together. At first the Beast House, scene of several earlier mysterious murders, is subordinate to the mayhem caused by Roy. Laymon appears to be suggesting that there is no one more inhuman than Roy, that there can be no greater evil than that inflicted by man upon man—or upon woman.

But there is.

What dwells in the cellar can snuff out Roy in an instant, can inflict infinitely worse terror than he ever could. At least Roy granted his victims the release of death. There is no such mercy for those who survive their ordeal in the Beast House.

This ultimate scene is written all in dialogue. We may not understand what has happened at first, but after a few lines there is no need for any description of the obvious. With several well-chosen words Laymon conjures up the truly horrifying fate which awaits those trapped in *The Cellar*.

—DAVID S. GARNETT

84 [1981]

THOMAS HARRIS
Red Dragon

Will Graham, a former FBI agent, is called out of early retirement when his special talents—he is an expert in tracking down apparently motiveless serial murderers—are required. Two middle-class families have been coolly wiped out by a killer who has been nicknamed 'The Tooth Fairy' and Graham hopes hopes to catch the psychopath before he strikes again. His problems are exacerbated by the malign influence of Dr Hannibal Lektor, the last murderer he put away, and by his suspicion that he can only do his job if he actually becomes as warped as his quarry. Meanwhile, Francis Dolarhyde— the killer—is furious about the demeaning 'Tooth Fairy' tag and tries to get his pseudonym changed by eating William Blake's painting 'The Red Dragon'. Harris' novel is a state-of-the-art police procedural, and an outstanding examination of the anatomy of madness as exemplified by its hero and villains alike. It was filmed by Michael Mann in 1986 as Manhunter, *with excellent performances from William L. Peterson, Brian Cox and Tom Noonan.*

*R*ed Dragon is, quite simply, the most frightening book I have ever read, and surely belongs in the best one hundred horror volumes. I'd be tempted to place it in the top ten, despite the fact that there is no supernatural element in the book. Believe me, it doesn't need one. Thomas Harris requires no vampires, werewolves, or any of the other stock spooks that make up a good percentage of the menaces of horror fiction. For him, as for William Blake in a quotation Harris uses as an epigraph, 'Cruelty has a Human Heart'.

Francis Dolarhyde, the monster of *Red Dragon*, is indeed human, pitiful, terrifying, sympathetic, and all too believable. He is a beast who murders entire families to feed a dark, sociopathic, psychosexual urge, the result of an upbringing nearly as hideous as his own responses to it. His personality and background are impeccably drawn, as are those of Will Graham, the investigator brought out of an early retirement to hunt down the Dragon.

For Graham, who in the past has caught serial killers by thinking the way they do, the greatest horror lies in the self-recognition that such an empathic projection causes, the distressing awareness of the magnitude and potential of the evil that lies in his own heart. It is the same horror that confronts Kurtz and Marlow in Conrad's *Heart of Darkness*.

The basic plot has been used before and since, but precursors of *Red Dragon* had pulled back, reluctant to expose and explore the cellars of the soul that Harris maps so vividly, while most of those who have followed in his footsteps have substituted either buckets of viscera or a barrage of verbal pyrotechnics for the true and terrifying confrontation that Harris offers.

And confrontation is the key word in discussing *Red Dragon*. To approach this book as an 'escape' novel, be it a police procedural or a slasher-on-the-loose story, is shortsighted, though it works on either of those levels. Unfortunately, so do half a hundred otherwise undistinguished novels to be found in any bookstore. Most of these books are content to splash the reader with stage blood and explore the first level of cellars, the most accessible part of the subconscious where the easily definable—and admissible—fears dwell. But the best horror fiction goes below to the sub-cellars, to the places in the mind that we dare not admit exist. *Red Dragon* is not an escape novel, for it refuses to let us escape. Instead, it makes us confront the worst in ourselves. It shows us the monster in the mirror, the one with our own face, smeared not with stage blood but with the naked emotions of hate and lust and murderous rage.

Along with its disturbing theme, *Red Dragon* is full of wicked pleasures. It is an intensely visual novel, rich with sound and color and telling use of small detail to make large points. All of its characters are brilliantly portrayed, and it is filled with gritty verisimilitude. Harris has done his homework, and it shows, but the fascinating investigative procedures never intrude upon the plot or slow the savage pace.

Awful and awesome things happen in this book, but we are not overwhelmed with descriptive and gory detail, for understatement is one of Harris's greatest virtues. He clearly understands the visions already resident in the imagination of his readers, so he tells us, simply and honestly, of the acts of Francis Dolarhyde. Then we move on, and the memories of what Harris may have allowed us to glimpse for only a moment resonate inside us for hours.

The book itself resonates far longer. I have read it three times, and every time I have found something new in it—more to admire in the craftsmanship of the writing, deeper levels, unexpected meanings. Indeed, this last time I saw parts of it as a parable for creating fiction, with Will Graham's struggles to put a face on the Dragon a metaphor for the writer's effort to assume multiple points of view and so delineate his characters.

But that, of course, is only the reaction of one writer, finding a more innocent reading in order to give his mind ease, to temporarily deny the uncomfortable truths at the book's core, truths that horror fiction and its readers must ultimately confront, and be richer for the knowledge and the recognition.

Buy *Red Dragon*, read it, shiver at it, remember it—for you will be unable to forget it. It is as real as fiction can be, and as frightening.

—CHET WILLIAMSON

85 [1981]

F. PAUL WILSON
The Keep

In 1941, a detachment of German soldiers led by Captain Klaus Woermann occupies the Keep, a strange structure which overlooks a pass in the Carpathians but which seems to have been built to keep something in rather than out. A looting sergeant pries a silver cross from the wall, and releases Molasar, an ancient and evil creature who begins killing the Nazis. German High Command sends in SS sadist Erich Kaempffer to sort the trouble out, and he is forced to call in a Jewish historian to explain to the Germans what they are up against. Glaeken, an immortal warrior, is psychically summoned to do battle with Molasar, but arrives to find that the monster has found human allies among those who would see the Nazis out of Romania. A spirited and horrific thriller which declares its debt to Lovecraft, Clark Ashton

186

Smith and Robert E. Howard, The Keep also flirts with the Dracula myth by creating a monster who seems to be a Transylvanian vampire but is actually something much worse! The novel was filmed with bizarre and arty results by Michael Mann in 1985.

It is difficult, when one has finished reading F. Paul Wilson's *The Keep*, to imagine anything essential to the genre's form which was omitted. Whatever a reader or reviewer of horror fiction thinks primary—necessary in the sense of originality of idea, basic to tight plotting and its progression, desirable in characterization and imperative in terms of suspense, surprise, and the inexorable build-up of the total storyline from event to event, chapter to chapter—seems to me present in Dr Wilson's masterwork. I include the qualifying 'seems to me' from a sense of fealty to the proprieties, but I will be inclined toward becoming passionately disagreeable if anyone wishes to quarrel over this admittedly extreme viewpoint.

More a matter of sheer opinion, I think, is the further thought that this novel wouldn't be the worst choice in the world as an exemplar held up for would-be novelists working in any modern genre (including the mainstream—which could use an infusion of originality, plot, suspense and so forth). Many new writers who have the good sense to check into what's selling in the realm of their literary bent are often heard (when one listens) to remark, 'Even *I* can write something better than that!' It would make a pleasant change if novices were exposed to a novel which elicits a sense of respect for the writing craft.

And the overwhelming majority of newcomers to any sort of novel writing are not about to write a book even fractionally so fine as *The Keep*. The fact that it was conceived and brought to full term by a young man who is a full-time, practicing physician—who was also engaged in creating richly-inventive science fiction—causes a lifelong Sherlockian to reflect about reincarnation, and to wonder, 'Whatever happened to Sir Arthur Conan Doyle?'

Not that it was Dr Conan Doyle whom Paul Wilson cited on his acknowledgments page; those fantasists were Lovecraft, Howard and Clark Ashton Smith, undeniably with sound and sometimes-obvious reason. Yet it's just as true that Wilson, as was true of Sir Arthur in detective fiction, is one of the few frequent practitioners of horror who deals conspicuously with questions of good versus evil; with mythology and the supernatural.

Unlike many popular authors—some of whom object to the 'horror' label mainly because it's *de rigueur* to do so—Dr Wilson often permits his characters the motivation of morality or immorality, self-identification with entrenched rules of faith and decent conduct, nihilism and sin. He thereby endows them with a timelessness absent from much of modern fiction. 'Molasar was evil,' Theodor Cuza concludes, in *The Keep*: 'That was given: Any entity that leaves a trail of corpses in order to continue its own existence is inherently evil.'

Which is not at all to say that his supremely well-crafted novel advances the simplistic notion that its characters (mirroring real people) are all black or all white, virtuously—devoid of those psychological shadings so dear to those engaged unceasingly in a sentimental search for better ways to forgive the unforgivable. From the start of his book, Paul Wilson uses as his viewpoint character Captain Klaus Woermann. The period is the Second World War, a time when, as a small boy, I believed all living Germans were Nazis and that Nazis were the embodiment of evil. It's hard for me to conceive of a protagonist for whom, as a reader, I was less likely to care; when I read Woermann's message, '*Something is murdering my men,*' I thought, *Good!*

But this German officer is not one 'to abandon a position'; the fight has 'gone out of his heart', he paints, he has two sons and detests the SS, he is 'intelligent and precise', and he's 'no longer in command of the Keep' because 'something dark and awful' has 'taken over'. And when, at the end for Klaus Woermann, he prays, '*Dear God, if you are my God*', I was reminded that human beings may work for or ruefully support endeavors of evil, but that its source, and the origins of its opposite, stem from elsewhere.

Let us not make too much, however, of the serious intent or elements of *The Keep*; not when it is the perfect product of a master storyteller who is here at his endlessly entertaining best. Instead, let's refer again to the echoes of the great storyteller Conan Doyle to which I listened raptly right up to the penultimate period of this readable book. Good Glaeken, running through Dr Wilson's symbol of evil, grapples with his opposite number on the parapet of the Keep. 'Together,' he writes, 'they toppled over the edge and plummeted down.' Sherlock Holmes and Professor Moriarty 'tottered together upon the brink of the fall' and Dr Watson believed they went 'reeling over, locked in each other's arms ... deep down in that dreadful cauldron of swirling water'. Wilson's contrasting pair awaited 'the shattering impact with the stones invisible below'; Holmes saw Moriarty when 'he struck a rock'. Ultimately, both figures of courage and goodness—each in his own way immortal—triumph.

Contemporary horror, in common with most so-called 'modern fiction' regardless of the year of publication, is written to sell, be read, establish the author, and persuade the powers that be—readers among them, if he or she is fortunate—to allow the cycle to occur all over again. And there is nothing wrong with that, I suppose; it's far worse when the author is merely an imitator or sets out to craft a classic and falls woefully short. Novels that last, particularly in that which is too loosely called 'genre fiction', are the soul of serendipity; delightful happenstance as the product of immense creative effort.

I feel sure *The Keep* is one of the only four or five such enduring novels I've read in contemporary horror.

—J. N. WILLIAMSON

86   [1982]

DENNIS ETCHISON

The Dark Country

A collection of short material written between 1972 and 1981, The Dark Country *demonstrates the quiet, modern American Gothic strain of which Etchison is a master. Typically, he writes of the horrors that stalk motel car parks ('It Only Comes Out at Night'), laundromats ('Sitting in the Corner, Whimpering Quietly'), or all-night drug stores ('The Late Shift'). This volume also contains a loosely connected series of science fiction horror stories ('The Machine Demands a Sacrifice', 'Calling All Monsters', 'The Dead Line') about organ transplants. Etchison is among the most exquisitely depressing voices in modern horror.*

In a world brutalized by televised overkill from Beirut and Northern Ireland, it takes a Master of the Horror Genre to set his stories in the late 20th century and come up with anything more gut-churning than what passes for everyday life.

Dennis Etchison is such a Master and *The Dark Country* is such a collection. Eschewing the gore of the Texas Chainsaw set he gives us instead the understated atrocity—the inference rather than the actuality, the razor-blade as opposed to the hatchet.

Just beneath the surface of his stultifyingly ordinary world something unspeakable is going on. Victim and reader alike are lulled into a sense of false security, only to be caught on the hop by the unexpected outrage. For Etchison works on two levels. In reading him we become his victim and he plays us like the expert angler plays the fish. One moment we are swimming, womb-warm in well-known waters, the next we are hoist on the impaling hook, torn into the killing air and left to thrash out an agonized death in an alien world where even the elements conspire against us.

189

There are echoes of Poe in these first-person narratives and yet the subjects are uncomfortably contemporary. The preoccupation with premature burial is replaced by an equally chilling but updated terror, felt at some time by all of us, that when our time comes to go, gently or otherwise, into that dark night, we might instead be prevented and preserved, quail's eggs in aspic, brain-dead yet breathing, so that our vital organs may be torn from our shuddering flesh and sewn into other bodies, other lives. Read 'The Dead Line' before you sign that Donor Card. Or, on second thoughts . . . don't.

Each of these stories has been crafted with the delicacy of a miniaturist so that what we end up with is a series of small, disturbing masterpieces. From 'The Pitch', in which a super salesman slices off his own particular corner of the food processing market to 'We Have Been Here Before', which reminds us that not all psychics are saintly souls, each is a tiny gem.

Most of the tales begin innocuously enough, the settings mundane in their normality—the supermarket, the laundrette, the motel bedroom. The characters are ordinary too. Rather like us. They leave us with the distinctly unpleasant feeling that anytime now . . . or at least one of these days . . . maybe. . . .

The Dark Country is the kind of book which, days after laying it aside, causes one to look more closely than usual at the parking attendant with the secret smile or draw back a hand from the waitress as she presents us with the cheque, for fear that her blood-red nails might be tipped with just that.

Etchison cradles us in the palm of his hand, almost persuading us that we are travelling well-trod ground, secure in the knowledge that we have read it all before. Only when our defences are down do his fingers tighten around our vulnerable flesh and begin to squeeze. . . . Like the hungry lips of the 'Daughter of the Golden West'.

I defy any red-blooded male, having read that one, to ever again submit to a fellatious tongue without at least a frisson of apprehension.

—SAMANTHA LEE

KARL EDWARD WAGNER

In a Lonely Place

Although best known for his violent and sophisticated series of heroic fantasy tales featuring Kane, the immortal Mystic Swordsman, Karl Edward Wagner has been contributing a number of highly original horror stories to small press magazines and anthologies throughout the 1970s and 1980s. His first collection, In a Lonely Place, *was published as a paperback original in 1983 with an introduction by Peter Straub, and contains 'In the Pines', 'Where the Summer Ends', 'Sticks', 'The Fourth Seal', '.220 Swift', 'The River of Night's Dreaming' and 'Beyond Any Measure'. It was reprinted the following year in hardcover by Scream/Press with an extra story, 'More Sinned Against', and a new afterword by the author. Winner of both the British and World Fantasy Awards, Wagner has edited DAW Books'* Year's Best Horror Stories *anthology since volume VIII.*

K arl Edward Wagner is among the most important and accomplished contemporary writers to have emerged from the tradition of the horror story, and *In a Lonely Place* (graced with delicately menacing illustrations by Ron and Val Lakey Lindahn) is one of the most impressive horror collections to have appeared for quite some time. Where many recent horror writers appear to have learned too much of their craft from their own generation, Wagner draws strength from his considerable knowledge of the history of the field. Indeed, *In a Lonely Place* demonstrates the development of the genre from the landscapes of the Gothic novel through the ghost story and pulp fiction to the modern self-consciously psychological horror story, and does so with a good deal of individuality and unexpectedness.

Wagner isn't a writer who seeks to conceal his influences, as the title of the book—with its clustering references to Bogart, Nicholas Ray, Dorothy B. Hughes and Walter de la Mare—makes clear. (The assumption that the reader will note the references also implies that Wagner is a writer to be read attentively.) Thus the earliest tale, 'In the Pines', a ghost story which perhaps isn't only that, acknowledges its echo of 'The Beckoning Fair One', though the reader may be more struck by the ways in which it prefigures 'The Shining', published three years later. 'In the Pines' is the first statement of one of Wagner's recurring themes, the swallowing up of characters and their psychological conflicts by a vividly imagined, almost hallucinatory landscape.

If 'In the Pines' incorporates Wagner's tributes to several aspects of British supernatural fiction, not least a piny whiff of Algernon Blackwood, 'The Fourth Seal' both reaches further back, to Faust, and deserves to be hailed as a progenitor of the modern tale of medical horror where the mad doctors are not so much visionaries, misguided or otherwise, as professionals who have sold their souls to the job. That the tale derives from Wagner's observations of medical school makes it even more dismaying. The reader may turn with some relief to 'Sticks', one of the few original Lovecraftian stories of the seventies, a witty and touching tribute to *Weird Tales* and in particular to the artist Lee Brown Coye. With its enigmatic landscape strewn with lattices that seem on the point of turning into symbols, the story also reinvents the Gothic in terms of the psychedelic decade.

'.220 Swift' was written partly with a Lovecraftian anthology in mind, but found a home in an anthology of newer terrors. Though both Lovecraft and Machen loom in its shadows, it reaches back to an earlier myth, and its scenes of underground terror are all Wagner's own. 'Where the Summer Ends' is the most sustained tale of terror in the book, but 'The River of Night's Dreaming' may be the finest story; it is certainly the most variously disturbing, and a masterpiece. In this story Wagner uses Robert W. Chambers' mysterious symbol *The King in Yellow* as personally as Lovecraft did in reconceiving it as 'The Necronomicon'. 'The River of Night's Dreaming' repays especially attentive reading, and offers Wagner's finest nightmare landscape to put the reader in the mood.

'Beyond Any Measure' is both an unusually powerful treatment of the confrontation with the Other and an enviably original variation on the theme of vampirism, firmly rooted in the conventions of such stories. With their erotic explicitness, these last two tales might have had difficulty being published until recently, and the story that followed, 'More Sinned Against', was rejected by a horror anthologist who lacked the courage of his genre on the grounds that the drugs used by the characters were insufficiently disapproved of, a doubly absurd objection to the story. 'More Sinned Against' is the first example of a bleaker phase of Wagner's work, where the landscape is mostly psychological. Other examples may be found in his later collection, *Why Not You And I?*, alongside such stories as 'Sign of the Salamander' and its oblique sequel, 'Blue Lady, Come Back', remarkable rediscoveries of the merits of pulp writing.

Lately Wagner's short fiction has seemed limited by a bitterness akin to that apparent in Cronenberg's *The Brood* and Amis's *Stanley and the Women*, and it is to be hoped this is a darkness he needs to live through in order to emerge refreshed. The contemporary horror story would be much poorer without the full range of his intelligence and imagination and often audacious originality.

—RAMSEY CAMPBELL

TIM POWERS

The Anubis Gates

Brendan Doyle, an academic and expert on the poet William Ashbless—a contemporary of Coleridge's—is hired by millionaire J. Cochran Darrow to act as an expert guide on a time travel field trip to 1810 in order to attend one of Coleridge's lectures. Once in the past, things go awry and Doyle finds himself lost and caught up in a complex series of plots involving ancient Egyptian gods, sinister travelling showmen, a body-hopping spirit whose victims turn into hairy apes, various literary notables, mad scientists, and a community of artificially created mutants living under the streets of 19th-century London. Among other things, Doyle is tricked into another body and forced to live out the life of the little-known Ashbless, a fictional but convincing character who also figures briefly in James Blaylock's Homunculus *(1985). The* Anubis Gates *is the ideal post-modernist genre novel, at once science fiction, horror, literary fantasy, historical recreation, swashbuckling thriller and comic apocalypse: it was awarded the Philip K. Dick Memorial Award in 1984.*

There is no getting away from the man who invented steampunk. Charles Dickens (1812–70) may not be mentioned by name anywhere in *The Anubis Gates*, but his shaping presence can be felt everywhere in the populous chortling shadows of the London of 1810 to which the 20th-century hero of Tim Powers' time-travel fantasy travels, never to return. It does not much matter that Powers sets his tale in a time Dickens could never have experienced, and of which he never wrote, because novels like *Oliver Twist* (1837–9), which depicts a London not dissimilar to that explored by Brendan Doyle, are a kind of apothesis of the supernatural melodramas popular at the beginning of the 19th century, so that Dickens' Fagin and Powers' Horrabin share a common source in *grand guignol*. Similarly, the Gothic fever-dreams of such writers as Monk Lewis or Charles Maturin can be seen to underpin the oneiric inscapes of the greatest achievements of Dickens—*Bleak House* (1852–3) or *Little Dorrit* (1855–7) or *Our Mutual Friend* (1864–5)—those novels in which the nightmare of London attains lasting and definitive and horrific form. For Dickens that nightmare of London may be a prophetic vision of humanity knotted into the subterranean entrails of the city machine, while for Powers the London of 1810 may be a form of nostalgia, a dream theatre for the elect to star in, buskined and immune; but at the heart of both writers' work glow the lineaments of the last world city.

Between Dickens and Powers, of course, much water has flowed down the filthy Thames. Between steampunk—a term which can be used to describe any sf novel set in any version of the previous century, from which entropy has been banned—and the desolate expressionism of its true founder lies what one might call Babylon-upon-Thames-punk. *Fin de siècle* writers like Robert Louis Stevenson, Arthur Conan Doyle, and G. K. Chesterton attempted to domesticate Dickens' London by transforming it into a kind of Arabian Nights theme park capable of encompassing (and taming) all the strangenesses that an Empire in pullulant decline could possibly import. Even H. G. Wells was sometimes capable of quasi-Dickensian sentiment (as in novels like *Love and Mr Lewisham*, 1900) about the London he more normally destroyed utterly.

That this enterprise of domestication was deeply suspect, most writers of Babylon-upon-Thames-punk knew full well, and as a result much of what they wrote gave off an air of bad-faith complacency, uneasy nostalgia, weird inanition. It is from their doomed enterprise (and from other sources as well) that contemporary steampunk authors like K. W. Jeter and Powers and James Blaylock and others have borrowed not only a vision of a talismanic city, but also (it must be said) some of the complacency and diseased nostalgia of the epigones who thought to tame Dickens.

But there is no getting away from Dickens, and *The Anubis Gates*, despite the occasional chilling Chestertonian whimsy, is radiant with the ambience of his genius. The villains of the piece—like Horrabin, the beggar-king on stilts, half-immolated by the energy of his own self-depiction, or Dog-Faced Joe, or the Spoon-Sized Boys—strut through Powers' pages with a grotesque theatricality that is proudly Dickensian. The geography of London—from the Avernal Thames to the underground cathedrals whose crepuscular Romantic arches evoke thoughts of Henry Fuseli in at least one character—has all the inspired animism of Dickens at his most convinced. And the inturning twists of plot—fumbled, as so often in Dickens, only in the final pages—seem to tell the tale of a country in which anything can happen, and not decay; in which entropy is reversed. This—it must be said—is not the message of Charles Dickens.

An inextricable compact between world and self ordinates the whole of Dickens' work, a rhetoric of entailment. If his London is glowing and corrupt, multitudinous and confining, star-shot and subaqueous, then it is so by reason of the human soul, which it expresses. In *The Anubis Gates*, on the other hand, world and self are carefully separated from one another. As they twist and dance through the long theatre of their tale, Powers' protagonists—Brendan Doyle and Elizabeth Tichy—are like

194

tourists in an enchanted wonderland; they are like readers of *The Anubis Gates*. We do not enter their interior lives, nor are we meant to, and the novel only fails when, by all rights, we *should* come to grips with some soul in extremis, as in the final pages when, after innumerable adventures and scrapes, Doyle is finally tortured to death—or so close to actual death as makes no difference. We hear his screams, but from off-stage. Before he can die of his terrible wounds, the barge of Ra surfaces into the world to encompass his fallen form, and to deliver him, like a new-born child, to the waters of old Father Thames, whole again and baptized. To understand the superflux of implications unleashed at this point, perhaps unwittingly, we must enter Doyle's transfigured mind; but of the resurrection and epiphany of the hero we are tendered nothing but a brief passage of hearsay, offhandedly couched. Powers' strategy has allowed him no choice in the matter.

Terrible monsters do lurk in the cellars of *The Anubis Gates*, and fever-dream hints are dropped of circumstances in which it is possible for the hero truly to die. But after all, steampunk is a form of theodicy, and Powers displaces these intimations of the revolution-and-*Frankenstein*-haunted exterior world on to a harlequinade of magicians and other villains who know their place, generically familiar templates whose attempts to spook England into decline and corruption and despair are constantly thwarted by the invulnerable Adamic Doyle. In externalizing the horrors of the world of change, Powers has invented a tale of paradise, where entropy lies down with the lamb and the steam yachts run on time. In *The Anubis Gates* he has written a book of almost preternatural geniality, a book which it is possible (rare praise) to love. Let us all, it suggests, co-inhabit the Christmas London of Brendan Doyle, and gape like children at the pageant of the world-stage of his triumphs. We do. He is having the time of his life. We join him.

—JOHN CLUTE

89 [1983]

ROBERT IRWIN

The Arabian Nightmare

Cairo, 1486. Dirty Yoll, the story-teller, relates a series of adventures that mainly befall Balian of Norwich, an ostensible pilgrim who has been sent to the Holy Land as a spy for the Franks. Balian encounters Michael Vane, an English alchemist, and his sorcerer colleague, the King of Cats, and comes to suspect that he is suffering from a mysterious, deadly curse, The Arabian Nightmare. Stories unfold within stories, in which talking apes, murderous courtesans, an order of leprous crusaders, insoluable riddles, demons, and curses figure heavily. Yoll dies, but the stories continue, and a plot to bring about the end of the world is uncovered. A dense, witty, erotic, imaginative and macabre fantasy, The Arabian Nightmare *is one of the most original works in its many genres to appear in the '80s. Irwin, a former teacher of medieval history, is also the author of* History of the Mamluk Sultanate of Egypt and Syria *(1984) and a novel about the Wars of the Roses,* The Dreadlord *(1984).*

*T*he Arabian Nightmare is a thoroughly modern fantasy cast in a classical mould. Its literary antecedents are the *Thousand-and-One Nights*, which first came to Europe in the French edition issued between 1704 and 1717, and *The Saragossa Manuscript*, written by the Polish count Jan Potocki and first published (likewise in French) in 1804. Each of these makes use of a discursive and convoluted narrative structure in which tales are embedded within other tales; the first displayed for fascinated Europeans an exotic, mysterious and highly intriguing Eastern world; the second has a most effective recurrent motif in that its hero, who goes to sleep beneath a gallows-tree, is victim of a terrible dream and then awakes, only to find that this awakening is but the first of many illusory moments of relief in a nightmare which will never let him go. Irwin takes up this theme, of a man quite lost in a dream so tortuous he can never be certain that he has awakened, or ever will awake; and populates that dream with the phantasmagoria of that mythical Orient which so obsessed the French Romantic writers of the 19th century. He brings to this task a remarkable freshness, enlivening his consideration of the nature of dreams with ideas drawn from modern psychological inquiry, filling out his marvellous descriptions of 15th-century Cairo and its dream-analogue with detail drawn from the perspective of modern history.

It is typical of such a deceptive scheme that the nightmare into which Balian delivers himself might or might not be the Arabian Nightmare of the title, for that is a nightmare which can never be remembered; each time Balian thinks he awakes, he may reassure himself that he has not, after all, suffered *that* dread fate ... but then, he only *thinks* that he awakes. In much the same way, we are invited to wonder who, within the tale, is its true teller ... but every time we think we know, we are confounded; the text is engaged in a constant game of self-deconstruction which links it to the fancies of those more recent French Romantics, the Barthesian mythologies and Derridaesque post-structuralists.

There never was another tale as self-conscious in its convolutions as this one, and never one which brought the unease of the dream-state into such seductively sinister intercourse with the intelligence of the reader. It is a tale of horror because it reminds us, unremittingly, of the precariousness of our identity in the face of a world whose solidity and predictability might at any moment dissolve, and abandon us to be rent upon the rack of our anxieties. And yet, even while he taunts and undermines us with this cognitive vertigo, Irwin writes with great charm and suave wit, and almost compels us to believe that in nightmare—though nightmare it is—there is such wonder and such plenitude as would make a fool of any man who preferred jejune reality. There is no greater achievement at which the literary fantasist might aim.

—BRIAN STABLEFORD

90 [1984]

IAIN BANKS

The Wasp Factory

Frank, the sixteen year-old narrator, lives on an island off the coast of Scotland. Between accounts of his militarist fantasies—which involve murdering various animals—and various forays to the pub with his midget best friend, Frank reminisces about his farcical killings of his cousins Blyth and Esmerelda and his younger brother Paul. Meanwhile, Frank's unbalanced brother Eric has escaped from an institution and is travelling back to the island. Castrated, as he has been told by his reclusive father, in infancy by a dog, Frank makes discoveries about himself that exceed in strangeness anything that has gone before in his life. Iain Banks followed up this extraordinary and controversial first novel—typically, British readers were more offended by the cruelty to animals than the murdering of children— with the equally strange Walking on Glass *(1985) and* The Bridge *(1986).*

*T*he Wasp Factory was Iain Banks' first novel, and became an immediate literary *cause célèbre* on its first publication in 1984. Reactions ranged from extravagant praise to expressions of baffled disgust. It is debatable whether or not *The Wasp Factory* is a horror novel—it is not fuelled by any vision of a malign universe, or any sense of Evil—but it certainly fixes on horrific incidents, and it has found a

197

following among horror readers. Banks has published several books since, ranging from a rock-'n'-roll novel (*Espedair Street*) to an extravagant space opera (*Consider Phlebas*), but though they have generally been well received, and in some cases have reached the bestseller list, none has had quite the impact of *The Wasp Factory*.

The novel is set in the present day on a small Scottish island connected by a bridge to the mainland. The only inhabitants are the teenage narrator, Frank Cauldhame, and his eccentric ex-hippie father. Frank apparently suffered a bizarre accident when only three: he was attacked by the family sheepdog, which bit off his genitals. When he was five he murdered his cousin by placing an adder inside his artificial leg, and before he was ten he also killed his younger brother Paul (whom he persuaded to attack an unexploded bomb with a plank) and his cousin Esmerelda (attached to a giant kite and never seen again). Each of the deaths was seen as a bizarre accident, and Frank tells us that this was just a phase he was going through at the time.

By contrast his older half-brother Eric was a good-natured and idealistic child, who went away to study medicine, only to be sent insane by the discovery in a hospital ward of an infant child whose brain was being eaten alive by maggots (a fly having got under the metal plate in its skull). Eric took to feeding worms to children and setting dogs on fire, and was institutionalized. The novel's plot (such as it is) is triggered by Eric's escape: Frank's account to the reader of his life is punctuated by Eric's deranged phone calls as he gets nearer the island.

Since Frank gave up murder his defences against the rest of the world have taken the form of a bizarre series of rituals and totems: animal heads mounted on 'Sacrifice Poles' around the island; a kind of temple in a Second World War bunker whose altarpiece is the skull of the dog which unmanned him; and the Wasp Factory itself, an elaborate construction centred on an old clock face, in which wasps are murdered (depending on which way they wander) in any one of a dozen different ways, which are interpreted by Frank much as an astrologer or tarot reader would interpret signs. The ritual murder of small animals is another essential part of Frank's invented symbol system for understanding and guarding himself against the world.

This may sound absurd in summary, but the novel's strength is that it pursues its central character's obsessions unflinchingly, and never steps outside Frank's skull to allow in conventional reality or perception. Its weakest moment is its denouement, where we learn that Frank's father has been lying to him all his life: he isn't a mutilated boy, but a more or less normal girl, dosed with male hormones by his father, partly as an experiment, partly as a sort of practical joke. The problem with this is that it reduces the situation from an obsessional reality to a puzzle with a solution—which ties up the novel, but is less interesting than what has gone before.

Still, *The Wasp Factory* is a remarkably sustained performance; for all the grotesquerie of its content Frank's narrative is written with tight control and a notable absence of sensationalism, and is sometimes very funny. Unsurprisingly, one of its greatest admirers is J. G. Ballard, himself probably the foremost chronicler of obsession in contemporary British fiction; like Ballard's *Crash*, Banks' novel shows the power of obsession to reform the world in its own distorted image.

—MALCOLM EDWARDS

91 [1984]

T. E. D. KLEIN

The Ceremonies

Academic Jeremy Friers spends the summer in Gilead, N.Y., renting a house on the Poroth Farm, preparing to teach a course in supernatural literature. Along with Carol Conklin, a girl he has recently met, and the dourly religious Sarr and Deborah Poroth, Friers is manipulated by the Old One, a sorcerer who hopes to bring about the return to Earth of an unimaginably vast and evil entity. The four characters are tricked into taking part in a series of obscure rituals that pave the way for the return of the monster. Elaborating upon the habitual themes of Arthur Machen and H. P. Lovecraft, Klein here delves deep into folklore and literary history to provide a richly detailed variation on the Return of the Elder Gods theme. The novel grew upon the skeleton of the story originally published as 'The Events at Poroth Farm' (1974). Klein has since worked similar shivers in his collection of novellas, Dark Gods (1985), which also deal with the connections between godhood, monstrousness and the artistic imagination.

*T*he Ceremonies is a carefully wrought book, excelling in the areas of characterization, style, and plot.

Klein assumes a leisurely pace in introducing and fleshing out the principle characters in his book. No sketches or convenient labels here—you get to know everyone thoroughly and believably. The protagonists become warm, likeable friends and the villain slowly assumes a mantle of wonderful despicability.

The beauty of this gradual process is achieved through a style and structure which adds layer upon layer of awareness into the story. Klein

199

steadily apprises the reader of the enormity of the evil waiting to engulf
our world, but he leaves out just enough to keep things enigmatic,
unfamiliar. For a long time, you know there is something terrible about
to happen, but you are never told the particulars. By keeping things
mysterious, Klein achieves a subtle momentum, which carries you
through the novel effectively as any collection of cheap narrative tricks
encountered in many commercially oriented novels. His style is an
interesting combination of both modern and traditional elements used in
the telling of a supernatural tale.

But it is the plot of *The Ceremonies* which most marks it as a
distinctive novel. The historical and literary references to the work of
Arthur Machen give the story an authentic feel, a true legitimacy. The
idea of a cyclic structure for catastrophe and apocalyptic resolution,
while not new in horror fiction, is given new meaning in Klein's tale.
While there are resonances with Lovecraft's Cthulhu Mythos and even
the Bible, there are also references to other far more arcane belief-
systems and world-views. Klein creates a conception of the world which
comprises the simplest terms of Absolute Good and Absolute Evil, but
he also suggests a hideously complex set of rules which govern the
Universe as it chugs merrily along towards its ultimate fate. In essence,
the plot of *The Ceremonies* is unique. It is shot full of menace and a
looming sense of inevitability which suggests that Evil is never successfully vanquished. The book's final image of a great and hideous force in
the earth is extremely powerful and, for me at least, unforgettable.

The Ceremonies is a book of many levels. It depends as much on
philosophy as it does on suspense. It is written with a standard of craft
and care rarely seen in the horror and dark fantasy genres, and deserves
recognition as modern classic.

—THOMAS F. MONTELEONE

92 [1984]

ROBERT HOLDSTOCK

Mythago Wood

*Just after the Second World War, Steven Huxley returns to the Gloucester
countryside where he grew up. He discovers that his brother Christian has
inherited their father's obsession with Ryhope Wood, a vast tract of primal*

forest he believes to be inhabited by 'mythagos'. These are folkloric archetypes created by the collective imaginings of the human race, who are compelled to live and relive their legends. Christian disappears into the wood, and Steven sets off after him with the lovely mythago Guiwenneth and ex-flier Harry Keeton in tow. Within the woods, Steven encounters a giant demon pig, Robin Hood, a First World War battlefield mythago, among other creatures, before he confronts his brother in a Neolithic village. Expanded from Holdstock's 1981 Magazine of Science Fiction and Fantasy *novella,* Mythago Wood *is a fantasy adventure story and an examination of the roots of England's rich native mythology. It won the 1985 World Fantasy Award for Best Novel. Holdstock has since returned to the Ryhope Wood with* Lavondyss *(1988).*

There is a type of English fantasy story which for me holds a special fascination. It can loosely be described, I suppose, as the 'haunted wood' fantasy. The haunted wood is that place where England's most ancient history impinges upon the modern world, where prehistoric spirits still live, sometimes yearning for their old power in the world, sometimes merely content to be left alone to hide from the new creatures, the human creatures, whose religions and realities have overwhelmed their own. In the haunted wood magic still persists. Sometimes it is little more than a faint aura, a hint of what it once was. Sometimes it is concentrated, merely awaiting the right catalyst to set it loose, to wreak revenge upon those who opposed it, imprisoned it or sent it into hiding.

Various authors have produced fine examples of this kind of story. Machen, Blackwood and Buchan spring immediately to mind, as well as E. F. Benson, M. R. James and several other outstanding English horror writers. For me, Barrie's *Dear Brutus* has much of the atmosphere I have described.

In recent years, however, only Robert Holdstock has been able to recreate this special *frisson* for me, in his marvellous fantasy *Mythago Wood*.

Mythago Wood has much of the feel of a classic horror story, both in its elegant style and in its choice of form. Holdstock uses traditional devices to draw us into his tale—mysterious activities, leaves torn from a journal, cryptic letters, discovered objects—until slowly we are as hooked, as obsessed with curiosity, as the protagonists themselves. By the time we begin our expedition into the magic wood we share the same compulsions to searh for the truth.

Again, as in the very best stories of this kind, the truth is not immediately definable. Indeed Holdstock uses all these traditional devices to his own ends, to discuss the nature of our perceptions, of our understanding of what truth actually is. While with one hand he offers us an answer to a mystery, an explanation for certain events, identification of shadowy characters, with the other he compounds the mysteries. With every revelation comes a fresh doubt until by the end of the novel we know a great deal about Mythago Wood but are left with an entirely new set of questions. Some of these, one hopes, will be answered in the author's follow-up, *Lavondyss*.

The story concerns two generations of the Huxley family, who live at Oak Lodge, an old country house situated at the edge of three square miles of post-Ice Age forest known as Ryhope Wood and which, by chance, has been left uncleared, undeveloped and largely unexplored for centuries. The sons, somewhat embittered with their father, who tended to ignore them and their mother in favour of his obsession with the wood and its 'mythago' inhabitants, are gradually also hooked on the wood's mysteries. Their father's journals and letters provide some of the narrative, while the younger brother Steven's first-person story provides most of the rest.

The wood has a cryptic geography. Its boundaries expand the deeper one goes into it; it seems impossible ever to reach the far side. Within it dwell the 'mythagos'—whole tribes, whole civilizations, as well as individuals, representing the British racial unconscious. Familiar figures of myth and legend exist here, frequently in their purest or most primitive personae—Hern the Hunter, King Arthur, Robin Hood and many others—while the explorer is apt to come upon the ruins of a Tudor manor farm, a Celtic stone fort or an 11th-century castle. And meanwhile, wandering the trails of this infinite place, are men and women, some 'real' and some little more than memories, following desires and urges which even they are scarcely able to describe or define. It is a dangerous place, the mythago wood, where it is perfectly possible for an explorer to be cut down by a Stone Age axe or a Bronze Age sword, to be killed by warriors brought into reality by his own racial memory. These archetypes as described by Holdstock have all the power that genuine archetypes should possess. Even the woman whom Steven falls in love with and who, it seems, falls in love with him, probably has only as much substance as his own longings can provide.

The genuine pathos of Holdstock's love story again has similarities with the theme of *Dear Brutus* and its heroine's desperate final cry that she does not want to be a 'might have been'. Holdstock avoids the sentimentality which some detect in Barry by offering us tougher questions, moral dilemmas, an imagined world far more complex than anything found in the wood's precursors. For me, this is the outstanding fantasy book of the 1980s; something to read several times and to rediscover the same delight with every new reading.

—MICHAEL MOORCOCK

MICHAEL BISHOP

Who Made Stevie Crye?

Mary Stevenson ('Stevie') Crye, a young widow trying to make a living as a freelance writer, faces a crisis when her typewriter breaks down. The machine is repaired by Seaton Benecke, a strange young man whose pet/familiar is a sinister capuchin monkey, but it develops the habit of writing on its own, interrupting the narrative with its own additions, side-tracks, dreams and nightmares. Stevie tries to deal with the havoc wrought by the typewriter's imaginings, and becomes convinced that Seaton is horribly involved in what is happening to her. She also retaliates by becoming a writer of fiction herself, and twisting her real life into a fairytale, 'The Monkey's Bride'. The punch line is a black joke twisting the cliché of the infinite number of monkeys with the infinite number of typewriters. Best known for his idiosyncratic science fiction, which includes A Funeral for the Eyes of Fire *(1975) and* And Strange at Ectaban the Trees *(1976), Michael Bishop here enters the horror genre with a playful, incisive, tricksy novel. Its impact is considerably enhanced by the photographic illustrations of J. K. Potter.*

Although contemporary horror at its best is a true home for valid insights into the psychopathology of modern life as well as for genuine experimental writing, yet many ghastly events in horror novels are fundamentally absurd if you stop to think. The writerly trick is to persuade readers through mimesis, compelling style, and tension (alias fear) not to think with their reason, their day-mind, but with their night-mind, their dream-mind. The ludicrous still peeps through, and some of the most effective grotesque horror (such as Stephen King's) actually uses and forefronts the joky ludicrous—before ripping the carpet of hilarity and sanity away again to commit abominations.

Who Made Stevie Crye? had a rough ride to publication, being bounced by big American commercial houses as impossible to classify, hence difficult to market. That was because it is a unique parody of the horror genre itself, funny, savage, and compellingly believable rather than flipply comic. Thanks to Jim Turner, astute editor at Arkham House, *Stevie* finally appeared from that vintage source of Lovecraftiana, native home of cherished genre horrors predating the mass cloning of schlock horror—there to be graced with notably more elegant production than most books.

Stevie is more than parody. It's meta-horror, perhaps the first application of meta-fiction to horror. It's a fiction which self-consciously constructs itself and critiques itself, and its adoptive genre; wherein the heroine's scary, hallucinatory experiences are written for her by a spooked typewriter, and where a delirious melting of reality occurs akin to Philip Dick's weirdest sf drug-fugues, terminating in the philosophic surrealism of a team of monkeys tapping typewriters in the attic.

En route, delicious moments of parody abound, both chilling and archly wry, such as Cujo's vehicle siege re-enacted by a goofy basset hound whose dementia is that of 'a desperate rush-hour commuter'. Ludic metaphors proliferate as part of the roguish, folksy, though also hyper-literate tone. 'Where were today's Faulkners?' complains Stevie after wading through book reviews of such titles as *Afterbirth* and *Shudderville*, irked by the spectre of writers 'whoring' into horror for the big bucks. This possible angry motive for undertaking *Stevie* is quite transcended by the author's humour, elegance, serious playfulness, and love, an alchemic transmutation of gut-themes into artistic gold.

Yet *Stevie* is truly scary, and the story makes pungent psychological sense even as it swallows its own tail (and tale). It is also decent and empathic, with believable, quirky, three-dimensional, Southern small town characters, especially Stevie herself, courageous, sad, bitterly good-humoured, whose reality may be torn apart, though her flesh and sanity are not ripped. 'Not merely horrifying but fundamentally contemptuous of civilized human feeling', is the comment on the hexed typewriter's narrative of Stevie's loved daughter melted in bed, the slasher side of horror; an important distinction, this. As for salvation, the repair of the daughter's gutted toys by the little girl in trance—out of parodied Disney as much as *Poltergeist*—is glossed by the motherly black roadside prophetess as a product of 'subliterary paranormal energies'.

Here is a humane, trickster kaleidoscope questioning a genre and a market, and fiction, and reality too—yet exquisitely spiced with human reality—and delivering the eerie chill of the occult and the illicit, curdling the blood but also warming the heart.

—IAN WATSON

DAN SIMMONS

Song of Kali

American poet Robert Luczak arrives in Calcutta, with his Indian wife and baby daughter, to meet Bengali poet M. Das, who has long been thought dead, and pick up for publication Das' latest work, an epic poem cycle about the goddess Kali. Although he is given the poem, various sinister forces prevent him initially from meeting Das, and he is told by a renegade member of the Kalipalakas, the Kali cult, that the poet is indeed dead and has been brought back to life by the evil goddess in order that he write a celebration of her which will spread her malign influence throughout the world. Although he disbelieves the story, Luczak presses his contacts to arrange a meeting with Das, and his encounter with what remains of the poet has tragic consequences for his family and perhaps the world. The winner of a World Fantasy Award, Song of Kali is a rich and evocative novel. Subsequently, F. Paul Wilson's The Tomb (1985) and Noel Scanlon's Black Ashes (1986) have echoed its themes, suggesting the presence of an Indian trend within modern horror.

Song of Kali is a finely crafted novel of psychological terror in which overt supernatural elements figure but subtly. The author's aim is to construct a crucible in which human toleration for and ability to deal with violence can be dissected. As an experimental laboratory in which the human psyche can be 'tested to destruction', modern India works just fine.

Sense of place, of *location*, is paramount in much horror fiction. It lies at the very core of *Song of Kali*. Simmons' novel demonstrates the horrendous effect setting has upon the human soul. It is an exactingly constructed, brutal, and uncompromising study of the degree to which an evil place may permeate and steep all that makes us human.

Song of Kali is set in modern Calcutta, where the author depicts a teeming, festering metropolis far darker and more sinister than any dozen Gothic castles. The novel begins, 'Some places are too evil to be allowed to exist. Some *cities* are too wicked to be suffered.'

In precise, darkly lyrical detail, Simmons delineates an urban horror story in which the city itself is the monster. That Calcutta is so vividly realized is an astonishing literary feat. Simmons spent ten weeks traveling through India on a Fulbright Fellowship tour. He spent a grand total of two and a half days in Calcutta. To attempt to write a major novel on so complex a subject after so brief an experience would seem, for most writers, to be the height of presumption. Apparently Simmons was exposed to precisely the right stimuli. He was powerfully struck by the suppurating urban environment in which he became immersed.

He came away from the city with voluminous notebooks filled with details, most valuable of which was a book of sketches (Simmons is a graphic artist as well as a writer). He took copious notes on such experiences as meeting with the Bengali poet P. Lal, a protégé of Tagore. Lal became an inspiration for the novel's mysterious poet, M. Das.

While the exotic and powerfully realized setting is integral to the events which befall Simmons' hapless journalist protagonist, it is not the sole outstanding attribute to which the novel lays claim. *Song of Kali*, while much honored and admired, has not met with universal acclaim from its readers. The reason seems to be that some come away from the novel not only disappointed by what Simmons seems to be saying, but actively resistant to the author's thesis.

The book's horrendous climax at first seems to revolve around protagonist Robert Luczak's discovery that his infant daughter has been murdered solely for the purpose of stuffing the child with contraband gems to be smuggled out of India. Luczak and his wife do what has to be done to return the corpse of their child home for burial. Little is done—or perhaps *can* be done about the killers. The second climax comes soon after in the book when Luczak, letting himself be swept into the seductive maelstrom of Kali's violent song, buys a gun and impulsively returns to India, bent on revenge.

This is potentially the stuff of melodrama. Fortunately the author no more yields to the siren call of cheap and exploitative violence than does his protagonist. Much along the line of the similar moral choice posed in David Morrell's *Testament*, Robert makes a conscious determination at the final moment not to opt for violence as a tactic. No Rambo, Robert Luczak. He discards his pistol and flies home to his wife and, ultimately, his new family. The insidious seduction of the death goddess has been spurned by a conscious moral act.

This is not, it would seem, a wide-screen, Technicolor crowd pleaser. But it does reify the stance of a psychologically violent novel about a violent society as a defensible and indisputably moral work of art.

—EDWARD BRYANT

CLIVE BARKER

The Damnation Game

Convict Marty Strauss is offered parole on the condition that he takes a job as bodyguard with multi-millionaire Joseph Whitehead. Whitehead has made a fortune through his association with Mamoulian, an immortal Faust-turned-Mephistopheles who now wants to back out of the bargain he has made. Strauss and Whitehead's daughter Carys are caught up in the struggle between the tycoon and the human monster, and realize that something apocalyptic is in the offing. Meanwhile, Mamoulian's zombie associate Breer—The Razor Eater—lurks threateningly in the background, and a pair of comic relief American evangelists are co-opted into the service of Evil. Clive Barker's dense and complicated first novel is a variant on the themes of Dr Faustus and Melmoth the Wanderer, and established him as one of the genre's leading lights.

The book opens with an extraordinarily perceptive description of Warsaw in the Second World War, ravaged and mutilated, a dreadful, devastated landscape, a microcosmic hell. It is just such a terrain that Clive Barker traverses so painstakingly in his work, a terrain that is both provocative and dangerous. Yet it is a mark of his skill that he does so without falling into the trap that has claimed so many of his contemporaries, that of self-indulgence, the cult of the cheap thrill. Although his reputation has inevitably grown to some extent around obvious hype, his work cuts far below the surface of superficial ugliness and violence to expose deeper layers of human suffering beneath. In *The Damnation Game* he is uncompromising and ruthless in his examination of the human condition, and the result is at once electrifying, horrifying and compelling.

There are five meticulously drawn principal characters, each interlinking in the Damnation Game scenario, which is their own personal Apocalypse, the torment they endure as a result of their own sin. 'Everything's chance,' says Marty Strauss, a gambler and thief who has sacrificed all he possessed to feed his hunger. On parole from prison, he is to act as bodyguard to the multi-millionaire Joseph Whitehead, whose huge empire grew up from his own scavenging, gambling days in the Warsaw of the opening scenes. Whitehead tells Marty that there is no external God, and no Hell: there is only our own appetite, to which we are all slaves, although there is always a price. Our soul is the stake in this Game.

In *The Damnation Game* this retribution is largely epitomized by Mamoulian, the self-styled Last European, who is many things: the personification of our worst fears and our darkest desires, guilt incarnate, the very Devil. He is almost vampiric in his power, able to raise the dead, forcing them to serve him without a shred of compassion, torturing and manipulating to satisfy his own insatiable greed. His main servant is the resurrected Breer, the Razor-Eater, whose gradual disintegration is both appalling and pitiful, his guilt eating into him physically, cancer-like. Breer is one of the most remarkable creations in modern fiction, his humanity, though like his body victim to damnation, giving him a dimension that makes him far more abhorrent than any vampire or demon.

It is against Mamoulian that Marty has to pit himself, gradually realizing that this is no ordinary opponent, but one of supernatural magnitude. Whitehead's daughter, Carys, controlled by her decadent father through heroin, is also the victim of the Game, and Marty finds in his love for her a fresh purpose, a will to break free of the impending Deluge.

Clive Barker draws on the human fears of his creations, their frailties (fear of loneliness, of age, of death) as well as the more visceral terrors, exposing them to the nerve equally as effectively. The physical horrors are at times obscene, though the book is designed to shock, to put before us the excesses of the psyche, the darkside of the soul. There may not be an external Creator, but built into us, Barker asserts, is a leveller, and we are the instruments of our own judgement, our own executioners.

Like Kubrick's *Clockwork Orange*, *The Damnation Game* faces us with truths we may not want to know: it is not a book to be taken lightly.

—ADRIAN COLE

96   [1985]

PETER ACKROYD

Hawksmoor

In the early 18th century, Nicholas Dyer, an architect and associate of Sir Christopher Wren and Sir John Vanbrugh, is commissioned to design and erect seven churches around London. Dyer, who has made an ambiguously Faustian bargain with a man named Mirabilis, uses his churches to write a mystic design across the map of the city. In the late 20th century, a series of murders by strangulation are taking place in Dyer's churches, baffling the police. Inspector Nicholas Hawksmoor, whose life parallels Dyer's in many details, becomes obsessively interested in the case, to the dismay of his superiors. Hawksmoor is certain that an answer lies among the city's vagrant population and within the walls of the churches. Peter Ackroyd's Whitbread Award-winning novel is a dazzling mix of literary pastiche, historical recreation, subtle ghost story and metaphysical detective story. Ackroyd is a novelist, historian and biographer whose other subjects include Oscar Wilde, T. S. Eliot, Thomas Chatterton and the Great Fire of London.

In the company of 99 horror novels, an appreciation of Peter Ackroyd's *Hawksmoor* could simply linger over its catalogue of horrors, for it offers horrors aplenty both of the flesh and of the spirit. The awful things limned therein, brutality and madness lapped in ordure, are but surface eruptions, however, signals of more truly awe-full mysteries.

For indeed, *Hawksmoor* is a Mystery in the archaic sense, embracing as it does a sense of the writer's craft cunningly displayed while hinting at more arcane matters, for this Mystery is not least a sombre meditation on the occult in all shades of meaning. More than one genre mingles in the overall design, police procedural and historical melding with supernatural horror; each follows its own receipts yet the whole transcends its parts, attaining a literary form splendidly *sui generis*.

Ackroyd has an authentic genius for literary pastiche, best demonstrated in Dyer's confessions, which restore in vivid Baroque prose the full 'Terrour and Magnificence' of Augustan London. The cold austerity of the modern passages corresponds accordingly to Hawksmoor's bleak alienation, but his London remains one with Dyer's, a haunted labyrinth where past and present flow into one another in intricate patterns of recurrence.

Many voices clamour therein, addressing the author's concerns; one that rather speaks through him is T. S. Eliot, most clearly in the obsession with physical corruption, coupled with sexual loathing, and the vision of London as a 'whited sepulchre'. Images and events, be they a catch phrase, a murdered child's name, even a plot twist, echo across the centuries, as do subtler adumbrations of character, in a psychotic tramp's sufferings and, more significantly, in the duality of Dyer/Hawksmoor. Within this skein of resonances stand fixed constants: Dyer's churches, built by the Light of Reason to celebrate Darkness.

Ackroyd's novel is itself a masterpiece of construction opening on many perspectives, yet though he lets the arguments of Reason shine, the Shaddowes are not dispelled. Senseless horrors, too, remain constant in Time. Time is, indeed, the essence of the Mystery, the contemplation of an unfathomable void. This is truly a work of suspense, for even as the author cunningly unfolds the pattern of the Mystery by degrees, he reveals the surrounding Abyss without illuminating its depths. *Hawksmoor* is much more than an intellectual entertainment, however. Its power, and greatness, lie not so much in brilliant technique as in sombre tone.

If there is a coda to *Hawksmoor*, then Dyer states it early on when he declares 'There is no Light without Darkness, and no Substance without Shaddowe.' A Metaphysical melancholy pervades the work, and more than this, deep tragedy in the suffering of its lost souls, caught in the unseen meshes of time. There is much irony, but little humour in *Hawksmoor*, save that as black as night.

Indeed, the Darkness so overwhelms *Hawksmoor* as to exceed even Ackroyd's stated intentions, fashioning a Dark Glass in which we the readers see ourselves, each caught in Time like ants in amber. Such Shaddowes as these pall the lowest depths of filth and cruelty; if this is not horror, I do not know the meaning of the word.

—R. S. HADJI

97   [1986]

LISA TUTTLE

A Nest of Nightmares

Although it includes the author's first published story, 'Stranger in the House' (1972), this collection consists mainly of short horror stories written between 1980 and 1985. Lisa Tuttle's speciality is domestic terror, frequently with a feminist slant, focusing on families breaking up, women under pressure and the insidious intrusion of supernatural evil into an already fractured normality. The pieces, many of which originally appeared in The Magazine of Fantasy and Science Fiction *and* The Twilight Zone Magazine *include 'Bug House', 'Dollburger', 'Flying to Byzantium', 'The Horse Lord', 'The Other Mother', 'A Friend in Need', 'Sun City' and 'The Nest'.*

I had always thought of Lisa Tuttle as a science fiction writer—until I read 'The Nest': in manuscript form, at the 1981 Milford writer's workshop. 'The Nest' is now the final story in Lisa's 'horror' collection, *A Nest of Nightmares*. One of its two nightmare images is the glimpsed figure of something manlike, black, and flapping like a garbage bag, a figure which appears from, and disappears into, the roof of Pamela's newly acquired, ramshackle country house; it seems to be constructing a vast nest out of detritus in the loft. At the end of the workshop session on the story, fellow writer Garry Kilworth re-entered the room wearing nothing but a black dustbin-liner, with appropriate head and arm holes. He leapt into Lisa's lap; she made nervous sounds. It was a very funny moment; it was also one of the most horrifying sights I have ever seen. That said, the spectacle was nowhere near as disturbing as the story itself.

In 'The Nest', the 'monster' never appears on full stage. Everything that happens, or appears to be happening in the attic, is glimpsed out of the corner of an eye, or from a distant hill; Pam's sister Sylvia, who has agreed to share the house, is drawn to the loft, to the nest of rubbish, to the creature, but what happens to her there is reflected only in the sounds of her body being rhythmically moved against that attic's creaking floorboards. This is extremely effective and the stories in A Nest of Nightmares are, on the whole, strong, scary and impressive for just this controlled use of nightmare imagery.

Lisa Tuttle is a writer who moulds *tension* to create the effect of horror, rather than shaping direct and horrific narrative image. And that tension is expertly drawn not just from the interaction of the main character with the supernatural but also by focusing on the main character and her 'real-time' agonies. Nearly all the stories in the collection are centred around women. Nearly all the women are in pain. The pain is real, realistic and recognizable. Few of the characters are happy in their personal lives: men have left them; they have left men; fiancés are fickle; dreams of sharing a new house founder on the question of privacy in life; one-parent families have career difficulties and guiltily acknowledge that they are neglecting their children ('The Other Mother'); suitors turn out to be corpses ('Need'); hosts in far-off, lonely towns become dedicated to belittling their author-guest out of simple jealousy ('Flying to Byzantium').

Add a secondary supernatural element: horses possessed by ancient shaman forces ('The Horse Lord'); Celtic goddesses, complete with boar avatars, who fulfil neglected children's needs ('The Other Mother'); dark men who prowl the house at night stealing dolls for nourishment ('Dollburger'), and you have a collection of stories that work on level after level, teasing out recognition of childhood (in particular those awful family mythologies which can be so frightening to a child), fear of the unknown, and guilty acknowledgement of familiar weaknesses in our own personal lives.

This is horror at its best because it addresses more than the supernatural. It is good horror, too, because it acknowledges that nightmares are real only in a simple, subjective dimension. There *are* no ghosts, no living corpses, no skin-robed spirits of old ('Sun City'), no worlds created from imagination in which the imaginer gets trapped ('Flying to Byzantium') ... not for *you* or *me* ... but there *are* for the fevered, oppressed minds that might create them. Which is why 'The Nest' and 'The Other Mother' stand out so well as elegant psychological studies of disturbed minds: the attic, with its pile of rubbish, has become a haven for Sylvia, away from the cloying dependency of her older sibling; the white goddess is an actualizing of the guilt that has been so well suppressed by a mother's selfishness.

The stories in *A Nest of Nightmares* work on a variety of levels, and are deeply disturbing.

—ROBERT HOLDSTOCK

98 [1986]

CHARLES L. GRANT

The Pet

—

Ashford, New Jersey. Donald 'Duck' Boyd, a mixed-up adolescent, discovers that he has the power to wish into existence the animals whose pictures cover his bedroom walls. When Don faces down The Howler, a homicidal maniac who murders only teenagers, he manages to summon up a huge stallion who tramples the killer to death. Don takes the credit and briefly becomes a local hero, but is still subject to intensive persecution at school. His notoriety only gives the community's bullies another incentive to pick on him, and his parents—his father is also his high school principal, which adds to the all-round awkwardness of his situation—consistently fail to understand his problems. As his home and school life becomes unbearable, the stallion returns to carry out Don's increasingly angry and violent wishes. Although obviously influenced by the plot and background details of Stephen King's Carrie, *Grant cites Bill Forsyth's film* Gregory's Girl, *a somewhat gentler picture of confused teenagers, as the inspiration for the novel.*

Once in a while a real blockbuster of a horror novel hits the bookstalls. *The Pet* falls into this category and it is one of the few books in recent years which has left a lasting impression with me. Sometimes the 'big' book with its hype and 500 or so pages does not live up to its reputation; all too often size seems to be the criterion and when one gets down to reading it one is sadly disillusioned. The work is

212

padded out for the sake of it and instead of a scary bedtime read guaranteed to give you nightmares it soon has your eyelids closing, and more than likely you will wake up the next morning, tread on the book as you leap out of bed and try to remember where you got to. You can't because it is but a hazy memory of incidents unrelated to the main theme and in all probability you won't try again. But not *The Pet*, you won't sleep over this one because you won't be able to put it down until you have finished it, and when you have finally reached page 343 you won't dare to sleep!

It would be unfair to the reader for me to dwell too much on the plot; suffice to say that the Howler, a Jack the Ripper-type killer who murders teenagers, has moved into the village of Ashford, New Jersey. I think that a small community as a setting for any book has a greater impact than a city one. If the author has done his job, and Grant certainly has, you feel that you are part of that small community, an unseen observer, and there is always the lurking fear that the Howler might seek YOU out!

Grant is also a master of the sudden unexpected shock, a vital ingredient in any horror novel; however gruesome a book, however shocking, that necessary element is lacking if the next move is telegraphed. There is plenty in this book to make you jump, however hardened a reader of the horror genre you are.

I bought *The Pet* for two reasons. First, I am an admirer of Charles L. Grant's work and guessed it would be good. Secondly, I had enjoyed *Pet Sematary* by Stephen King and the word 'pet' had suddenly taken on a new meaning for me. Of course, there is no similarity between the two books—I did not for one moment expect there to be—but I suspected that Grant's novel might just top my league of favourite horror novels.

The characterization is strong and the reader at once identifies with the characters. It could all just as easily be happening to YOU, not to some silhouette who flits in and out of situations and you don't even know what he or she looks like. You know them almost as well as you know yourself, and their terror becomes very much your terror.

The style is appealing. Grant's short sentences create a sense of pace. The whole atmosphere of a book can be lost if the style is pedestrian. If a lengthy book is racy then it will grip you because the author has not had to pad it out. He has not needed to; the plot is full, there is no room for irrelevant sub-plots. We move on from one macabre scene to the next with barely a pause for breath.

Today's horror readership is discerning. Gone are the days when a mediocre novel could go to a reprint. Only the best is acceptable and *The Pet* is certainly among the front-runners. Having finished reading it, I was left with much to think about. Uneasy thoughts. But that's the way it should be.

—GUY N. SMITH

ROBERT McCAMMON

Swan Song

***

America, after a cataclysmic nuclear war. Swan, a scarred nine-year-old, has mystic powers which could provide a new hope for the ravaged world. However 'Friend', an evil force who can assume many forms, is out to prevent Swan from saving anyone. Swan and 'Friend' both pick up allies and associates, with ex-wrestler Josh and bag-lady Sister Creep opting to fight for Good, and Colonel Macklin, a rabid militarist, and Roland Croniger, a young man with delusions of knightly splendour, on the side of Evil. Longer even than Stephen King's similarly themed The Stand, Swan Song *is an epic which combines nuclear nightmare with fantastical adventure, and is McCammon's most ambitious work to date.*

R obert Bloch once wrote that the most frightening thing was 'the clown at midnight', the smiling face of innocence hiding whatever evil we care to imagine. *Swan Song* is in several ways a novel about masks: the mask of make-believe society under which man tries to hide what he has done to the world and himself, and the mutation mask nine-year-old Sue Wanda ('Swan') grows on her mutilated face, turning her into an abomination. Meet the adversaries for the final Armageddon: a sick nine-year-old who is slowly changing into a monster, and is aided by a group of weird characters, and a sadistic and utterly crazy creature which acts like a clown. Good survives under a mask of horror, while Evil wears a clown's mask: the Man with the Scarlet Eye, the Man with Many Faces, our old friend Satan himself.

Robert R. McCammon has taken on the most ambitious theme of dark fantasy: the ultimate confrontation of Good and Evil, using mankind as pawns. A theme worked to death by countless others, but McCammon manages to make it something unique and special, keeping his readers entranced through all the 956 small-print pages of this meganovel of multiple disaster. There are hundreds of plot twists, but what keeps the reader turning the pages is the way McCammon blends mood and atmosphere with characters which are alive, no matter how bizarre they are.

The post-nuclear war setting has its drawbacks: some of the situations are familiar stuff (the Survivalists, the warring armies, the crazies and cultists), but McCammon manages to give new flavour to old concepts, and turn them into something original. The occult themes (the powers of the spiked ring, the mental communication by 'dreamwalking', all leading to the quest of Swan and her friends) are developed parallel with the more 'realistic' adventures and horrors in the post-war societies.

McCammon shows all his strength in characterization: the first several hundred pages show us the cataclysm and destruction, including some really remarkable scenes, but mainly they serve to introduce the many people who will aid Swan unselfishly, unaware of the importance of what they are doing. These are scenes of great power, tragedy and compassion, but also scenes of utter horror: McCammon doesn't shy away from graphic descriptions, and some are real stomach-turners. *Swan Song* may be called fantasy or even sf, but it delivers more than its share of gory horror and straight terror. The survivors first have to learn to stay alive, and then learn that survival alone means nothing if it means losing their humanity, compassion and hope.

This feeling extends itself to the adversary: the Man with Many Faces (who is never really called Satan) is evil incarnate, and he knows it. This gives him his power: a terrifying shape-changing being, feeding on its own insane hatred of mankind. At the same time, however, this self-knowledge hurts him, constantly showing him what he can never be, and this makes this sociopathic and murderous creature at the same time a pathetic, sad and lonely being.

When Swan's change is completed and the mask goes off her face, we not only witness a symbolic revelation of the beauty of the 'inner face' of mankind, but also a mystical transformation which transcends her humanity. The very earth becomes a real power which cleans itself of the horrors inflicted by the stupidity of mankind. This is utter abomination to the Man with Many Faces: no longer is he just fighting his old opponent (there are a few references to his past, and to God) but the power of life itself. A 'God' of a kind makes a rather unexpected stage-appearance, but the final fight is not between God and Satan but becomes the struggle of mankind cleaning itself of its inborn evil.

Swan Song is a rollercoaster ride into a world of terror and horror, but also of wonder and beauty, a story which is cruel and compassionate, a novel of eternal struggle, and eternal hope.

—EDDY C. BERTIN

RAMSEY CAMPBELL

Dark Feasts

This collection demonstrates why Campbell has been hailed as Britain's foremost horror writer. Assembling the pick of Campbell's earlier collections—The Inhabitant of the Lake and Less Welcome Tenants *(1964),* Demons by Daylight *(1973),* The Height of the Scream *(1976) and* Dark Companions *(1982)—plus other outstanding pieces from various original anthologies and magazines,* Dark Feasts *represents the author's own choice from the first 25 years of his writing career. Campbell began as a self-confessed disciple of H. P. Lovecraft ('The Room in the Castle'), gradually expanded within the Lovecraftian vein to find his own subjects ('Cold Print', 'The Voice of the Beach'), and then emerged as a distressingly original voice in his own right. His speciality is urban* Angst *and horror as supernatural nastiness stalks the inner cities ('The Man in the Underpass', 'Mackintosh Willy', 'The Midnight Hobo', 'Boiled Alive'), but he also includes EC-comic-style black jokes ('Call First'), several evocative stories about childhood ('Apples', 'The Guy', 'Just Waiting'), and dark visions of a twisted religion ('The Words That Count', 'The Hands').*

A dozen years ago, in a little piece for *Harper's* on neglected spook masters, I sang the praises of an unknown named Ramsey Campbell, 'a young British writer who is probably the best living creator of supernatural horror'. Robert Aickman was still alive, so the statement was perhaps a reckless one, but my friend Ted Klein had put me on to a book called *Demons by Daylight*, and I was in that peculiarly heightened state one experiences when discovering an utterly new literary voice.

Here at last, I thought, was a horror writer who could really write, who was scarier than anyone in the business and whose scares were earned, who brought the same intelligence and verbal sophistication to the creation of terror as Le Fanu, M. R. James, and other past masters, but who did so in uncompromisingly contemporary terms.

Since 1976, Campbell has gained steadily in popularity and critical acclaim, and others have made similarly sweeping generalizations about his work. He has even survived the trappings of success in the genre—the lurid paperback covers, the claustrophobic thrall of fandom, the suspicious promotional blurbs—that have reduced so many others to self-parody.

Campbell's newest volume, *Dark Feasts: The World of Ramsey*

Campbell, is dedicated to T. E. D. Klein, 'who helped launch me and wrote tales for me to aspire to'. This is an entirely fitting dedication since Klein, now a prominent writer himself, has often confessed to being inspired by Campbell, and whose prose has raised the standards of the genre in America much the way Campbell's has done in Britain.

For anyone who has not sampled the dark delights of Campbell's short fiction, *Dark Feasts* is the book to get, for the simple reason that it has more first-rate Campbell tales than any other single volume. Campbell aficionados will want to have the book too, because of its chronological range and stylistic variety. It takes in everything from early masterpieces like 'The Scar' (surely the most terrifying doppelgänger tale ever written) to recent tales like the Halloween treat, 'Apples', a story which demonstrates Campbell's peerless ability to get inside a frightened child's sensibility. For those who enjoy Campbell at his most relentless, there is 'The Hands', which revives the anti-cleric (in this case, anti-nun) tradition of Gothic horror with a vengeance. For those who prefer a lighter touch, there is the creepily delightful 'Seeing the World', which reveals a terseness and satirical flair that constitute a new direction in Campbell's work. For those who prefer brooding atmosphere to terse repartee, there is 'The Brood' (like 'The Scar', an inventive variation on *Invasion of the Body Snatchers*). And for those who still delight in a dollop of Lovecraft there is 'The Voice of the Beach', which manages to avoid the Lovecraftian mannerisms of *The Inhabitant of the Lake*.

As the subtitle promises, this book thus encompasses a large portion of Ramsey Campbell's 'world'. It is unmistakably a modern one: dislocated, disorienting, and alienating. Campbell is a master of capturing that world and the myriad ways it makes us feel vulnerable. Long before Stephen King made it fashionable, Campbell was writing about ordinary people and settings, capturing a moment of anxiety or panic in their lives and thickening it into nightmare horror. The heroes in this book are alienated college students, harassed secretaries, anxious parents, lonely children, and struggling middle-class families. The epiphany these characters invariably experience is the realization that the world is even more awful than they thought it was, so much so that positing supernatural conspiracies seems an utterly sensible and fitting thing to do.

Campbell's style is a perfect embodiment of his vision. He is a master of spectral atmosphere, but also very good at hard realism. His jagged, hallucinatory prose is exactly in touch with the reality he depicts, both psychological and physical. He knows how to inject just a drop of paranoia or dream sensation and let it either spread out to engulf an entire tale (as in the delectably wacky 'Boiled Alive') or remain in a state of deeply unsettling ambiguity (as in 'The End of a Summer's Day'). At his very best, in 'The Chimney', his most moving and personal story, he is capable of creating something as multi-layered and exquisitely disturbing as anything by Hartley or de la Mare.

In the introduction to *Dark Feasts*, Campbell writes that his purpose has always been to disturb. Disturb, you notice, not disgust: 'Many horror stories communicate awe as well as (sometimes instead of) shock, and it is surely inadequate to lump these stories together with fiction that seeks only to disgust, in a category regarded as the deplorable relative of the ghost story.' This statement needs to be made again and again, especially in the current market, where sadism and misogyny are regularly confused with 'horror'. Even in the most physically jolting tales, such as the notorious 'Again', Campbell hopes to communicate 'a little of that quality that has always appealed to me in the best horror fiction, a sense of something larger than is shown'.

It is precisely this sense—that something lurks in the corner of the page even more chilling than what is so vividly shown—that makes Campbell's fiction so memorable.

—JACK SULLIVAN

THE CONTRIBUTORS

FORREST J ACKERMAN (b. 1917) has inspired several generations of writers and film-makers—from Stephen King to Steven Spielberg. He is the world's premier fan of science fiction, fantasy and horror. He has spent a lifetime building a priceless collection of books, magazines and movie memorabilia which he displays throughout his home, the 'Ackermansion', in 'Hollyweird, Karloffornia'. He won the first Hugo Award, coined the term 'sci-fi' and in 1958 created the monster movie magazine field with *Famous Monsters of Filmland*. He has known many of the great film stars and technicians personally, been a literary agent for more than forty years, written countless articles and numerous books and has appeared in over twenty films, including *Dracula vs. Frankenstein*, *The Howling* and *Michael Jackson's Thriller*. After many years of tireless effort, he is still waiting to see the permanent establishment of the Ackerman Science Fiction Museum.

BRIAN W. (WILSON) ALDISS (b. 1925) is one of Britain's most important and prolific science fiction authors. He was born in East Anglia but now lives in Oxford with his wife Margaret. Aldiss' first sf story, 'Criminal Record' appeared in *Science Fantasy* (1954) and his first novel, *Non-Stop* (US: *Starship*) followed four years later. Writer, editor and critic, Aldiss has produced a rich and varied stream of novels, stories, articles and non-fiction books over the years. His most recent work includes the *Helliconia* trilogy and a revised edition of his landmark history of science fiction, *Trillion Year Spree*. He has won the Hugo Award, the Nebula, the British Science Fiction Award and the first James Blish Award for excellence in sf criticism. Aldiss' 1973 time-travel adventure *Frankenstein Unbound* is a tribute to Mary Shelley's 1818 classic and features the young authoress as a major character; however, he declined to write about the original book as he firmly considers it science fiction—not a horror novel

MIKE ASHLEY (b. 1948) was born in Middlesex, England, and now lives in Kent, where by day he is an auditor with the Kent County Council. By night he researches the related fields of science fiction, fantasy and weird fiction and is the author of more than twenty books and some two hundred articles. He has edited such anthologies as *Souls in Metal*, *Weird Legacies* and *The Best of British SF*, while his non-fiction books include the four-volume *History of the Science Fiction Magazine*, *Who's Who In Horror and Fantasy Fiction*, *The Illustrated Book of Science Fiction Lists* and *Algernon Blackwood: A Bio-Bibliography*. Amongst his current projects, Ashley is working on a full biography on Blackwood, and a book about Hugo Gernsback and the pioneer days of the science fiction magazines.

CLIVE BARKER (b. 1952) was born in Liverpool and moved to London in the early 1970s. An award-winning short-story writer, best-selling novelist, illustrator, playwright, screenwriter and film director, after his early success with plays like *The History of the Devil*, *Frankenstein in Love*, *Colossus* and *The Secret Life of Cartoons*, he made an impressive début as a horror writer in 1984 with the publication of the first three volumes of *Clive Barker's*

Books of Blood. A further trio of *Books of Blood* followed, along with the novels *The Damnation Game*, *Weaveworld* and *Cabal*. Barker also scripted the movies *Underworld*, *Rawhead Rex* and *Hellraiser* (based on his own novella, *The Hellbound Heart*), the latter also marking his successful début as a director. More recent projects have included the role as executive producer on *Hellbound: Hellraiser II* and his second outing as a writer/ director, based on the supernatural exploits of his fictional private eye, Harry D'Amour. Barker has won both the British Fantasy Award and World Fantasy Award for Best Short Fiction.

HILAIRE BELLOC (1870–1953) was a French-born English writer, best known for his poetry, political satires, and vindicatory essays about the Roman Catholic church. A number of his books, such as *But Soft We Are Observed!* (1928), a satirical suspense novel set in 1979, are borderline science fiction or fantasy: others are *Mr. Petre* (1925), *The Man Who Made Gold* (1930) and *The Postmaster-General* (1932). The piece reprinted here was published anonymously in *The Morning Post* for September 17th, 1908. At the time, Belloc was the literary editor and internal evidence in the review, as well as references in correspondence between Belloc and Algernon Blackwood, strongly suggest that he was the author of the piece.

EDDY C. (CHARLY) BERTIN (b. 1944) was born in Hamburg-Altona, Germany, but at a very early age he moved to Belgium, where he still lives. He started writing horror stories at the age of 13 and began selling fiction to British anthologies and American magazines in 1967. Bertin's first professional collection, *De Achtjaarlijkse God* (*The Eight-Yearly God*) was published in the Netherlands in 1970, and he has subsequently published one or more books each year in Holland, Belgium, France, Germany and Poland. More than fifty short stories have been translated into English (including three chosen by Richard Davis for his original *Year's Best Horror* series) and his best-known work includes a massive science fiction trilogy known as *Membrane Universe* and a dark fantasy novel about Edgar Allan Poe. His most recent books in the field are two juvenile horror novels, *The House Wants Blood* and *Witchcraft at Midnight* (both in Dutch) and the adult collection *Demon's Triad*, published in France. An as-yet-untitled collection of realistic horror and crime stories is due in the Netherlands as a follow-up to *The Most Gruesome Stories of Eddy C. Bertin* (1984).

JOHN BLACKBURN (b. 1923) has been described as 'today's master of horror' and 'the best British novelist in his field'. Born in Northumberland, Blackburn served in the merchant navy during World War II and prior to becoming a full-time writer he worked as a lorry diver, a teacher in London and Berlin, and the owner of an antiquarian bookshop. His first novel, *A Scent of New-Mown Hay* (1958), was an instant success, and he has followed it with more than thirty books, most of them in the horror genre. Among his best-known titles are *A Ring of Roses*, *Children of the Night*, *Nothing But the Night* (atmospherically filmed in 1972, starring Christopher Lee and Peter Cushing), *Bury Him Darkly*, *Blow the House Down*, *For Fear of Little Men*, *Devil Daddy*, *Our Lady of Pain* and *The Cyclops Goblet*. Blackburn's short fiction has appeared in such original anthologies as *Cold Fear*, *The Taste of Fear* and *The Devil's Kisses*.

ROBERT BLOCH (b. 1917) was born in Chicago and has lived in Los Angeles, California, for many years. His interest in horror first blossomed after he was frightened by Lon Chaney's classic 1925 portrayal of *The Phantom of the Opera*. A young devotee of the pulp magazine *Weird Tales*, he began corresponding with author H. P. Lovecraft, who advised him to try his own hand at writing fiction. Bloch's first story was 'Lilies' (1934) and a year later he made his professional début with 'The Secret of the Tomb'. Quickly establishing himself as a popular and prolific short-story writer, Bloch's early work obviously emulated Lovecraft's own distinctive style and themes, but by the early 1940s he had developed a unique blend of twisted psychological horror and grim graveyard humour (perhaps best exemplified by one of his most famous tales, 'Yours Truly, Jack the Ripper'). However, despite having two dozen novels and hundreds of short stories to his credit, he will always be identified with his 1959 book, *Psycho*, successfully filmed by Alfred Hitchcock the following year. Bloch has often scripted adaptations of his own work, starting with the radio show *Stay Tuned for Terror* in 1944, and including the television series *Alfred Hitchcock Presents*, *Star Trek* and *Tales from the Darkside*, and such movies as *Torture Garden*, *The House That Dripped Blood* and *Asylum*. His most recent novel is *The Night of the Ripper* and 500,000 words comprising *The Selected Stories of Robert Bloch* recently appeared in three volumes. He won the science fiction field's Hugo Award in 1959 for 'The Hell-Bound Train' and was the first recipient of The World Fantasy Award for Life Achievement in 1975.

SCOTT BRADFIELD (b. 1955) was born in California and divides his time between the American West Coast and London. He received his Ph.D in American Literature from the University of California, where he taught for five years. Bradfield's stories, essays and reviews have appeared in a wide variety of magazines and anthologies, including *Omni*, *Ambit*, *The Year's Best Horror Stories*, *The Year's Best Fantasy Stories*, *Interzone*, *New Statesman*, *The Listener*, *The Evening Standard*, *Other Edens 2* and *The Times Literary Supplement*. His first collection of short fiction, *The Secret Life of Houses*, was published in 1988 and he has recently completed a novel, *The History of Luminous Motion*, and a study of American colonial and revolutionary narrative entitled *Dreaming Revolution*.

EDWARD BRYANT (b. 1945) was born in White Plains, New York, and grew up on a cattle ranch in Southern Wyoming. He met Harlan Ellison, who assisted his early career, at the Clarion SF Writer's Workshop in 1968 and 1969 and Bryant sold his first short story, 'They Come Only in Dreams', to *Adam* in 1970. His fiction has appeared in a wide variety of magazines and anthologies and two stories, 'Stone' (1978) and 'giANTS' (1979), both won the Nebula Award. Bryant's collections include *Among the Dead and Other Events Leading Up to the Apocalypse*, *Cinnabar*, *Wyoming Sun*, *Particle Theory* and one-third (seven new stories) of *Night Visions 4*. He collaborated with Ellison on the short novel *Phoenix Without Ashes* and edited the original anthology *2076: The American Tricentennial*. Currently the books review editor for *Twilight Zone Magazine*, Bryant continues to write superior short stories for such anthologies as *Book of the Dead* and *Blood is Not Enough*.

RAMSEY CAMPBELL (b. 1946) has been justly described as 'perhaps the finest living exponent of the British weird fiction tradition' and last year he celebrated twenty-five years of chilling spines with a bumper collection, *Dark Feasts*. A life-long resident of Liverpool, John Ramsey Campbell sold his first story, 'The Church in the High Street', to August Derleth in 1962. Leaving school that same year, his first collection, *The Inhabitant of the Lake and Other Less Welcome Tenants* appeared from Derleth's Arkham House imprint two years later. Campbell worked for the Inland Revenue and later in a library until he became a full-time writer and reviewer in 1973. Although his early fiction was heavily influenced by H. P. Lovecraft's Cthulhu Mythos (yet set in a distinctly British milieu), his subsequent books and stories have revealed him to be a unique voice in horror fiction—whether as an anthologist (*Superhorror*, or *The Far Reaches of Fear, New Tales of the Cthulhu Mythos, New Terrors, The Gruesome Book, Fine Frights*), in his collections of short fiction (*Demons By Daylight, The Height of the Scream, Dark Companions, Cold Print, Scared Stiff*), or as a novelist (*The Doll Who Ate His Mother, To Wake the Dead* (US: *The Parasite*), *The Nameless, The Face That Must Die, Incarnate, Obsession, The Hungry Moon, The Influence, Ancient Images*). A winner of both the British and World Fantasy Awards, Campbell has also completed several of Robert E. Howard's stories of Solomon Kane, written the novelizations of *The Wolf Man, Bride of Frankenstein* and *Dracula's Daughter* under the house name 'Carl Dreadstone' and is the author of *Claw* (US: *Night of the Claw*) behind the somewhat obvious alias of 'Jay Ramsey'.

HUGH B. (BARNETT) CAVE (b. 1910) was born in Chester, England, but emigrated to America with his family when he was five. While editing trade journals he sold his first story, 'Corpse on the Grating', to the pulp magazines in 1930. He quickly established himself as an inventive and prolific writer and became a regular contributor to *Strange Tales, Weird Tales, Ghost Stories, Black Book Detective Magazine, Thrilling Mysteries, Spicy Mystery Stories*, and the so-called 'shudder pulps', *Horror Stories* and *Terror Tales*. Cave left the field for almost three decades, moving to Haiti and later Jamaica, where he established a coffee plantation and wrote a number of books about voodoo and tribal magic. Karl Edward Wagner's Carcosa imprint published a hefty volume of Cave's best horror tales, *Murgunstrumm and Others*, in 1977 and he returned to the genre with stories in *Whispers* and *Fantasy Tales* and a string of modern horror novels: *Legion of the Dead, The Nebulon Horror, The Evil* and *Shades of Evil*. More recently, he has written two new horror novels, tentatively titled *Disciples of Dread* and *The Lower Depths*, a couple of young adult novels, *The Voyage* and *The Wild One*, and a new collection—*The Corpse Maker*—has been edited by Sheldon Jaffery. Also in 1988, Starmont published a biography by Audrey Parente, titled *Pulp Man's Odyssey: The Hugh B. Cave Story*.

SUZY McKEE CHARNAS (b. 1939) was born in New York City but currently lives in Albuquerque, New Mexico, where she moved with her husband and two step-children in 1969. After working in Nigeria with the Peace Corps from 1961–63, she returned to New York to tour suburban high schools as part of a drug abuse treatment team. Her first novel was published in 1974: *Walk to the End of the World*, a feminist view of futuristic amazons, it won the John W. Campbell Award. A sequel, *Motherlines*, followed four years later. Two vampire stories, 'The Ancient Mind at Work' and 'Unicorn Tapestry' (winner of the 1980 Nebula Award for best novella), led to her acclaimed novel *The Vampire Tapestry*. It has been followed by three fantasy books: *The Bronze King*, *Dorothea Dreams* and *The Silver Glove*.

R. (RONALD) CHETWYND-HAYES (b. 1919) was born in Isleworth, West London. His first book was *The Man from the Bomb*, an undistinguished science fiction novel published in 1959. A supernatural thriller, *The Dark Man*, followed in 1964, and by the early 1970s he was turning out a prolific number of ghost stories and gentle tales of terror, tinged with a disarming sense of humour. These have been collected in numerous volumes, such as *The Unbidden*, *The Elemental*, *The Night Ghouls*, *A Quiver of Ghosts*, *Tales from the Dark Lands* and *Tales from the Other Side*. He has edited *Cornish Tales of Terror*, *Scottish Tales of Terror*, twelve volumes of *Fontana Book of Great Ghost Stories* and the *Armada Monster Books* series for children. Chetwynd-Hayes is the author of two film novelizations, *Dominique* and *The Awakening* (the latter based on Bram Stoker's *The Jewel of Seven Stars*), and his own stories have been adapted for the screen in *From Beyond the Grave* and *The Monster Club* (in which the author was portrayed by actor John Carradine).

JOHN CLUTE (b. 1940) was born in Toronto and grew up in Canada and America. His first science fiction story, 'A Man Must Die', was published in *New Worlds* (1966) and he moved to London in 1969. Author of the novel *The Disinheriting Party* (1977) and Associate Editor of *The Encyclopedia of Science Fiction* (1979), Clute is a co-editor of the three *Interzone* anthologies and his collection of sf essays, *Strokes*, was published in 1988. He has been the reviews editor of *Foundation* since 1980 and his reviews and essays have been published regularly in *The Times Literary Supplement*, *The Guardian*, *New Statesman*, *New Scientist*, *Omni*, *The Washington Post* and *The New York Times*.

ADRIAN COLE (b. 1949) was born in Plymouth and worked for a number of years as a librarian in Birmingham before moving to Devon with his family. He began writing for the small press magazines in the early 1970s, creating a series of adventures about a cursed warrior, The Voidal. His early books include *Madness Emerging* (1976), *The Lucifer Experiment*, *Wargods of Ludorbis* and 'The Dream Lords' trilogy. More recently he has published two children's books, *Moorstones* and *The Sleep of Giants*, and an ambitious adult fantasy series started in 1986 with *A Place Among the Fallen* and has continued through *Throne of Fools*, *The King of Light and Shadows* and *The Gods in Anger*.

BASIL COPPER (b. 1924) was born in London and for thirty years he worked as a journalist and editor of a local newspaper before becoming a full-time writer in 1970. His first story in the horror field was 'The Spider' in the *5th Pan Book of Horror Stories* (1964), and among his most-reprinted tales are 'Camera Obscura' and 'Amber Print'. Besides writing two non-fiction studies of the vampire and werewolf in legend, fact and art, his novels of the macabre and gaslight gothic include *The Great White Space*, *The Curse of the Fleers*, *Necropolis*, *The Black Death* and *House of the Wolf* (described by Peter Haining as 'the most imaginately plotted and stylishly written' of all the novels on the theme published in recent years). Copper's short fiction has been collected in *Not After Nightfall*, *From Evil's Pillow*, *When Footsteps Echo* and *And Afterward, the Dark*. He has written more than fifty hard-boiled thrillers about Los Angeles private detective Mike Faraday, and his *Solar Pons* collections have successfully continued the exploits of August Derleth's Holmes-like consulting detective. Basil Copper is also one of Britain's leading film collectors, with a private archive containing more than a thousand titles.

RICHARD DALBY (b. 1949) is a London-born author, bibliographer, researcher and bookdealer specializing in supernatural fiction. In 1971 he unearthed a previously unreprinted M. R. James story which he included in his anthology, *The Sorceress in Stained Glass*. His other anthologies include *The Best Ghost Stories of H. Russell Wakefield*, *Dracula's Blood*, *Ghosts and Scholars* (with Rosemary Pardoe), *The Virago Book of Ghost Stories* and *The Virago Book of Victorian Ghost Stories*. Dalby is also the author/compiler of *Bram Stoker: A Bibliography of First Editions* (1983).

LES DANIELS (b. 1943) was born in Providence, Rhode Island, and graduated from Brown University with honours in English Literature. He received an M.A. in English in 1968 from Brown, since when he has been a freelance writer, composer, film buff and musician. He has performed with such groups as Soop, Snake and The Snatch, The Swamp Steppers and The Local Yokels. His first book was *Comix: A History of Comic Books in America* (1971), and he went on to write *Living in Fear: A History of Horror in the Mass Media* and edit *Dying of Fright: Masterpieces of the Macabre*. His début novel, *The Black Castle*, was published in 1978 and introduced readers to Don Sebastian de Villanueva, the enigmatic vampire-hero whose adventures span the centuries in a series of superior horror novels: *The Silver Skull*, *Citizen Vampire* and *Yellow Fog*. Daniels is currently working on a new novel, *No Blood Spilled*, in which Sebastian is revived in India.

JACK DANN (b. 1945) lives in Binghamton, New York. A writer and anthologist with a BA in social and political science, he began publishing science fiction in 1970 with two stories in *Worlds of If*, 'Dark, Dark, the Dead Star' and 'Traps', co-written with George Zebrowski. His short fiction has been published in most of the leading sf magazines, plus *Playboy*, *Penthouse*, *Omni*, *Gallery*, *Shadows*, *After Midnight* and *A Gallery of Horror*. The author of such books as *Starhiker*, *The Man Who Melted*, and the collection *Timetipping*, he has edited several anthologies, including the acclaimed *Wandering Stars, More Wandering Stars,* and, with Gardner Dozois, *Future Power, Aliens!, Unicorns!, Magicats!, Bestiary!, Mermaids!* and *Sorcerers!* He has been a Nebula Award finalist five times, as well as a finalist for the World Fantasy Award and The British Science Fiction Association Award. He is currently working on novels about Leonardo Da Vinci and Josef Mengele, and tells us he has been inspired by re-reading *The Painted Bird* to plan his next book, based on a quote from Kosinski's introduction: 'They blamed me for watering down historical truth and accused me of pandering to an Anglo-Saxon sensibility whose only confrontation with national cataclysm had been the Civil War a century earlier, when bands of abandoned children roamed through the devastated South.'

CHARLES DE LINT (b. 1951) was born in Bussum, the Netherlands, but his father's job with a surveying company allowed him to grow up in places as diverse as the Yukon, Turkey, Lebanon and Canada, where he currently lives as a full-time writer and musician with his wife, MaryAnn Harris. His first two books, *The Riddle of the Wren* and *Moonheart: A Romance,* won him the 1984 William L. Crawford Award for Best New Fantasy Writer. More recently he has published *Mulengro: A Romany Tale, Yarrow: An Autumn Tale, Jack the Giant Killer, Greenmantle* and *Wolf Moon.* De Lint also writes regular horror fiction columns for the trade journals *Short Form* and *Horrorstruck,* and he contributes book reviews to *OtherRealms.* He has served as a judge for the Theodore Sturgeon Memorial Short Fiction Award, the 1986 World Fantasy Awards, the 1987 Horror Writers of America Awards and the 1988 Nebula Awards. His short fiction has appeared extensively in magazines and anthologies.

THOMAS M. DISCH (b. 1940) was raised in Arizona and has been a resident of New York, England, Turkey, Italy and Mexico. Poet, reviewer, short-story writer and novelist, Disch has been described by David Hartwell as producing 'a body of work that seems of growing importance to the contemporary horror field'. His first science fiction story, 'The Double-Timer', appeared in *Fantastic* in 1962, and his highly-regarded output includes such books as *One Hundred and Two H Bombs, The Genocides, Camp Concentration, The Prisoner* (based on the cult TV series), *334, Fun With Your New Head, Getting Into Death* and *The Businessman.* Disch also collaborated with John Sladek on a mystery novel, *Black Alice* (1968) and a Gothic, *The House that Fear Built* (1966).

MALCOLM EDWARDS (b. 1949) was born in London, where he has lived his entire life, except for three years at King's College, Cambridge, He has an M.A. in social anthropology which he has 'never put to any constructive use'. Formerly Administrator of the Science Fiction Foundation and editor of *Vector* and *Foundation,* Edwards is founding co-editor of *Interzone.* He was a Contributing Editor to *The Encyclopedia of Science Fiction* and co-author (with Maxim Jakubowski) of the *Complete Book of SF and Fantasy Lists.* He has also co-written six illustrated books, one with Harry Harrison and five with Robert Holdstock, and his first published short story, 'After-Images' (*Interzone,* 1983), was reprinted in *The Year's Best Horror Stories* and won the British Science Fiction Association Award for Best Short Story 1984. Malcom Edwards is currently the Publishing Director of Victor Gollancz Ltd., sf and fantasy division.

HARLAN ELLISON (b. 1934), author, essayist and screenwriter, was born and raised in Ohio and moved to Los Angeles in 1962, where he has remained. Probably one of the field's most controversial yet talented writers, Ellison made his professional début with 'Glowworm' in *Infinity Science Fiction* (1956). After several books based on his experiences with New York street gangs (*Rumble, The Juvies* etc.) and a stint as editor of *Rogue Magazine*, he firmly established himself as a maverick sf/horror writer with a string of powerful short stories and the occasional novel. In 1963 he started writing for television, contributing scripts to such popular shows as *The Alfred Hitchcock Hour, The Outer Limits, The Man from U.N.C.L.E.*, *Star Trek* and the revived *Twilight Zone*. His 1969 novella *A Boy and His Dog* was filmed with reasonable success in 1975. Ellison has won both the Hugo and Nebula Awards a number of times and he is the editor on the New Wave sf anthologies *Dangerous Visions* (1967) and *Again, Dangerous Visions* (1972); a third volume, *Last Dangerous Visions*, is still awaiting publication.

DENNIS ETCHISON (b. 1943) was born in Stockton, California. Described as the best short-story writer in the horror field today, he started writing before his teens, winning $250 for an essay 'What America Means to Me' at the age of twelve. His first professional sale was a science fiction story, 'Odd Boy Out', in *Escapade* (1961), since when he has contributed fiction to a wide variety of magazines and anthologies. Etchison has had three major collections of short stories published, *The Dark Country, Red Dreams* and *The Blood Kiss*, a novel, *Darkside*, and he has edited *Cutting Edge* and *Masters of Darkness* volumes I and II. His novelizations include *The Fog* and, under his 'Jack Martin' pseudonym, *Halloween II, Halloween III* and *Videodrome*. He has written several unproduced screenplays, including Ray Bradbury's *The Fox and the Forest*, Stéphen King's *The Mist* and *Halloween IV*, was a staff writer for the HBO TV series *The Hitch Hiker*, and adapted his own story 'The Late Shift' for a short film entitled *Killing Time*. His story 'The Dark Country' won both the British Fantasy Award and The World Fantasy Award in 1982.

CHRISTOPHER EVANS (b. 1951) was born in Tredegar, South Wales, and has been a London-based freelance writer since 1979. He has written science fiction, fantasy, horror, TV and film novelizations, non-fiction and reviews under various pen-names. His most recent books under his own name are *In Limbo* (1985) and *Writing Science Fiction* (1988). With Robert Holdstock, Evans co-edited *Other Edens* (1987), an anthology of new science fiction and fantasy stores, and followed it with a second volume in 1988.

LIONEL FANTHORPE (b. 1935) was born in Dareham, Norfolk, and for a period of fifteen years was Britain's most prolific science fiction, fantasy and horror author. While working as a full-time teacher, Fanthorpe wrote his first published story for the John Spencer imprint in 1952 and until 1966 he produced almost 200 books for them with titles like *The Macabre Ones*, *Softly By Moonlight*, *The Immortals*, *Valley of the Vampire*, *The Crawling Fiend*, *The Loch Ness Terror*, *Fingers of Darkness* and *Rodent Mutation*. He almost single-handedly filled all the issues of *Supernatural Stories*, using a multitude of pseudonyms, and created a series about occult investigator Val Stearman and his wife La Noire. In 1979 he co-authored *The Black Lion* with his wife Patricia and they also collaborated on *The Holy Grail Revealed* (1982). In 1987 Fanthorpe was Ordained as a Minister in the Church of Wales, serving as non-stipendiary assistant curate at St German's, Roath, Cardiff, and he is also Headmaster of Glyn Derw Comprehensive High School in Cardiff. His most recent book is *God in all Things*, a collection of Christian pieces, published in 1987.

JOHN M. FORD (b. 1957) was born in East Chicago, Indiana. He began writing in 1974 and sold his first science fiction story, 'This, Too Reconcile', to *Analog* the following year. Since then, his short fiction has appeared in several anthologies and such magazines as *Amazing*, *Omni* and *Asimov's*. Ford published his first novel, *Web of Angels*, in 1980, and followed it with *Princes of the Air*, the World Fantasy Award-winning *The Dragon Waiting*, *The Illusionist*, and two best-selling *Star Trek* volumes, *The Final Reflection* and *How Much For Just the Planet?* He has also contributed the novella *Fuge State* to the anthology *Under the Wheel*, written children's fiction under a pseudonym, and is the author of the spy/thriller *The Scholars of Night*.

NEIL GAIMAN (b. 1960) was born in Portchester, England. Interested in books and comics at an early age, he was twelve when he was told by a school advisor that it would be impossible to become a comics writer. His articles, interviews and reviews have appeared in a wide variety of periodicals, including *Today*, *Time Out*, *The Good Book Guide*, *Foundation*, *Knave*, *News on Sunday*, *You*, *American Fantasy*, *Publishing News*, *Observer Colour Supplement*, *The Sunday Times Magazine* and *Penthouse*. Gaiman's short fiction has been published in *Knave*, *Imagine*, *Penthouse*, *Dragon*, *Winter Chills* and *Tales from the Forbidden Planet 2*, and his comic scripts have appeared in *2000 AD*, *Outrageous Tales from the Old Testament* and DC Comics' *Black Orchid* and *The Sandman*. He is the author of *The Official Hitch-Hiker's Guide to the Galaxy Companion* and *Violent Cases*, co-compiler (with Kim Newman) of *Ghastly Beyond Belief*, and co-editor (with Stephen Jones) of *Now We Are Sick*. He no longer admits to having written various pop group biographies.

STEPHEN GALLAGHER (b. 1954) was born in Salford, Lancashire, and currently lives in Blackburn with his wife and daughter. He graduated with Joint Honours in Drama and English from Hull University in 1975 and worked for a number of British television companies before making his first professional sale as a writer to commercial radio. Gallagher became a full-time freelance writer in 1980, and he went on to script two serials for BBC-TV's popular *Doctor Who* series, *Warrior's Gate* and *Terminus* (which he subsequently novelized under the pseudonym 'John Lydecker'). His short fiction has mostly appeared in America in *The Magazine of Fantasy and Science Fiction* and *Asimov's*, or such anthologies as *Ripper* and *Shadows 9*. Gallagher wrote the novelization of the sf movie *Saturn 3*, and his horror novels include *Chimera* (in development as a TV serial), *Follower*, *Oktober* and *Valley of Lights* (optioned for filming and described by Ramsey Campbell as 'a treat—a suspensful and terrifying tale, compellingly told'). His latest novel is *Down River*, which Gallagher describes as a cross-over between horror and mainstream fiction.

CRAIG SHAW GARDNER (b. 1949) was born in Rochester, New York, the home of the Eastman Kodak Company ('thus I was able to obtain large amounts of free film at an early age'). He was introduced to science fiction at the age of ten and he wrote *Frankenstein meets Juliet* for his grammar school paper. After majoring in 'Broadcasting and Film' at Boston University ('a degree with absolutely no worth in the real world') he worked in public relations while writing short stories in his spare time. In 1978 he sold 'A Malady of Magicks' to *Fantastic Stories* and within a couple of years his fiction was appearing regularly in such anthologies as *Horrors*, *Shadows*, *Halloween Horrors*, *Midnight* and *Doom City*. His first novel, *A Malady of Magicks* (1986), was a humorous fantasy filled with tap-dancing dragons, magical virgins and used weapons sales-demons, which was followed by *A Multitude of Monsters* and *A Night in the Netherhells*. A second trilogy involving the same characters began in 1987 with *A Difficulty with Dwarves*. Gardner's other books include *Wishbringer*, the novelization of *The Lost Boys* and a horror novel tentatively titled *Blood for the Master*. He currently lives in 'artsy' Cambridge, Massachusetts, with his third wife, Elisabeth.

FRANCES GARFIELD (b. 1908) was born in Texas and has lived in Chapel Hill, North Carolina, since 1951 where she moved with her husband, Manly Wade Wellman. During the late 1930s and early '40s she had three stories published in *Weird Tales* and another in *Amazing Stories*. After retiring from her job as a secretary in a school of public health, she kept thinking up ideas for horror stories and telling them to Wellman. He said they were 'women's stories' and she would have to write them herself. So Garfield returned to her typewriter, and over the past decade the results have appeared in such magazines as *Fantasy Tales*, *Whispers*, *Fantasy Book*, *Kadath* and several anthologies, including *The Year's Best Horror Stories*.

DAVID S. GARNETT (b. 1947) was born in Liverpool and currently lives in West Sussex. He has written six science fiction novels under his own name, the first, *Mirror in the Sky*, when he was nineteen. Garnett is also the author of numerous other books under various psuedonyms—including novelizations of *The Hills Have Eyes* and its sequel. A 1986 Hugo Award nominee for his story 'Still Life', his short fiction has been published in *Interzone*, *Mayfair*, *The Magazine of Fantasy and Science Fiction* and such anthologies as *Other Edens*, *Shadows* and *The Year's Best Horror Stories*.

CHARLES L. GRANT (b. 1942) has lived most his life in northwestern New Jersey. In 1964 he graduated from Trinity College, Connecticut, with a

B.A. in History and English. A prolific editor, short-story writer and novelist, he sold his first story, 'The House of Evil', to *Fantasy and Science Fiction* in 1968. After publishing a number of science fictions novels like *The Shadow of Alpha*, *Ascention* and *The Ravens of the Moon*, he began to develop his unique brand of 'quiet' horror in more than thirty novels, such as *The Curse* (1977), *The Hour of the Oxrun Dead*, *The Soft Whisper of the Dead*, *The Nestling*, *The Tea Party*, *The Pet*, *For Fear of the Night* and *In a Dark Dream*. His stories have been collected in *Tales from the Nightside*, *A Glow of Candles* and *Nightmare Seasons* and he is the editor of the popular *Shadows*, *Midnight* and *Greystone Bay* anthologies, amongst others. Grant has won the Nebula Award, the British Fantasy Award and the World Fantasy Award and published more than 100 short stories.

COLIN GREENLAND (b. 1954) holds a doctorate in English Literature from Pembroke College, Oxford, and lives and works in Essex and Colorado. From 1980 to 1982 he was the Arts Council Writer in Residence at the Science Fiction Foundation and *The Entropy Exhibition*, his study of Michael Moorcock's *New Worlds* magazine, won the University of California's Eaton Award for Science Fiction Criticism in 1985. Greenland's reviews appear in *The Times Literary Supplement*, the *New Statesman*, *Foundation* and Channel Four TV's *Book Choice*, he is the co-editor of *Interzone: The First Anthology*, and his fantasy novels include *Daybreak on a Different Mountain*, *The Hour of the Thin Ox* and *Other Voices*.

ROBERT STEPHEN HADJI (b. 1953) was born in London, Ontario, Canada, where he admits he enjoyed 'an idyllic childhood roaming the woods in search of salamanders'. Eventually moving to Toronto, Hadji has become a noted authority on horror fiction, with articles published in *Myriad*, *Twilight Zone Magazine*, *American Fantasy* and *The Penguin Book of Horror and the Supernatural*. He was the founding editor of the Canadian magazine *Borderland*, is currently employed as one-half of Hadji & Sherlock Books Inc., and was appointed as a judge for the 1988 World Fantasy Awards.

PETER HAINING (b. 1940) was born in Middlesex, England, and now lives in a sixteenth-century house (sadly, not haunted!) in Suffolk with his wife and children. Haining has been described as 'the most prolific anthologist of horror fiction in the world', and certainly the number of volumes he has compiled since his first in 1965, *The Hell of Mirrors*, supports this view. He began his career as a journalist in Essex and a story about Satanic desecration sparked his interest in the occult, resulting in his first book, *Devil Worship in Britain* (1964). Since then he has edited numerous collections and anthologies, selecting lesser-known tales for such volumes as *The Craft of Terror*, *The Evil People*, *The Hollywood Nightmare*, *The Ghouls*, *Great British Tales of Terror*, *The Fantastic Pulps*, *Weird Tales*, *The Black Magic Omnibus* and *M. R. James—Book of the Supernatural*, amongst many others.

JOE HALDEMAN (b. 1943) sold his first story, 'Out of Phase', to *Galaxy* in 1969) He took a BS in physics and astronomy, doing postgraduate work in mathematics and computer science before being drafted to Vietnam as a combat engineer. His first science fiction novel, *The Forever War*, proved to be a popular and critical success, and he followed it with *Mindbridge*, *All My Sins Remembered*, a *Star Trek* novel: *Planet of Judgment*, *Into the Out Of*, *Tool of the Trade* and *The Long Habit of Living*. He has edited the sf anthologies *Cosmic Laughter* and *Study War No More* and his short fiction has appeared in *Playboy*, *Omni* and Dennis Etchison's *Cutting Edge* anthology. Haldeman has won both the Hugo and Nebula Awards. Recently, he has scripted *Robojox* for director Stuart Gordon.

DAVID G. HARTWELL (b. 1941) is a four-time Hugo Award nominee for Best Editor. In 1963 he received a B.A. from Williams College, followed by an M.A. in English from Colgate University (1965) and a Ph.D. in Comparative Medieval Literature from Columbia University (1973). A reviewer, columnist and awards administrator, Hartwell has edited such publications as *The Little Magazine* and *Cosmos*. He was a consulting science fiction editor at New American Library, Gregg Press and Waldenbooks Otherworlds Club, Editor-in-Chief of Berkeley sf and Director of Science Fiction for Timescape/Pocket Books before becoming a consulting editor at Tor Books and Director of sf at Arbor House. Hartwell lives in Pleasantville, New York, and is the author of *Age of Wonders*, a non-fiction study of the science fiction field, and has edited such anthologies as *Christmas Ghosts* (with Kathryn Cramer), *The Dark Descent* and *Masterpieces of Fantasy and Enchantment*.

GEORGE HAY (b. 1922) was born in Chelsea, London. Author, editor and science fiction enthusiast, he is a Council member of the Science Fiction Foundation, of which he was the founder. Hay's novels include *Man, Woman and Android* (1951) and *This Planet for Sale* (1952), and he has been responsible for the reprinting of fantasy novels, plays and stories by such authors as Lord Dunsany, Walter de la Mare, Robert Aickman, Iaian Sinclair etc. In 1978 he edited *The Necronomicon*—a spoof edition of H. P. Lovecraft's fabled forbidden book, and he is currently campaigning to get Applied Science Fiction accepted in the educational curriculum in Britain. He keeps trying to retire, but . . .

ROBERT HOLDSTOCK (b. 1948) was born in a remote corner of Kent and currently lives in London. The eldest of five children, he read Applied Zoology at the University College of North Wales and holds a Master's degree in Medical Zoology. His first published story was 'Pauper's Plot' in *New Worlds* (1968) and he became a full-time writer in 1976. Among the novels published under his own name are *Eye Among the Blind* (1976), *Earthwind*, *Necromancer*, *Where Time Winds Blow*, *In the Valley of the Statues*, *The Emerald Forest*, the World Fantasy Award-winning *Mythago Wood* and its follow-up, *Lavondyss*. He has co-written the text (with Malcolm Edwards) of five illustrated books, co-edited *Stars of Albion* with Christopher Priest and *Other Edens* and *Other Edens 2* with Christopher Evans, and produced a bewildering array of novels under a variety of pseudonyms, including *Legend of the Werewolf*, *The Satanists*, and series such as 'The Professionals', 'Berserker', 'Raven', 'Bulman' and 'Night Hunter'.

ROBERT E. (ERVIN) HOWARD (1906–1936) was born and lived all his life in a Texas not far removed from Pioneer days. He began writing at the age of 15, and although considered something of a misfit by his friends and neighbours, he made his first professional sale with 'Spear and Fang' in the July 1925 *Weird Tales*. Responsible for almost single-handedly popularizing the heroic fantasy genre, he soon became one of the most prolific contributors to the pulp magazines, creating such memorable characters as Bran Mak Morn, Solomon Kane, King Kull and, his most famous, Conan the Cimmerian. Besides his fantasy fiction and verse, Howard wrote about a wide range of topics, including sports stories, historical adventure, western, pirate, detective and Oriental mystery. His best-known horror tales include 'Black Canaan', 'Worms of the Earth', 'Pigeons from Hell' and the Lovecraft-inspired 'The Thing on the Roof'. On the morning of June 11th, 1936, the thirty-year-old author ascertained that his mother (to whom he was devoted) would not regain consciousness from a coma. He calmly got into his car, rolled up the window, and shot himself in the head. As an epitaph, he left the following couplet in his typewriter:

> 'All fled—all done, so lift me on the pyre:
> The Feast is over and the lamps expire.'

Robert E. Howard's continued influence on new generations of writers cannot be undervalued, and his books reached a peak of popularity during the mid-1970s.

SHAUN HUTSON (b. 1958) lives and writes in Milton Keynes, Buckinghamshire. Described as 'the sort of writer who inspires kindly old grannies to lobby their local library to remove his books from the shelves', the self-confessed heavy metal music fan and frustrated drummer published his first novel in 1980. With the publication of *Slugs* (1982), an audacious blend of explicit sex and gratuitous violence, Hutson's work met with instant popular appeal, and he has subsequently produced a steady stream of best-selling horror books with titles like *Spawn*, *Shadows*, *Erebus*, *Deathday*, *Breeding Ground*, *Relics*, *Victims*, *Assassin*, *Nemesis* and *Monolith*. *Slugs:The Movie* was produced in 1988 by Spanish director Juan Piquer Simon, and Hutson lists among his hobbies 'irritating and annoying people' and a desire 'to see euthanasia introduced for critics . . .'

MAXIM JAKUBOWSKI (b. 1944) was born in Barnet, Hertfordshire, but was educated and lived in France for more than twenty years. Publisher, critic, translator, anthologist and author of more than twenty books (not always in the sf and fantasy field), he has continued the exploits of Michael Moorcock's character Jerry Cornelius in a number of stories, and is the editor of *Travelling Towards Epsilon*, *The Complete Book of SF and Fantasy Lists*, *Lands of Never* and *Beyond Lands of Never*. A series of fantasy novels has appeared under a pseudonym.

(MR) MONTAGUE RHODES JAMES (1862–1936) was born at Goodnestone Parsonage in Kent, where his father was curate. A serious child, he developed a life-long interest in medieval books and antiquities at an early age. He was educated at Eton and later King's College, Cambridge, where he declined to follow his father and eldest brother into the Church. In 1905 he became Provost of King's and was Vice-Chancellor of the University from 1913–15 before returning to Eton as Provost in 1918. He has been described as 'an unlikely author of some of the most alarming and unforgettable ghost stories in the English language', most of them occasional pieces, written for friends or college magazines. Among his most famous tales are such subtle chillers as 'Lost Hearts', 'Canon Alberic's Scrap-Book', 'The Mezzotint', 'Casting the Runes' and the classic 'Oh, Whistle, and I'll Come to You, My Lad'. The first collection of James' tales was *Ghost Stories of an Antiquary*, published in 1904, and an omnibus volume entitled the *The Collected Ghost Stories of M. R. James* appeared in 1931. His favourite author was J. Sheridan Le Fanu, whom he described as 'absolutely in the first rank as a writer of ghost stories', and in 1923 he collected and reprinted some of Le Fanu's stories from forgotten Victorian periodicals in *Madam Crowl's Ghost*.

DIANA WYNNE JONES (b. 1934) was born in London and currently lives in Bristol with her husband, a professor of English at Bristol University, and their sons. Jones is half-Welsh, of a family which reputedly descends from Morgan the Pirate. She decided to be a writer at the age of eight, and her stories of witches, hobgoblins and magic have delighted young readers and adults since *Changeover* in 1970. Her other books include *The Ogre Downstairs*, *Dogsbody*, *Power of Three*, *Charmed Life*, *The Magicians of Caprona*, *Archer's Goon*, *Fire and Hemlock* and *Howl's Moving Castle*. She won the Guardian Award in 1977, was runner-up for the Children's Book Award in 1981, and was runner-up for the Carnegie Medal three times—in 1975, 1977 and 1984.

MARVIN KAYE (b. 1938) was born in Philadelphia and currently lives in New York City. A graduate of Pennsylvania State University and the University of Denver, he has a B.A. in Theatre and an M.A. in English Literature. His short fiction has appeared in *Amazing*, *Fantastic*, *Fantasy Macabre*, *Galileo*, *Night Cry*, *Weird Tales*, and such anthologies as *Arabesque II*, *Magical Wishes* and *The Year's Best Fantasy Stories*. Kaye is the author of a number of horror, mystery, science-fantasy and suspense novels (often in collaboration with Parke Godwin). These include *Ghosts of Night and Morning*, *A Cold Blue Light*, *The Masters of Solitude*, *Wintermind*, *The Incredible Umbrella*, *The Soap Opera Slaughters*, *The Laurel and Hardy Murders* and *Bullets for Macbeth*. He has also edited such fantasy anthologies as *Devils and Demons*, *Masterpieces of Terror & the Supernatural*, *Ghosts*, *Brother Theodore's Chamber of Horrors*, *Fiends and Creatures* and *Weird Tales: The Magazine That Never Dies*. Kaye's non-fiction volumes include *The Histrionic Holmes* and three handbooks of Magic.

GARRY KILWORTH (b. 1924) was born in York and spent his formative years in Aden. He studied English at King's College London after twenty years of global travel with the Royal Air Force and, later, Cable and Wireless. He now lives with his wife Annette in rural Essex, home of his forebears. Kilworth's first science fiction story, 'Let's Go to Golgotha', was published in *The Gollancz/Sunday Times Best SF Stories* anthology in 1975, having won the competition. His first sf novel, *In Solitary*, appeared two years later. The author of more than fifty short stories, he has written a number of science fiction and fantasy books, the most recent of which are the haunting *Witchwater Country*, *Cloudrock* and his acclaimed collection, *The Songbirds of Pain*. An urban horror novel, *The Street*, was recently published under the psuedonym 'Garry Douglas'.

STEPHEN KING (b. 1947) is arguably the most popular novelist in the history of American fiction and is indisputably the most successful horror writer of all time, with around 100 million copies of his books in print. Born in Portland, Maine, he currently lives in Bangor with his wife, Tabitha, and their three children. His first published story was 'I Was a Teenage Graverobber' in a 1965 comic book fan magazine. He made his first professional sale with 'The Glass Floor' in *Startling Mystery Stories* (1967), which was quickly followed by sales to better-paying markets. King's first novel, *Carrie*, appeared in 1974, since when he has published a phenomenal string of best-sellers: *'Salem's Lot, The Shining, Night Shift, The Stand, The Dead Zone, Firestarter, Danse Macabre, Cujo, Different Seasons, The Dark Tower: The Gunslinger, Creepshow, Christine, Cycle of the Werewolf, Pet Sematary, The Talisman* (with Peter Straub), *The Eyes of the Dragon, Skeleton Crew, It, The Dark Tower II: The Drawing of Three, Misery* and *The Tommyknockers*. As 'Richard Bachman' he has also published *Rage, The Long Walk, Roadwork, The Running Man* and *Thinner*, and there are numerous books available dissecting his work. Most of his books and stories have already been filmed or optioned by Hollywood.

T. E. D. KLEIN (b. 1947) is a native New Yorker who has been descibed as 'one of the finest stylists among modern horror writers'. He became a horror enthusiast after discovering the works of H. P. Lovecraft while studying at Brown University. His blending of themes found in Lovecraft and Machen's fiction resulted in the acclaimed short story 'The Events at Poroth Farm', first published in *The Year's Best Horror Stories: Series II* (1974). This was expanded to novel-length in the British Fantasy Award-winning *The Ceremonies* (1984), which he followed with *Dark Gods* (collecting three novelettes: 'Petey', 'Nadelman's God', 'Black Man with a Horn', and the short novel, 'Children of the Kingdom') and *Nightdown*. For five years Klein was editor of the successful *Rod Sterling's Twilight Zone Magazine*.

HUGH LAMB (b. 1946) was born in Sutton, Surrey. A journalist by profession, Hugh Charles Lamb is one of Britain's most diligent and accomplished anthologists of ghost and horror fiction, unearthing obscure tales by Victorian and Edwardian writers. His first anthology, *A Tide of Terror* (1972), was compiled to show that the same stories need not be reprinted endlessly. His collections have often included original fiction by some of the genre's leading contemporary writers, and he has also edited volumes by individual neglected authors (*The Best Tales of Erckmann-Chatrian* and *E. Nesbit's Tales of Terror*). Lamb discovered a lost M. R. James story for his 1975 anthology *The Thrill of Horror*, and his numerous other books include: *Victorian Tales of Terror, Star Book of Horror* volumes 1 and 2, *Terror by Gaslight, The Taste of Fear, Cold Fear, Forgotten Tales of Terror, The Man Wolf and Other Horrors, New Tales of Terror* and the recent *Gaslit Nightmares*.

DAVID LANGFORD (b. 1953) was born in Newport, Gwent, South Wales. He graduated from Oxford University and between 1975–1980 worked as a weapons physicist at the Atomic Weapons Research Establishment in Aldermaston. Since then he has been a freelance writer, critic, and software consultant, dividing his creative endeavours between books and sf fandom. His novels include *The Leaky Establishment* (based on his experiences at Aldermaston), *The Space Eater, The Wilderness of Mirrors, Earthdoom* and *Guts!* (the latter two spoof disaster and spoof horror, respectively, both co-written with John Grant). As well as short fiction, Langford also writes futurological non-fiction studies such as *War in 2080* and, in collaboration with Brian Stableford, *The Third Millennium*. He has won the Hugo Award three times.

JOE R. LANSDALE (b. 1951) was born in Gladewater, Texas, and now lives in Nacogdoches with his wife and children. He has been writing since he was nine, but only started taking it seriously around the age of twenty-five, when he admits to once getting one thousand rejection slips for three months' work! Nowadays he is less prolific but more successful, with early articles appearing—often under a pseudonym—in *Frontier Times, True West* and *Farm Journal*. A member of both the Mystery and Western Writers of America, Lansdale's short horror stories have appeared in such magazines as *Twilight Zone, Fantasy Tales, Mike Shayne* and *Cavalier*, as well as the anthologies *Masques, A Necropolis of Horror, Shadows, Fears, Mummy!, Creature!, Ghoul!* and *Spectre!*. His first novel, *Act of Love*, was a psychosexual thriller that revealed the influence of his self-confessed 'role models': Matheson, Nolan, King, Bloch and McCammon. More recent books, such as *Dead in the West, The Magic Wagon, The Nightrunners* and *The Drive-In*, have reflected Lansdale's own unique voice.

STEPHEN LAWS (b. 1952) lives in Gateshead, with his wife Lyn and young daughter Ellen, and works as a committee administrator at Newcastle Civic Centre. He has been writing since he was eight, and while at school he became a great fan of Hammer Films and actor Peter Cushing. At 27 he was writing television plays and his short stories of the supernatural were published locally and broadcast on radio. After winning a fiction competition in 1981, Laws decided to attempt his first novel. The result was *Ghost Train*, published in 1985, which received enthusiastic reviews in America and led to him being described as 'England's answer to Stephen King'. This initial success continued with two further novels, *Spectre* and *The Wyrm*, and to date his books are also published in Spain, Germany, Japan, Canada, France and Norway.

SAMAMTHA LEE (b. 1940) was born in Londonderry, Northern Ireland, but currently spends her time commuting between London and her home in Aberdeen, Scotland. Her short stories have appeared in a number of anthologies and magazines, including *The Pan Book of Horror Stories, Spectre, Nightmare, The Fontana Book of Monsters* and *Fantasy Tales*. She has also had several tales broadcast on Capital Radio's *Moment of Terror* series and her original screenplay, *The Gingerbread House*, was optioned by Orion Pictures. Lee's novels consist of 'The Lightbringer Trilogy'—*The Quest for the Sword of Infinity, The Land Where Serpents Rule* and *The Path Through the Circle of Time*—and a retelling of *Dr. Jekyll and Mr. Hyde*, to which she added a number of gruesome murders for the juvenile readers to enjoy!

H. P. (HOWARD PHILLIPS) LOVECRAFT (1890–1937) is probably the most important and influential author of supernatural fiction in the twentieth century. A life-long resident of Providence, Rhode Island, he remained a studious antiquarian and virtual recluse until his untimely death. Poor health as a young boy led him to read voluminously, and the stories of Poe, Dunsany and Machen inspired his own writing career. Although he was never prolific, Lovecraft's fiction, poems and essays received popular acclaim in the amateur press and through such pulp magazines as *Weird Tales* and *Astounding Stories*. In 1939 August Derleth and Donald Wandrei established their own imprint, Arkham House, to publish a posthumous collection, *The Outsider and Others*, and eventually bring all Lovecraft's work back into print. Many of his tales are set in the fear-haunted towns of an imaginary area of Massachusetts or in the cosmic vistas that exist beyond space and time, and a number of loosely-connected stories have become identified as 'The Cthulhu Mythos'. During the decades since his death, H. P. Lovecraft has become acknowledged as a master of modern horror and a mainstream American writer second only to Poe, while his relatively small body of work has influenced countless imitators and formed the basis of a world-wide industry of books, games and movies based on his concepts.

BRIAN LUMLEY (b. 1937) was born in Horden, on England's northeast coast just nine months after the death of H. P. Lovecraft. He claims that's just a coincidence. He joined the Army when he was twenty-one and was stationed in Germany and Cyprus, where he fell under Lovecraft's spell. He decided to try his own hand at writing horror tales, initially updating the Cthulhu Mythos, starting with his first sale, 'The Cyprus Shell' (1968). Arkham House published two collections of short stories, *The Caller of the Black* (1971) and *The Horror at Oakdene* (1977), and the novel *Beneath the Moors* (1974). He has continued Lovecraft's themes in two series of novels: *The Burrowers Beneath, The Transition of Titus Crow, Spawn of the Winds, The Clock of Dreams, In the Moons of Borea, Elysia, The Compleat Crow,* and the trilogy *Hero of Dreams, Ship of Dreams* and *Mad Moon of Dreams*. His other books include the fantasy *Khai of Ancient Khem, Psychomech, Psychosphere, Psychamok, Necroscope, Necroscope II: Wamphyri!* and a poetry collection, *Ghoul Warning*. Lumley's short fiction appears in a wide variety of small press and professional magazines and his work has been widely translated.

GRAHAM MASTERTON (b. 1946) was born in Edinburgh, exactly nine months after VE Day: 'I was a typical, miserable 1950s British schoolboy (grey flannel shorts, short-back-and-sides) but I was interested in fantasy and horror from an early age, writing my first full-length horror novel at the age of fourteen. It was about a vampire who fed on himself.' Trained as a newspaper reporter, Masterton moved on to edit *Mayfair* in the days of the mini-skirt, where his experience with tongue-in-cheek dialogue formed the basis of his first published book, *Your Erotic Fantasies*. Appointed to the executive editorship of *Penthouse*, he wrote more how-to sex books, such as *How To Drive Your Man Wild in Bed* (all of which are still selling phenomenally). His first horror novel was *The Manitou* (filmed in 1978 with Tony Curtis as the hero), followed by *Charnel House*, *Tengu*, *Mirror*, *Feast* (about gourmet cannibals), *Night Warriors*, and *Death Dreams*, amongst many others. He also writes historical sagas (*Solitaire*, *Maiden Voyage*, *Lords of the Air*) and has recently compiled *Scare Care*, an anthology of horror stories to benefit abused and needy children, which includes 38 tales from new and established authors on both sides of the Atlantic.

RICHARD CHRISTIAN MATHESON (b. 1953) is the son of acclaimed fantasist Richard Matheson. Born in Santa Monica, California, he left high school to work as an advertising copywriter. He also wrote material for stand-up comedians, played the drums, taught creative writing, freelanced as a reviewer for innumerable magazines and worked as a researcher/investigator at the Parapsychology Labs in UCLA. At the age of seventeen he sold his first short story to a hardcover anthology and four years later be became the youngest TV writer ever employed by Universal Studios. Matheson wrote more than 250 shows as diverse as *Knightrider*, *The Incredible Hulk* and *Three's Company*. He served as story editor on *The A-Team*, *Hardcastle and McCormick*, *Quincy* and *Hunter*, and recently produced and wrote the CBS-TV series *Stir Crazy*. His often short, but very sharp fiction has appeared in such magazines and anthologies as *Whispers*, *Gallery*, *Twilight Zone Magazine*, *Night Cry*, *Fantasy Tales*, *Shadows*, *Dark Forces* and *Cutting Edge*, while a collection entitled *Scars and other Distinguishing Marks* appeared from Scream/Press in 1987. Matheson is currently involved in projects with Steven Spielberg, Tobe Hooper, Dustin Hoffman and Barbara Striesand, is writing and producing a number of films and TV series, and has formed his own production company.

ROBERT R. McCAMMON (b. 1952) was born in Birmingham, Alabama, where he lives with his wife Sally. He was only 26 years old when his first novel, *Baal*, was published. Since then, he has followed it with a string of commercially successful books, including *Bethany's Sin*, *They Thirst*, *Night Boat*, *Mystery Walk*, *Usher's Passing*, *Swan Song* and *Stinger*. His shorter fiction has been collected in *Blue World* and his 1984 novelette, 'Nightcrawlers', was adapted into one of the most successful episodes on the revived *Twilight Zone* television series.

MICHAEL McDOWELL (b. 1950) was born in Alabama, and currently divides his time between Boston and Los Angeles. He is the author of more than thirty books, published under his own name and four different pseudonyms. His first horror novel, *The Amulet*, was published in 1979, and has been followed by *Cold Moon Over Babylon*, *The Elementals* and the six-volume *Blackwater* saga. Other books under his real name include the historical melodramas *Katie* and *Gilded Needles*, the macabre/surreal *Toplin* (illustrated by Harry O. Morris), and the *Jack and Susan* series of romantic adventures. He has written more than a dozen half-hour scripts for anthology TV shows like *Tales From the Darkside*, and has turned to the cinema with the Neil Jordan ghost comedy *High Spirits* and Tim Burton's box-office hit *Beetlejuice*. His hobbies include collecting American sheet music, 18th and 19th Century death memorabilia, the documentation of American crime, and photographs of corpses, criminals and atrocities.

THOMAS F. MONTELEONE (b. 1946) was born in Baltimore, Maryland, and has been a professional writer since 1972. He has published sixteen novels, a collection of short stories and edited two anthologies. His short stories and articles have appeared in more than a hundred anthologies and magazines. Monteleone's recent novels include *Night Train*, *Lyrica*, *The Magnificent Gallery*, *The Crooked House*, *Fantasma*, *Dragonstar Destiny* and *The Apocalypse Man*. Two of his stage plays have been produced professionally, and he has written several screenplays for television—one of which, *Mister Magister*, won the Gabriel Award and the Bronze Award from the International Film and Television Festival of New York.

MICHAEL MOORCOCK (b. 1939) was born in London and is one of Britain's most popular and prolific authors. He became involved with science fiction and fantasy at an early age, editing *Tarzan Adventures* when he was seventeen, and was the guiding hand behind the British sf magazine *New Worlds* from 1964. A major influence in the growing development of 'New Wave' fiction throughout the 'sixties, Moorcock's enormous output includes more than sixty novels, innumerable short stories, a rock album, numerous individual rock songs, and the screen play for *The Land That Time Forgot* (1974). Best known for his heroic fantasy series using the notion of a multiverse, his series characters include Elric of Melnibone, Corum, Dorian Hawkmoon, Count Brass, Jerry Cornelius and the Eternal Champion. His recent books include *Letters from Hollywood*, *The Dragon and the Sword*, *The City of the Autumn Stars*, *Wizardry and Wild Romance* and the partly autobiographical *Mother London*. A multiple winner of the British Fantasy Award for his novels and short fiction, Moorcock has also won the Nebula Award (for *Behold the Man*), the Guardian Fiction Award (*The Condition of Muzak*) and the World Fantasy Award (*Gloriana*).

PETER NICHOLLS (b. 1939) was born in Australia, where he lived for almost thirty years before moving to Britain in 1970. His adult life has oscillated cunningly between academic work (lecturing in English Literature at several Universities, the first administrator of the Science Fiction Foundation, 1971–77), media work (award-winning television documentary scripts, studied film writing in Hollywood), and freelance writing and editing. He edited *Foundation: The Review of Science Fiction* from 1974–78 and his books as editor or part-author include *Science Fiction at Large* (or *Explorations of the Marvellous*), *The Science Fiction Encyclopedia*, and *The Science in Science Fiction*; he is also the author of *Fantastic Cinema*. A regular reviewer of science fiction, fantasy and horror, both books and films, for BBC radio for several years, Nicholls returned to Australia to live in 1988. He is currently planning a critical and historical study of fantasy fiction for children.

WILLIAM F. (FRANCIS) NOLAN (b. 1928) was born in Kansas City and moved to California when he was nineteen. The author of more than forty-five books and more than 600 short stories, he has been a commercial artist, racing car driver, publisher of *The Ray Bradbury Review* and a friend of Steve McQueen. Nolan's first sf story, 'The Joy of Living', appeared in *If*, (1954), and his books include the novels *Logan's Run* (co-written with George Clayton Johnson) and its two sequels, *Space for Hire*, and the collections *Aliens Horizons*, *Wonderworlds*, *Things Beyond Midnight* and *Nightshapes*. He has twice won the Mystery Writers of America Edgar Allan Poe Award, and his biographies include McQueen, Dashiell Hammett and racing speed king Barney Oldfield. Nolan has also written a number of film scripts for both the cinema and television, including *Logan's Run*, *Burnt Offerings*, *Trilogy of Terror*, *The Norliss Tapes* and *Bridge Across Time*. He is currently scripting a CBS-TV Movie of the Week and writing a new horror novel.

GERALD W. PAGE (b. 1939) was born in Chattanooga, Tennessee, but has lived most of his life in Atlanta, Georgia. He has been interested in fantastic fiction for as long as he can remember and sold his first story to John Campbell's *Analog* in 1963. He continued to turn out the occasional sf and horror story for a variety of magazines while being employed for several years as a programming editor in *TV Guide*'s Atlanta office and teaching a course in Modern Science Fiction at the Atlanta College of Art. In 1970 Page became editor of *Witchcraft and Sorcery* (a short-lived magazine that had started life as *Coven 13*), and went on to edit the original Arkham House anthology *Nameless Places* (1975) and volumes IV–VII of DAW Books' *The Year's Best Horror Stories Series*.

MICHEL PARRY (b. 1947) was born in Brussels, Belgium of a Welsh father. His first published writings were contributions to magazines such as *Castle of Frankenstein* and *Famous Monsters of Filmland* in the early 1960s. In 1969 he produced his own short surreal film, *Hex* and his script for *The Uncanny* was filmed in 1977 with an all-star cast. A prolific anthologist, his numerous books include six volumes of *The Mayflower Book of Black Magic* (1974–77), the four-volume *Reign of Terror* (1976–78), *Rivals of Dracula*, *Rivals of Frankenstein*, *Rivals of King Kong*, *Christopher Lee's 'X' Certificate*, *Christopher Lee's Omnibus of Evil*, *Savage Heroes*, *Strange Ecstasies*, *Dream Trips*, *Spaced Out*, *Jack the Knife*, and two books of sex and horror stories, *The Devil's Kisses* and *More Devil's Kisses*, edited under the pseudonym 'Linda Lovecraft'. Parry has also written the novelization of *Countess Dracula*, several western novels under the pen name of Steve Lee, and a non-fiction book about mercenaries, *Fire Power*. His most recent screenplays include a short fantasy, *The Zip*, and a supernatural adventure set in Mexico, *Falco*. He is currently working on the screenplay for a comedy fantasy set in Los Angeles.

DAVID PIRIE (b. 1946) was born and grew up in Scotland. He began his writing career as a film critic for the London listings magazine *Time Out* and he is the author of several critical studies like *A Heritage of Horror* (about English Gothic cinema) *The Vampire Cinema* and *Anatomy of the Movies* (about Hollywood finance). He began writing screenplays in 1984 with the prize-winning BBC-TV film *Rainy Day Women* starring Charles Dance and Lindsay Duncan. His subsequent screenplays have included an adaptation of his own novel, *Mystery Story*, for Barry Hanson and *Total Eclipse of the Heart* for David Puttnam and Warner Bros. In 1988 he delivered *Love-Act* for producer Michael White and MGM, and *Wild Things* for BBC's 'Screen Two' series. Pirie is currently working on an original financial thriller called *Treasure* for HBO.

EDGAR ALLAN POE (1809–1849) has been described as 'the father of modern horror' (and of scientific and detective fiction as well). He was born in Boston to parents who were itinerant actors, but the death of his mother and desertion of his father resulted in Poe, aged three, being made the ward of Virginia merchant John Allan, who later disowned him. Expelled from the University of Virginia for not paying his gambling debts and dismissed from the West Point military academy for deliberate neglect of duty, Poe finally embarked on a literary career. In 1836 he married his 13-year-old cousin Virginia Clemm, who burst a blood vessel in 1842 and remained a virtual invalid until her death from tuberculosis five years later. Poe suffered from bouts of depression and madness and in 1848 he attempted suicide. In September 1849, on his way to visit his new fiancée in Richmond, he vanished for three days, and inexplicably turned up in a delirious condition in Baltimore, where he died a few days later. Poe had published a volume of poetry, *Tamerlane*, in 1827 but it wasn't until he wrote 'The Raven' (1845) that he became known as 'Mr. Poe the poet'. His first short story, 'Metzengerstein', appeared in 1832, and although his tales of madness and premature burial were admired, they never gained him wealth or recognition until after his death. His best stories include 'The Fall of the House of Usher' (1839), 'William Wilson' (1839), 'The Murders in the Rue Morgue' (1841), 'The Black Cat' (1843), 'The Gold Bug' (1843), 'The Tell-Tale Heart' (1843), 'The Pit and the Pendulum' (1842), 'The Premature Burial' (1844) and 'The Facts in the Case of M. Valdemar' (1845). Poe's only novel was *The Narrative of A. Gordon Pym* (1837).

TERRY PRATCHETT (b. 1948) was born in Beaconsfield, England, and moved to Winscombe in the early 1970s. He worked as a journalist before becoming Press Officer for the Central Electricity Board Western Region, with special responsibility for nuclear power. In 1987 he gave the CEGB three months' notice and became a full-time writer. Pratchett's early books include the children's novel *The Carpet People* (1970) and two science fiction adventures, *The Dark Side of the Sun* and *Strata*. In 1983 he scored an unexpected success with *The Colour of Magic*, a comedy-fantasy set in the mythical Discworld, that still sells a steady 2,000 copies a month in Britain alone! To date Pratchett has written five Discworld books: *The Light Fantastic*, *Equal Rites*, *Mort*, *Sourcery* and *Wyrd Sisters*, while he has another novel, *Pyramid*, forthcoming.

GEOFF RYMAN (b. 1951) was born in Canada and has lived in London since the early 1970s. He experienced a number of jobs while establishing himself as a full-time writer, and his first story was published in 1976. A successful playwright whose work includes an adaptation of Philip K. Dick's *The Transmigration of Timothy Archer* novel), his first novel, *The Warrior Who Carried Life*, appeared in 1985 and his story 'The Unconquered Country', which was originally published in *Interzone*, won the 1985 World Fantasy Award for Best Novella. His forthcoming novels include *A Low Comedy*.

JESSICA AMANDA SALMONSON (b. 1950) lives in Seattle, Washington, where she writes, edits and watches numerous samurai movies. In 1980 she won the World Fantasy Award for her anthology *Amazons!*, and followed it with *Amazons II* and *Tales By Moonlight*. An expert on the supernatural fiction of the last century, Salmonson's own novels reflect her love of Japanese culture and High Fantasy, with titles like *Tomoe Gozen*, *The Golden Naginata* and *The Swordswoman*.

AL SARRANTONIO (b. 1952) was born in Queens, New York, and currently lives in Putnam Valley, N.Y., with his wife and two sons. He has published more than forty short stories in such magazines as *Heavy Metal*, *Twilight Zone*, *Analog* and *Isaac Asimov's Science Fiction Magazine*, as well as in such anthologies as *Shadows*, *Whispers*, *Great Ghost Stories* and *The Year's Best Horror Stories*. He was a book reviewer for the late *Night Cry* magazine and currently reviews horror books for *Mystery Scene*. Sarrantonio's novels include *The Boy with Penny Eyes*, *Totentanz*, *Campbell Wood*, *The Worms*, *Moonbane*, *House Haunted* and *Cold Night*.

DAVID J. SCHOW (b. 1955) was born in Marburg, West Germany, and lived in Middlesex, England, until 1957 when he moved to the United States. In 1985 he won *Twilight Zone* magazine's Dimension Award for his short story, 'Coming Soon to a Theatre Near You'. Based on a reader poll, the prize was only given once as, shortly afte the ceremony, the organizer was sacked! However, Schow's stories continued to appear in a wide variety of magazines and anthologies—he is a regular contributor to Karl Edward Wagner's *Year's Best Horror Stories*—and in 1987 he won the World Fantasy Award for his tale, 'Red Light'. He is the author of several novelizations under a psuedonym, and is co-author of *The Outer Limits: The Official Companion*. His horror novel *The Kill Riff* appeared in 1988 along with his anthology of cinema horror stories, *Silver Scream*. A self-avowed 'Splatter Punk', Schow is currently working on two novels, *The Shaft* and *Gore Movie*, and a pair of collections, *Seeing Red* and *Lost Angels*.

DAN SIMMONS (b. 1948) was born in Peoria, Illinois. A teacher for eighteen years, he lives with his wife and daughter in Colorado. He began writing his first short fiction at the age of nine and in 1982 he won the Rod Sterling Memorial Award for his story 'The River Styx Runs Upstream'. He has also contributed to such magazines as *Omni, Twilight Zone* and *Asimov's*. Simmons' first novel, *Song of Kali*, won the 1986 World Fantasy Award for Best Novel and was described by Harlan Ellison as 'one of the most brilliant first novels I've read'. His subsequent books include the novels *Phases of Gravity, Carrion Comfort, Tales of Hyperion* and *The Fall of Hyperion*, the short-story collection *Eyes I Dare Not Meet in Dreams*, and one-third of *Night Vision 5* (with Stephen King and George R. R. Martin).

JOHN SKIPP (b. 1957) is one of a new breed of writers working at the cutting-edge of urban horror. He was born in Milwaukee, Wisconsin (the beer capital of the U.S.) and has lived in a variety of locations: Arlington, Va; Buenos Aires, Argentina; York, Pa; and New York City. He was forced to leave Buenos Aires at the age of thirteen when President Ongania was deposed and grew up with a healthy disrespect for authority, and a need to rock 'n' roll. Skipp started writing horror stories at the age of ten and had his first bestseller in 1986 with *The Light at the End* (co-written with Craig Spector). He has subsequently published *The Cleanup, The Scream, Dead Lines* and the novelization of *Fright Night*, as well as a number of shorter pieces, mostly in collaboration with Spector. Skipp's ambition is to be the Woody Allen of horror: 'To whit: To write, direct, produce, score and star in films where I play this nebbish who gets horribly murdered, then wanders around whining about how death is even worse than he thought it would be, and he still doesn't understand what it all means.'

JOHN SLADEK (b. 1937) was born in Iowa and lived in London for many years. He was educated at the University of Minnesota, where he studied mechanical engineering and English Literature. Since then he has worked as a technical writer, barman, draughtsman and railroadman. His first published story was 'The Poets of Milgrave, Iowa' in *New Worlds* (1966) and he started writing science fiction with 'The Happy Breed' in Harlan Ellison's *Dangerous Visions* anthology the following year. Sladek's first novel, *The Reproductive System*, was published to enormous critical acclaim in 1968, and his blend of black comedy and sf has been likened to Kurt Vonnegut at his best. The author's other books include *The Müller-Fokker Effect, The Steam-Driven Boy, Keep the Giraffe Burning, Roderick, Roderick At Random, Alien Accounts* and *Tik-Tok*. His detective novel *Black Aura* contains borderline sf elements, and he has collaborated with Thomas M. Disch on the Gothic novel *The House That Fear Built* (as 'Cassandra Knye', 1966) and *Black Alice*.

GUY N. SMITH (b. 1939) is the versatile and incredibly prolific author of more than fifty best-selling horror novels. He was born in Tamworth, Staffordshire, and currently resides in Shropshire with his wife Jean, where he works as a farmer, bookseller and writer of ecological/countryside books (with such titles as *The Rough Shooter's Handbook, Practical Country Living* and *Moles and their Control*). He began writing when he was twelve and entered the horror genre in 1974 with *Werewolf by Moonlight*. The following year he gave up his job in banking and became a full-time writer, turning out a remarkable number of lively novels with such colourful titles as *The Ghoul* (a film novelization), *The Sucking Pit*, *The Slime Beast*, *Night of the Crabs* (and its several sequels), *Abomination*, *Cannibals*, *The Festering*, *Carnivore*, *Mania*, and the *Sabat* series of pulp supernatural adventures. His major occult novel set in Russia, *Fiend*, recently appeared as a lead-title in Britain.

CRAIG SPECTOR (b. 1958) was born in the confederate capitol, Richmond, Virginia. Spector tells us 'Tom Robbins once described Richmond as a town "settled by a race of thin bony-faced psychopaths", who would "sell you anything they had, which was nothing, and kill you over anything they didn't understand, which was everything". Of course, he was referring to *South* Richmond, and I was in the West End, but there you are. Narrowly escaping a promising career of juvenile delinquency in Virginia Beach by being force-marched to Pennsylvania at the tender age of fifteen, where I shortly thereafter met John Skipp and began the series of creative mutations that led me to where I am today. Used to consider myself a cartoonist, until art school beat it out of me. Hands-down winner of *Most Surprising Mutation* award.' Like Stan Laurel and Lou Costello, Spector is condemned by alphabetical order in reference books to have all his works listed under his partner's name. For works, see under John Skipp.

BRIAN STABLEFORD (b. 1948), author, critic and academic, was born in Shipley, Yorkshire. In 1969 he graduated from the University of York with first class honours in Biology, and went on to complete postgraduate research in Biology and Sociology (a thesis on *The Sociology of Science Fiction* was presented in 1978). He is currently a lecturer in the Sociology Department of the University of Reading. Stableford began writing science fiction in his teens, and to date he is the author of more than thirty novels and a number of reference works. He won the European SF Award in 1984 for *The Science of Science Fiction* (written in collaboration with Peter Nicholls and David Langford). He has recently completed two novels: *The Centre Cannot Hold* concludes the trilogy begun with *Journey to the Centre* and *Invaders from the Centre*, set on a gigantic hollow world; while *The Empire of Fear* is an alternative history adventure, where the 17th-century empires established in Europe and Asia by a race of vampires begin to crumble following the revolution in scientific thought.

TIM STOUT (b. 1946) is a legal journalist who lives in Leigh-on-Sea, Essex, with his wife, son and daughter. His early work in the horror field included contributions to John Carpenter's fanzine *Fantastic Films Illustrated*, and editing two issues of the British film magazine *Supernatural* (1969). Becoming a writer of short stories, he published two collections—*Hollow Laughter* and *The Doomsdeath Chronicles*—before turning to novels with *The Raging*, the tale of a haunted Celtic statue. He admits to a preference for the restraints and polished style of such old masters as Stoker, Conan Doyle, Wells, Machen, and his all-time favourite author, H. Rider Haggard. Stout's most recent novels include *Dark Image*, a genetics mystery yarn, and *Green Blood*, a speculative look at the horrors of environmental pollution.

PETER STRAUB (b. 1943) is probably regarded second only to his friend Stephen King as America's most popular horror novelist. Born in Milwaukee, Wisconsin, he taught at a private Milwaukee school for boys, where he wrote poetry published in a number of British and American literary journals (eventually collected together in *Leeson Park and Belsize Square* (1983)). He began his first novel, *Marriages* (1973), while working on his doctorate at University College, Dublin, and he followed it with a string of popular best-sellers that include *Julia* (filmed in 1976 as *Full Circle*—a.k.a. *The Haunting of Julia*—starring Mia Farrow), *If You Could See Me Now*, *Ghost Story* (poorly filmed in 1981), *Shadow Land*, *Floating Dragon*, *Wild Animals* (containing *Julia*, *If You Could See Me Now* and the non-genre novel *Under Venus*) and *Koko*. In 1977 he collaborated with Stephen King on *The Talisman*, which combined a fantasy quest with elements of both authors' horror fiction.

MILTON SUBOTSKY (b. 1921) was born in New York City, and despite majoring in chemical engineering, he started writing, editing and directing educational, documentary and industrial films at the age of seventeen. After World War II he wrote scripts for such TV shows as *Lights Out*, *Danger*, *Suspense*, *The Clock* and *Mr. I Magination*. He teamed up with financier Max J. Rosenberg to make the feature musical *Rock, Rock, Rock* (1956), for which Subotsky wrote nine songs, including a No. 1 hit! He moved to England in 1959 to produce *City of the Dead* (a.k.a. *Horror Hotel*), a low-budget horror film starring Christopher Lee, and his successful 1964 production, *Dr. Terror's House of Horrors*, led to the formation of Amicus Productions. Second only to Hammer Films during the 1960s and early '70s, Amicus produced a string of horror and science fiction films, many scripted by Subotsky: *Dr. Who and the Daleks*, *The Skull*, *Torture Garden*, *Scream and Scream Again*, *The House That Dripped Blood*, *Tales from the Crypt* and *The Land That Time Forgot*, amongst numerous others. More recently he has produced *The Uncanny*, *Dominique*, *The Monster Club* and the TV mini-series of Ray Bradbury's *The Martian Chronicles*. An avid reader, Subotsky has also co-edited an anthology of science fiction stories and written the TV series and book *The Golden Treasury of Classic Fairy Tales*.

JACK SULLIVAN (b. 1946) lives in New York and is a teacher and lecturer on the ghost story, English and humanities. His short story, 'The Initiation', was published in Ramsey Campbell's anthology *New Terrors* (1980). Sullivan is the author of *Elegant Nightmares: The English Ghost Story from Le Fanu to Blackwood* (which develops Robert Aickman's insight that the ghost story is akin to poetry) and a book on music criticism, *Words on Music*; he has also edited *Lost Souls: A Collection of English Ghost Stories* and *The Penguin Encyclopedia of Horror and the Supernatural*. He reviews regularly for *The New York Times Book Review* and *Washington Post Book World*.

STEVE RASNIC TEM (b. 1950) was born in Pennington Gap, Virginia, in the heart of the Appalachian Mountains. He received his Masters in Creative Writing at Colorado State University and currently lives with his wife, the writer Melanie Tem, and two of his three children in a supposedly haunted Victorian house in Denver. Tem has sold more than a hundred poems and a similar number of short stories to such magazines and anthologies as *Fantasy Tales*, *Weirdbook*, *Whispers*, *Twilight Zone*, *Shadows*, *Cutting Edge*, *Halloween Horrors I* and *II*, *Tales By Moonlight I* and *II*, and *Tropical Chills*. His first novel, *Excavation*, appeared in 1987 and was followed by a second, *Deadfall Hotel*.

THOMAS TESSIER (b. 1947) was born in Connecticut, where he currently lives. Educated at University College, Dublin, he spent several years in London, where he was a regular contributor to *Vogue*. The author of three books of poems and three plays that were professionally staged, his novels include *The Fates*, *Shockwaves*, *The Nightwalker*, *Phantom* (nominated for the 1982 World Fantasy Award for Best Novel), *Finishing Touches* and *Rapture*.

PETER TREMAYNE (b. 1943) is the pseudonym of author and Celtic historian Peter Berresford Ellis. The youngest son of a journalist, he was born in Coventry, England, but because of his father's work received his education in a dozen different schools around the country. After studying at Brighton College of Art he tried his hand as a reporter, magazine editor, and lecturer. Being of Irish descent on his father's side, he travelled widely in Ireland, studying its history, politics, language and culture, later broadening his interest to all Celtic countries. Already the author of such political volumes as *Wales—A Nation Again* and *A History of the Irish Working Class*, Ellis used the 'Peter Tremayne' alias on his first horror novel, *Hound of Frankenstein*, published by Mills & Boon! Since then he has published more than a dozen horror and fantasy novels with such commercial titles as *Dracula Unborn*, *The Ants*, *The Curse of Loch Ness*, *Dracula, My Love*, *Zombie!*, *The Morgow Rises*, *Swamp!*, *Kiss of the Cobra*, *Angelus!* and *Ravenmoon*. Tremayne has edited *Masters of Terror: William Hope Hodgson* and *Irish Masters of Fantasy*, his infrequent short fiction appears in magazines and anthologies on both sides of the Atlantic, and six short horror stories are collected together in *My Lady of Hy-Brasil*.

LISA TUTTLE (b. 1952) was born in Texas but has lived in Britain since 1980. An early member of the Clarion SF Writers' Workshop, she won the John W. Campbell Award for best new science fiction writer in 1974. Her first book, *Windhaven*, was a collaboration with George R. R. Martin. Since then she has published two supernatural novels, *Familiar Spirit* and *Gabriel*, and the non-fiction studies, *Encyclopedia of Feminism* and *Heroines*. Her excellent short fiction has been collected in *A Spaceship Built of Stone* and *A Nest of Nightmares*.

KARL EDWARD WAGNER (b. 1945) was born in Knoxville, Tennessee, and trained as a psychiatrist before becoming a full-time writer and editor. His first novel, *Darkness Weaves With Many Shades* (which appeared in a much-butchered edition in 1970) introduced Kane the Mystic Swordsman, and was the first in an intelligent and often extremely brutal heroic fantasy series that continued with *Death Angel's Shadow*, *Bloodstone*, *Dark Crusade* and the collections *Night Winds* and *The Book of Kane*. Wagner also developed the exploits of two of Robert E. Howard's characters, Conan and Bran Mak Morn, in the novels *The Road of Kings* and *Legion from the Shadows*, and his other books include *Sign of the Salamander*, *Killer* (co-written with David Drake), *In A Lonely Place* and *Why Not You and I?* He has edited nine volumes of *The Year's Best Horror Stories* and three *Echoes of Valor* anthologies. A multiple British Fantasy Award winner for his stories 'Sticks' (1974), 'Two Suns Setting' (1976) and 'Neither Brute Nor Human' (1983), he also won the Special Award in 1982 and the World Fantasy Award the following year for his story 'Beyond Any Measure'.

IAN WATSON (b. 1943) was born and raised on Tyneside. After receiving a first class Honours degree in English and a research degree from Oxford, he lectured in literature for several years in Tanzania and Tokyo. Returning to teach future studies at Birmingham Polytechnic, he has been a full-time writer since 1976. His first sf story was 'Roof Garden Under Saturn' in *New Worlds* (1969), and although he has published numerous short stories since, it is as a novelist that he has gained his reputation: His novel *The Embedding* was nominated for the John W. Campbell Memorial Award in 1974 and won the Prix Apollo in its French translation the following year. Subsequent novels have included *The Jonah Kit* (winner of the British Science Fiction Award for 1978), *The Martian Inca*, *Alien Embassy*, *The Book of the River*, *Queenmagic*, *Kingmagic* and *Whores of Babylon*. More recently he has turned to horror with such novels as *The Power*, *The Fire Worm* and *Meat*. Watson lives with his wife and daughter in a small Northamptonshire village and is an active member of CND and the Labour Party.

TAD WILLIAMS (b. 1957) has been a rock and roll singer, a shoe salesman, a talk-show host, an insurance agent, a radio journalist and a commercial artist. Born in California, he grew up in Palo Alto, where he loved reading from an early age. He began writing at the age of 24 and his first novel, *Tailchaser's Song* (1985), became a bestseller. Moving from ginger tomcats to Heroic Fantasy, Williams' next book, *The Dragonbone Chair* (1988), is the first in a trilogy entitled 'Memory, Sorrow & Thorn'. He had a short story in the revived *Weird Tales* magazine and is currently producing a black comedy series for television about Valley Vision, a TV station situated in Silicon Valley.

CHET WILLIAMSON (b. 1948) was born in Lancaster, Pennsylvania. His first short story was published in 1981, and his fiction has appeared widely in such magazines as *Playboy*, *Twilight Zone*, *The Magazine of Fantasy and Science Fiction*, *Alfred Hitchcock Mystery Magazine*, *New Yorker*, *Games*, *New Black Mask* and *Skullduggery*. Williamson's first novel, *Soulstorm* (1986) was an inventive reworking of the traditional haunted house theme, and he has since published *Ash Wednesday* and *Lowland Rider*.

JACK WILLIAMSON (b. 1908) was born in Arizona and raised in New Mexico, where he still lives. After discovering *Amazing Stories* and being influenced by its 1927 serialization of *The Moon Pool* by A. Merritt, he decided to try writing stories for the magazine. His first published effort, 'The Metal Man' (1928) was obviously influenced by Merritt, but over the next couple of decades he produced a prolific amount of sf and fantasy fiction for the pulp magazines, including 'Golden Blood' (*Weird Tales*, 1933), 'The Reign of Wizardry' (*Unknown*, 1940) and the classic werewolf novel, 'Darker Than You Think' (*Unknown*, 1940). Early in his career he began writing his most famous work, the 'Legion of Space' series comprising *The Legion of Space* (1934), *The Cometeers* (1936), *One Against the Legion* (1939) and *Nowhere Near* (1967). Williamson's best-known novel, *The Humanoids*, was published in 1949 and he collaborated with Frederik Pohl on the 'Undersea' and 'Starchild' trilogies. Since 1960, Williamson has been actively involved in promoting sf as an academic subject, winning the Pilgrim Award in 1973 for his work. In 1976 he was awarded the second Grand Master Nebula.

J. (JERRY) N. WILLIAMSON (b. 1932) was born and raised in Indianapolis, where he still lives with his wife Mary and their six children. Since starting out as a horror writer in 1979, his incredibly prolific output has resulted in more than thirty novels, from publishers such as Leisure and Zebra Books, with colourful titles like *The Evil One, Death-Coach, Ghost Mansion, The Dentist, Babel's Children, The Offspring, The Houngan, Ghost, Dead to the World* and *The Black School*. More recently, his short fiction has appeared in *Night Cry* and *Twilight Zone* magazines and in such anthologies as *Phantom of the Opera Stories, Scare Care, Whispers IV* and *14 Vicious Valentines*. Williamson has also edited three volumes of the popular *Masques* anthologies, and also *How To Write Tales of Horror, Fantasy and Science Fiction* for Writer's Digest Books.

COLIN WILSON (b. 1931) was born in Leicester and is at once one of Britain's most respected and controversial literary figures. He left school at the age of sixteen and worked in a variety of jobs until he gained international recognition eight years later with his first book—an 'inquiry into the nature of the sickness of mankind'—titled *The Outsider*. Since then he has written more than fifty books on a diversity of subjects: psychosexual thrillers (*Ritual in the Dark, The Sex Diary of Gerard Sorme, Lingard*), non-fiction studies of literary creativity and the paranormal (*The Strength of Dream, The Occult, Mysteries, Poltergeist!*), H. P. Lovecraft-inspired horrors (*The Mind Parasites, The Philospher's Stone, The Return of Lloigor*) and straightforward science fiction adventures (*The Space Vampires*—filmed as *Lifeforce*, which he describes as 'the worst movie of all time!', and the *Spider World* series), as well as historical fiction, mysteries, spy stories, biographies and works on philosophy, psychology and sexuality.

F. PAUL WILSON (b. 1946) was born and raised in New Jersey, where he misspent his youth playing with matches, poring over E.C. and Uncle Scrooge Comics, listening to Chuck Berry and Alan Freed, and watching Soupy Sales and horror movies. (He would sneak off on Saturday afternoons to catch sf horror double features at the Oritani Theatre in Hackensack, stay up late to watch Zacherly on TV's *Shock Theatre*, and managed to see *King Kong* eleven times in one week on *Million Dollar Movie*). Eventually he learned to read, and even write. His short fiction first saw print in *Startling Mystery Stories 18* in 1971, while he was studying as a medical student, and since then he has appeared in all the major science fiction and fantasy magazines. He is the author of three sf novels (*Healer, Wheels Within Wheels, An Enemy of the State*), a trio of successful horror books (*The Keep, The Tomb, Black Wind*) and a supernatural medical thriller (*The Touch*). Over two million copies of his books are in print in America, and he hasn't the faintest idea how many are floating around overseas. Wilson describes the 1983 movie version of *The Keep* as 'visually striking but perfectly incomprehensible', and he currently resides at the Jersey Shore with his wife and two daughters.

DOUGLAS E. WINTER (b. 1950) is a Washington D.C. lawyer and probably the horror/fantasy genre's premièr critic. He is the author of the definitive biography and literary study, *Stephen King: The Art of Darkness* (1984), and a history of contemporary horror fiction, *Faces of Fear* (1985), and Winter's fiction, criticism and interviews have appeared in books and magazines as diverse as *Gallery, Harper's Bazaar, Saturday Review, Twilight Zone, Fantasy Newsletter/Review, Midnight* and *Greystone Bay*, as well as numerous major metropolitan newspapers. Also the editor of *Shadowings* and *Black Wine* and a major contributor to *The Penguin Encyclopedia of Horror and the Supernatural*, his most recent books include *Splatter: A Cautionary Tale*, the state-of-the-art anthology *Prime Evil*, and the novel *From Parts Unknown*, written with Charles L. Grant.

GENE WOLFE (b. 1931) was born in Brooklyn, New York, and raised mainly in Houston, Texas. He attended Texas A&M, the University of Houston and Miami University, and today he lives with his wife, Rosemary, in Barrington, Illinois. The author of more than a hundred science fiction and fantasy stories, he made his début with a supernatural thriller, 'The Dead Man', published in 1965 in *Sir* magazine. His first book, *Operation Ares*, appeared in 1970, and was followed by *The Fifth Head of Cerberus* (a collection of three linked novellas), *Peace, The Devil in a Forest, Free Live Free, Soldier of the Mist* and two collections of short stories, *The Island of Doctor Death and Other Stories and Other Stories* and *Gene Wolfe's Book of Days*. In 1980, the first volume in Wolfe's 'The Book of the New Sun' tetralogy was published to major acclaim: *The Shadow of the Torturer* was described by Ursula Le Guin as 'the first volume of a masterpiece' and won both the World Fantasy Award and the British Science Fiction Award. The second book, *The Claw of the Conciliator*, won the 1982 Nebula Award, and was followed by *The Sword of the Lictor* and *The Citadel of the Autarch*. The saga quickly attained a cult status as one of the most original and important works of modern sf and fantasy, and an eagerly-awaited coda to the series, *The Urth of the New Sun*, appeared in 1987.

DONALD A. (ALLEN) WOLLHEIM (b. 1914) was born in New York

City and together with Forrest J Ackerman was one of the leading members of the embryonic science fiction fandom during the 1930s. His first published story was 'The Man from Ariel' in *Wonder Stories* (1934), although his fiction didn't appear widely until the following decade. The author of more than twenty books and numerous short stories (often under the pseudonym 'David Grinnell'), Wollheim has been a professional editor since 1941, with such magazines as *Cosmic Stories*, *Stirring Science Stories* and the *Avon Fantasy Reader*, as well as a multitude of sf anthologies to his credit. After the Second World War he worked for Avon Books, before moving to Ace Books in 1952, where he edited their acclaimed sf list for twenty years. He formed his own highly successful imprint, DAW Books, in 1971, which is still going strong. Wollheim has been semi-retired since 1985, although he is still technically President and Publisher, and he continues to be a major editorial influence on the entire sf and fantasy field.

JANE YOLEN (b. 1939) was born in New York City, grew up in Westport, Connecticut and currently lives with her husband and children in the small New England town of Hatfield, Massachusetts. The author of more than ninety fantasy books for both children and adults, her output ranges from picture books (*Owl Moon*, *The Emperor & The Kite*, *An Invitation to the Butterfly Ball*) to fairy tale collections (*The Girl Who Cried Flowers*, *Merlin's Booke*, *Dragonfield*) to non-fiction (*Ring Out: A Books of Bells*) to novels (*Cards of Grief*, *Dragon's Blood*, *Children of the Wolf*) and poetry. Her most recent volumes include a sword-and-sorcery novel, *Sister Light, Sister Dark*; *The Devil's Arithmetic*, a time-travel adventure for young adults; *Were-wolves*, an anthology co-edited with Martin Greenberg, and a collection of Hallowe'en poems for children, *Best Witches*. She is the recipient of numerous awards, including the World Fantasy Award, The Caldecott Medal, The Christopher Medal and the 1988 Kerlan Award for attainments in children's literature.

ABOUT THE EDITORS

STEPHEN JONES (b. 1953) lives in Wembley, Middlesex. Winner of the 1984 World Fantasy Award and seven-time recipient of the British Fantasy Award for his fiction magazine *Fantasy Tales* (co-edited with David Sutton), he is also a full-time columnist, film-reviewer, illustrator, television producer/director and horror movie publicist (*Hellraiser*, *Hellraiser II*, etc.) His early interview with Stephen King was recently reprinted in the non-fiction volume *Bare Bones*, he is the co-author of a short horror story in the *Shadows 11* anthology, co-editor of the *Fantasy Tales* anthology *Best Horror* and *Now We Are Sick*, a collection of 'nasty' children's verse, and the compiler of *Clive Barker's Shadows in Eden*.

KIM NEWMAN (b. 1959) lives in Crouch End, London. Freelance writer, film critic, broadcaster and sometime kazoo-player, his reviews and essays appear regularly in *City Limits*, *The Monthly Film Bulletin*, *The New Statesman*, *Sheep Worrying*, *Shock Xpress* and other publications. A playwright whose works include the gruesome thriller *My One Little Murder Can't Do Any Harm* and the musical *The Gold Diggers of 1981*, his short fiction has appeared in both *Interzone* anthologies and *Best Horror* from 'Fantasy Tales'. He is a major contributor to *The Penguin Encyclopedia of Horror and the Supernatural, The Penguin Encyclopedia of Mystery and Suspense* and *The BFI Companion to the Western*, co-compiler of *Ghastly Beyond Belief*, the science fiction book of quotations, and the author of *Nightmare Movies*, an acclaimed critical history of the horror film since 1968.

LIST OF RECOMMENDED READING

Inevitably, in a work like this – with its more or less random sampling of 100 titles – certain important books and authors have unavoidably been overlooked or forgotten. Therefore, in collaboration with our distinguished line-up of contributors, we've compiled this list of recommended books. We could have presented a comprehensive listing, but that would have meant dropping everything else in the book, so regard this – unabashedly arbitrary – list as a guide to further reading in the genre rather than a pantheon of classics engraved in marble and handed down to posterity.

– THE EDITORS

458 BC:	*The Oresteia*, Aeschylus	1831:	*Notre Dame De Paris/*
1300:	*Inferno*, Dante		*The Hunchback of Notre*
1657:	*Paradise Lost*, John		*Dame*, Victor Hugo
	Milton	1834:	*Pikovaia Dama/Queen of*
1764:	*The Castle of Otranto*,		*Spades*, Aleksandr
	Horace Walpole		Pushkin
1776:	*Ugetsu Monogatari/*	1838:	*The Narrative of Arthur*
	Tales of The Pale Moon		*Gordon Pym*, Edgar Allan
	After Rain, Ueda Akinari		Poe
1778:	*The Old English Baron*,	1839:	*The Phantom Ship*,
	Clara Reeve		Frederick Marryat
1788:	*Vathek*, William Beckford	1843:	*A Christmas Carol*,
1794:	*The Mysteries of*		Charles Dickens
	Udolpho, Anne Radcliffe	1845:	*Varney The Vampire*,
1798:	*Weiland; or: The*		J. M. Rymer
	Transformation, Charles	1847:	*Jane Eyre*, Charlotte
	Brockden Brown		Brontë
	Lyrical Ballads, William		*Wuthering Heights*,
	Wordsworth and Samuel		Emily Brontë
	Taylor Coleridge	1850:	*Auriol; or: The Elixir of*
1815:	*Die Elixir Des Teufels/*		*Life*, W. Harrison
	The Devil's Elixirs,		Ainsworth
	E. T. A. Hoffmann	1851:	*House of The Seven*
1819:	*The Vampire*, John		*Gables*, Nathaniel
	Polidori		Hawthorne

The Piazza Tales,
Herman Melville

1857: *Les Fleurs Du Mal/*
Flowers of Evil, Charles
Beaudelaire

1860: *The Woman In White,*
Wilkie Collins

1870: *The Mystery of Edwin*
Drood, Charles Dickens

1872: *In A Glass Darkly,*
J. Sheridan leFanu

1883: *Contes Cruels,* Villiers de
l'Isle Adam

1887: *The Diamond Lens,* Fitz-
James O'Brien

1888: *The Phantom Rickshaw*
and Other Tales, Rudyard
Kipling

1890: *Hauntings,* Vernon Lee

1891: *La Bas/Down There,*
J. K. Huysmans
The Picture of Dorian
Gray, Oscar Wilde

1895: *A Bid For Fortune,* Guy
Boothby

1897: *The Hill of Dreams,*
Arthur Machen
The Beetle, Richard
Marsh

1898: *The War of the Worlds,*
H. G. Wells

1902: *The Hound of The*
Baskervilles, Arthur
Conan Doyle

1904: *Kwaidan,* Lafcadio Hearn

1906: *The Empty House and*
Other Ghost Stories,
Algernon Blackwood

1911: *Wandering Ghosts,*
F. Marion Crawford
Fantome De L'Opera/
The Phantom of The
Opera, Gaston Leroux

1912: *The Night Land,* William
Hope Hodgson

1913: *The Lodger,* Mrs Belloc
Lowndes
The Mystery of Dr Fu-
Manchu, Sax Rohmer

1914: *Beasts and Superbeasts,*
Saki
Dracula's Guest, Bram
Stoker

1915: *The Golem,* Gustav
Meyrink

1922: *The Undying Monster,*
Jessie Douglas Kerruish

1923: *Madame Crowl's Ghost,*
J. Sheridan LeFanu

1925: *The Smoking Leg and*
Other Stories, John
Metcalfe

1926: *The Ghost Book,* Lady
Cynthia Asquith (ed.)
Das Schloss/The Castle,
Franz Kafka

1927: *Benighted,* J. B. Priestley
Lukundoo and Other
Stories, Edward Lucas
White

1928: *The Beast With Five*
Fingers, W. F. Harvey

1930: *As I Lay Dying,* William
Faulkner

1931: *The Supernatural*
Omnibus, Montague
Summers

1933: *Burn, Witch Burn,*
A. Merritt
Miss Loneleyhearts,
Nathaniel West

1934: *The Cat Jumps,* Elizabeth
Bowen

1935: *The Circus of Dr Lao,*
Charles G. Finney
The Devil Rides Out,
Dennis Wheatley

1936: *Metamorphosis and*
Other Stories, Franz
Kafka

1937: *The Beast Must Die,*
Nicholas Blake

1938: *Rebecca,* Daphne Du
Maurier
Hangover Square, Patrick
Hamilton

1939: *Day of The Locust,*
Nathaniel West

1939:   *Gaslight*, Patrick
         Hamilton
         *The Edge of Running
         Water*, William Sloane
1940:   *Darker Than You Think*,
         Jack Williamson
1942:   *The Best Short Stories of
         Walter De La Mare*
         The Uninvited, Dorothy
         McCardle
         Black Alibi, Cornell
         Woolrich
1943:   *Donovan's Brain*, Curt
         Siodmak
         Malpertuis, Jean Ray
1944:   *Ficciones*, Jorge Luis
         Borges
1945:   *The Demon Lover*,
         Elizabeth Bowen
         Witch House, Evangeline
         Walton
         All Hallows' Eve, Charles
         Williams
1946/59: *The Gormenghast
         Trilogy*, Mervyn Peake
1946:   *Fearful Pleasures*, A. E.
         Coppard
         The Deadly Percheron,
         John Franklin Bardin
         Skull-Face and Others,
         Robert E. Howard
         The Hounds of Tindalos,
         Frank Belknap Long
         West India Lights, Henry
         S. Whitehead
1947:   *This Mortal Coil*, Cynthia
         Asquith
         Dark Carnival, Ray
         Bradbury
         Night's Black Agents,
         Fritz Leiber
         Bend Sinister, Vladimir
         Nabokov
1948:   *The Travelling Grave*, L.
         P. Hartley
1949:   *The Screaming Mimi*,
         Fredric Brown
         *Tomato Cain and Other
         Stories*, Nigel Kneale

         Nineteen Eighty-Four,
         George Orwell
1950–54: *Tales From The Crypt*,
         The Vault of Horror, *The
         Haunt of Fear*, William
         M. Gaines (publisher)
1951:   *Fancies and Goodnights*,
         John Collier
         *Ringstones and Other
         Curious Tales*, Sarban
1952:   *The Killer Inside Me*, Jim
         Thompson
1953:   *Night of The Hunter*,
         Davis Grubb
         *The Doll Maker and
         Other Tales*, Sarban
1954:   *Someone Like You*, Roald
         Dahl
1955:   *The Body Snatchers*, Jack
         Finney
         Men Without Bones,
         Gerald Kersh
         Satan In Goray, Isaac
         Beshevis Singer
1956:   *The Shrinking Man*,
         Richard Matheson
1957:   *The Cosmic Puppets*,
         Philip K. Dick
         The Midwich Cuckoos,
         John Wyndham
1958:   *A Scent of New-Mown
         Hay*, John Blackburn
         The Third Level, Jack
         Finney
         The Sundial, Shirley
         Jackson
1959:   *The Naked Lunch*,
         William S. Burroughs
         Night of The Big Heat,
         John Lymington
         Doctors Wear Scarlet,
         Simon Raven
         *The Pan Book of Horror
         Stories*, Herbert Van Thal
1961:   *Nightmares and
         Geezenstacks*, Fredrick
         Brown
         Some of Your Blood,
         Theodore Sturgeon

1962: *Yours Truly, Jack The Ripper*, Robert Bloch
A Clockwork Orange, Anthony Burgess
We Have Always Lived in The Castle, Shirley Jackson
The Surly Sullen Bell, Russell Kirk
The Case Against Satan, Ray Russell

1963: *Something Wicked This Way Comes*, Ray Bradbury
The Dark Man and Others, Robert E. Howard
Who Fears The Devil?, Manly Wade Wellman

1964: *The Kiss of Death*, Charles Birkin
Seconds, David Ely

1965–77: *The Dark Is Rising*, Susan Cooper

1965: *In Cold Blood*, Truman Capote
The Magic Man, Charles Beaumont
Something Breathing, Stanley McNail

1966: *Le Locutaire/The Tenant*, Roland Topor

1967: *Not After Nightfall*, Basil Copper
Camp Concentration, Thomas M. Disch
Rosemary's Baby, Ira Levin
The Playboy Book of Horror and The Supernatural,
Unholy Trinity, Ray Russell
The Mind Parasites, Colin Wilson

1968: *Dagon*, Fred Chappell
The Ring of Thoth, Arthur Conan Doyle
Dance of The Dwarfs,

Geoffrey Household

1971: *The Caller of The Black*, Brian Lumley
Hell House, Richard Matheson
The Other, Thomas Tryon

1972: *For Fear of Little Men*, John Blackburn
First Blood, David Morrell

1973: *Crash*, J. G. Ballard
Demons By Daylight, Ramsey Campbell
From Evil's Pillow, Basil Copper
Gravity's Rainbow, Thomas Pyncheon
Harvest Home, Thomas Tryon

1974: *The Elemental*, R. Chetwynd-Hayes
The Burrowers Beneath, Brian Lumley
The Black House, Paul Theroux
Collected Ghost Stories, Mary E. Wilkins-Freeman

1975: *Cold Hand In Mine*, Robert Aickman
The Fog, James Herbert
Testament, David Morrell
Nameless Places, Gerald W. Page (ed.)
The Auctioneer, Joan Samson
Julia, Peter Straub

1976: *Eaters of The Dead*, Michael Crichton
The Year of The Sex Olympics: 3 TV Plays, Nigel Kneale
Interview With A Vampire, Anne Rice
The Children of Dynmouth, William Trevor

1977: *Echoes From The Macabre*, Daphne Du

Maurier
Our Lady of Darkness,
Fritz Leiber
Night-Side, Joyce Carol
Oates
Blind Voices, Tom
Reamy
Nightwing, Martin Cruz
Smith

1978: *Half In Shadow*, Mary
Elizabeth Counselman
The Black Castle, Les
Daniels
The Cement Garden, Ian
McEwan
*San Diego Lightfoot Sue
and Other Stories*, Tom
Reamy
The House Next Door,
Anne Rivere Siddons

1979: *Flowers In The Attic*, V.
C. Andrews
The Lizard's Tail, Marc
Brendel
The Face That Must Die,
Ramsey Campbell
*Kiss of The Spider
Woman*, Manuel Puig
The Nightwalker,
Thomas Tessier

1980: *The Shapes of Midnight*,
Joseph Payne Brennan
New Terrors, Ramsey
Campbell (ed.)
The Vampire Tapestry,
Suzy McKee Charnas
*The Specialty of The
House and Other Stories*,
Stanley Ellin
The Voice of The Night,
Dean R. Koontz
Dark Forces, Kirby
McCauley (ed.)
*Cold Moon Over
Babylon*, Michael
McDowell
Shadowland, Peter Straub
Puffball, Fay Weldon

1981: *Tales From The*

Nightside, Charles L.
Grant
They Thirst, Robert R.
McCammon
The Elementals, Michael
McDowell

1982: *Psycho II*, Robert Bloch
The Nestling, Charles L.
Grant
Different Seasons,
Stephen King
Fevre Dream, George
R. R. Martin
Blackwater, Michael
McDowell
The Book of The Beast,
Robert Stallman

1983/87: *Nighthunter*, Robert
Faulcon (Robert
Holdstock)

1983: *The Ice Maiden*, Marc
Behm
Incarnate, Ramsey
Campbell
The Name of The Rose,
Umberto Eco
Flying To Nowhere, John
Fuller
*The Ice Monkey and
Other Stories*, M. John
Harrison
A Cold Blue Light,
Marvin Kaye and
Parke Godwin
Pet Sematary, Stephen
King
Mystery Walk, Robert R.
McCammon
Claw, Jay Ramsey
(Ramsey Campbell)
Dead White, Alan Ryan
Monkey Shines, Michael
Stewart
Phantom, Thomas
Tessier
Familiar Spirit, Lisa
Tuttle

1984/86: *The Books of Blood*,
Clive Barker

1984:   *The Voice of Our
        Shadow*, Jonathan Carroll
        *The Businessman: A Tale
        of Terror*, Tom Disch
        Red Dreams, Dennis
        Etchison
        Catch Your Death, John
        Gordon
        Domain, James Herbert
        The Ghost Light, Fritz
        Leiber
        Night Train, Thomas F.
        Monteleone
        Things Beyond Midnight,
        William F. Nolan
        Cast A Cold Eye, Alan
        Ryan
        Vampire Junction,
        S. P. Somtow
        (Somtow Sucharitkul)
        *A Manhattan Ghost
        Story*, T. M. Wright
1985:   *Death Is A Lonely
        Business*, Ray Bradbury
        Obsession, Ramsey
        Campbell
        *Son of The Endless
        Night*, John Farris
        Darklings, Ray Garton
        The Tea Party, Charles L.
        Grant
        Moon, James Herbert
        Dark Gods, T. E. D. Klein
        Angelus, Peter Tremayne
1986:   *The Cormorant*, Stephen
        Gregory
        Witchwater Country,
        Gary Kilworth
        *Dreams of Dark and
        Light*, Tanith Lee
        Time Out of Mind, John

R. Maxim
The Vampire Lestat,
Anne Rice
*The Unconquered
Country*, Geoff Ryman
Greey Eyes, Lucius
Shepard
The Light at The End,
John Skipp and Craig
Spector
1987:   *Weaveworld*, Clive Barker
        The Hungry Moon,
        Ramsey Campbell
        Bones of The Moon,
        Jonathan Carroll
        Valley of Lights, Stephen
        Gallagher
        Wildwood, John Farris
        Strange Toys, Patricia
        Geary
        The Dark Descent, David
        G. Hartwell (ed.)
        Dark Seeker, K. W. Jeter
        Mantis, K. W. Jeter
        Misery, Stephen King
        The Wyrm, Stephen Laws
        Slob, Rex Martin
        Scars, Richard Christian
        Matheson
        Finishing Touches,
        Thomas Tessier
        Why Not Your And I?,
        Karl Edward Wagner
        The Power, Ian Watson
1988:   *Fear of The Night*,
        Charles L. Grant
        The Kill Riff, David J.
        Schow
        Dark Winds, Graham
        Watkins

ACKNOWLEDGEMENTS

A project like this needs lots of friends. For books, information, advice, criticism and screaming abuse, we'd like to thank Forrest J Ackerman, Mike Ashley, Ramsey Campbell, John Clute, Richard Dalby, Meg Davis, Jo Fletcher, Stefan Jaworzyn, Tom Milne, Lisa Tuttle and our understanding editor, Richard Glyn Jones. Among many reference works, we found the most invaluable to be *The Encyclopedia of Science Fiction* edited by Peter Nicholls, *The Penguin Encyclopedia of Horror and the Supernatural* edited by Jack Sullivan, *Supernatural Horror in Literature* by H. P. Lovecraft and *Who's Who in Horror and Fantasy Fiction* by Mike Ashley. Of course, we'd also like to thank our contributors, whose self-sacrifice and dedication to this project is perhaps typified by Malcolm Edwards, who took time out from his honeymoon to write his piece.